Bryanston
reflections

Bryanston reflections

ET NOVA ET VETERA

Edited by Angela Holdsworth

THIRD MILLENNIUM
PUBLISHING, LONDON

First published in 2005 by Third Millennium Publishing Limited,
a subsidiary of Third Millennium Information Limited

Farringdon House
105–107 Farringdon Road
London
United Kingdom
EC1R 3BU
www.tmiltd.com

ISBN: 1 903942 38 1

Editor: Angela Holdsworth

Design: Helen Swansbourne

Produced by Third Millennium Publishing,
a subsidiary of Third Millennium Information Ltd

Printed and bound by MKT Press d.d., Slovenia

contents

part one : a changing picture

part two : at school

part three : the great outdoors

foreword

The publication of this wonderful celebration of Bryanston coincides, by chance, with the retirement of Tom Wheare after twenty-two years as its headmaster. If you know Tom you will have heard him speak of 'the Bryanston family'. His vision has always been that those who come to Bryanston join a family for life, whether they come to teach, to work in other ways, to learn or because they have had the wisdom to send their children there. And Tom, more than anyone, has made that vision a reality. Those who come to work at Bryanston are reluctant to leave and, for many, Bryanston becomes in truth the family home. Thorold Coade arrived as a young headmaster in 1932 and retired in 1959, a legend in his time. Tom's reign has been almost as long and will, I forecast, be no less legendary, for during his time the School has gone from strength to strength and he has earned the love and respect of the very large family of which he has been head.

It is not only the Bryanston staff who are reluctant to move on; the Bryanston governors are not known for their rapid turnover. There is only one essential qualification for a governor and that is dedication to the interests of the school. Governors who show that devotion are not encouraged to resign and their value grows with wisdom and experience – or so I hope. My predecessor, Geoff Udall, chaired the governors for twenty-two years, and I must confess to having been in the post even longer.

This continuity of staff and governors might be a bad thing in a traditional school, but Bryanston has never been that. Bryanston was founded for those who wanted an alternative to the traditional public school; a school that would not attempt to stamp its pupils into a mould, however admirable its features, but would enable each to find and develop his (alas then only his) particular talents and interests. Respect for one's own individuality and the individuality of others is the essence of the Bryanston ethos. The staff and governors have guarded that ethos and will continue to do so.

The face of Bryanston has changed over the years, and this book illustrates the changes. But the heart of the school is and will always be Norman Shaw's great building, albeit that the polish used on the floor no longer has that smell, which for many decades was so evocative. And the soul of the school has not changed, as will become apparent as you read the reminiscences of the many generations who have contributed to this book.

Bryanston has been a vital part of my family's world, and this book will tell my grandchildren about it. But I hope that in due course at least some of them will find themselves whiling away a rainy Bryanston afternoon by identifying their parents, uncles, aunts, grandfather and great-grandfather in the school photographs that line the corridor of the west wing.

Nicholas Phillips *(Connaught '56) has been Chairman of the Governors since 1981 and is Master of the Rolls.*

editor's note

The title of this book is carefully chosen. This is not a comprehensive history of Bryanston but rather a miscellany of memories brought together to create a picture of a school developing from infancy to maturity. It makes a compelling story. The founder of Bryanston set out to create something ground-breaking, a community with a different ethos from traditional public schools, and he succeeded. The diversity of Old Bryanstonians and their recollections of largely happy schooldays with physical and mental space to grow as individuals are a living memorial to that legendary first Staff Room and its successors.

Apart from breaking the mould, Bryanston had – and still has – a lot going for it. There are wonderful stories of hidden spaces, secret stairways and rooftop escapades which would have been impossible without Norman Shaw's extraordinary building. The size and richness of the grounds are eloquently described, with the sense of freedom and opportunities they brought. It is striking how often a hobby or extra-curricular activity shaped OBs' future lives. As have the opportunities to develop art, music and drama as careers or simply for fun.

War stories add fresh insights and colour to the social history of Dorset in those years. The countryside, transformed into a camouflaged military camp, delighted trophy-collecting schoolboys, some of whom stashed away alarming arsenals of ammunition. Tales from the austere post-war years, the rebellious sixties, the early years of co-education right through to what one OB describes as the wondercamp of recent years all make for a marvellous read. It is striking also how much affection is expressed not just for the School itself but for individual teachers.

Readers may occasionally be surprised by accounts which vary from their own recollections. Inevitably with such a multitude of personal views and perspectives recalled from a distance of many decades, there will be conflicting memories, but I hope the quintessence of the School comes across in every page.

Thank you to all of you who made this possible by contributing your reminiscences. The response was so good that not everything could be included but every single communication has helped to set the tone or direct my attention to something I may otherwise have missed. Anything not in the book will become part of the excellent Bryanston Archive, presided over by Alan Shrimpton. Alan has been a pivotal figure throughout. Having been a pupil, master, editor of the Yearbook and school archivist, his knowledge of Bryanston's history and OBs is formidable. He has given me a huge amount of his time and the benefit of his advice and support throughout. He has assiduously corrected the manuscript, picking up factual errors even to the point of spotting that one or two OBs had mistaken the year they actually left! For all this I owe him enormous gratitude. I should also like to thank Tom Wheare for giving me the freedom to get on with it, but providing inspiring ideas whenever they were needed, and Clare Price for her frequent input on the structure and appearance of the book.

Thanks also to Julian Platt's team at Third Millennium: Louise Wilson for her guidance on editing multi-authored books, Matt Wilson for his creative ideas and, especially, to Helen Swansbourne who designed such an imaginative and attractive book. It has been a pleasure to work with you all.

Angela Holdsworth
Abbotsbury
April 2005

part one : a changing picture

1

DOMESDAY TO DALTON

The Domesday Survey of 1087 records a 2,500-acre estate on the right bank of the River Stour just above Blandford, though not separating its name from Blanford [*sic*]. Camden's sixteenth-century 'Britannia' calls the estate Brientius Town, but Bryan de l'Isle's ownership in King John's reign more or less determined the present name of the settlement or 'ton'. Various families possessed it during the Middle Ages – the de Stephens, the Echinghams and the de Boxhalls and from 1415 onwards the Rogers, who held on to it for 247 years until, in about 1662, it was bought by Sir William Berkeley Portman, later famous for capturing the usurper Duke of Monmouth near Horton. His family retained ownership for the next 265 years.

Sir William contributed hugely to his descendants' wealth by another acquisition. When told that his wife's skin disease might benefit from bathing in asses' milk, he bought just over 100 acres of fields in the district of Marylebone to the west of London to graze the beasts during the London season. This land is still owned by the family, and extensive building during the late eighteenth century resulted in a substantial ground-rental income.

Left: the Tudor and Stuart house in an eighteenth-century etching

Above: Wyatt's 1780 house, in a print of 1811

Left: the Portman Chapel and Wyatt's house

Below: 'The new house took five hundred men and five years to build'

Not surprisingly, this part of the West End is full of addresses with Dorset associations – Blandford Street, Durweston Mews, Bryanston Square and of course Portman and Berkeley Squares.

The head of the family in the late eighteenth century was Henry William Portman who rebuilt Bryanston House, employing James Wyatt as his architect. The Wyatt house not only replaced an earlier jumble of Tudor and Stuart buildings, it also enabled the family to do the fashionable thing and remove the dwellings of their servants from the vicinity of the house, giving it a position of splendid isolation with a park that attractively sloped down to the Stour. The gateway at Blandford bridge is the main survivor of Wyatt's improvements, which also included the closing by Act of Parliament of the public highway through the grounds and its conversion to a private drive. To avoid serious inconvenience to local people, especially the inhabitants of Bryanston village, a new road was constructed parallel to the drive a mere 50 yards away behind a boundary wall. The Blandford to Sherborne highway was removed from the Bryanston grounds entirely by the building at Durweston of a fine new bridge (1795) to link with the road on the other bank of the Stour.

Wyatt's new Palladian house promised an elegant setting for the lifestyle of a grand family soon to be raised to the peerage. The 1st Lord Portman, Edward (1799–1888) was MP for the county after 1823 and later MP for Marylebone. But he inherited one insoluble problem – damp. Wyatt's builder had been a man for short cuts who not only acquired stone from Vanbrugh's Eastbury Park, of which parts were being pulled down, but also took sand from the coast which, being salt-impregnated, drew in moisture and made for perpetual discomfort, especially in winter.

His heir, William Henry (1829–1919), was the man who actually tackled the problem. Earlier attempts, like moving the River Stour to the far side of the valley, had made no difference, so the 2nd viscount and his wife, Mary Wentworth, decided to build a new Bryanston house on the higher, drier ground of what was called Middle Hill. Mary's family home, Wentworth Woodhouse, was one of England's most magnificent properties, and doubtless Mary encouraged her husband and his architect, Richard Norman Shaw, to build something outstandingly grand. French Renaissance style was chosen as appropriately noble. The 1660 Loire valley château at Menars was the model, with variations along the lines of Coleshill in Berkshire. The planned mansion was to be twice the size of these properties, and indeed more than twice the size of the existing Bryanston house. No expense was to be spared, and the cost passed beyond £200,000 – more than £10 million at early twenty-first-century prices. The new house took five hundred men and five years to build, but as the Marylebone ground rents produced over £100,000 per annum, Lord Portman had no difficulty in paying for it out of income. Even electric light was provided, a thoroughly modern touch, powered by a turbine generator built in the village – well out of earshot.

'With Norman Shaw's house the Portmans joined the great club of European aristocracy,' wrote Andrew Saint, in his biography of Norman Shaw. Lord Portman was not an easy client, and there was a prolonged building strike during construction. Shaw was dismissed before the design of the garden had been completed, but fortunately his plan of approaching the front courtyard through a cutting has always ensured a dramatic first impression for newcomers. Lady Portman is reputed to have manipulated the views from the house by standing at an upstairs window on the garden front and signalling with semaphore flags where she wanted trees planted. That the family disposed of most of their eighteenth-century furniture and equipped the house afresh through Maples of Tottenham Court Road seems to later generations oddly impetuous, but all their family portraits and most of their large collection of paintings were moved up from the old house, as well as many of the fine fireplaces now in the principal rooms.

Despite his great wealth, Lord Portman was not extravagant or wasteful. He arranged that the stone and timbers of the eighteenth-century house should be used again for the construction of a new church on the Wyatt site. The old chapel across the lawn to the north of the church is the original village church, but is known now as the Portman Chapel – looked after by the family and containing family remains in the vaults as well as monuments on its interior walls. The last surviving remnant of Wyatt's house is the kitchen wing, set into the hillside and largely hidden behind bushes: it now houses a protected colony of greater horseshoe bats.

The 2nd Lord Portman lived to be ninety, but even before his death in 1919 the old world was changing. The 1914–18 war had dragged most of the men away from the estate, many never to return. The experiences of those who did come back had unsettled their acceptance of the old ways with a feudal family ruling the roost, albeit generously. Most specifically, death duties, begun by the Budget of 1894, meant that Lord Portman's successor would incur a forty per cent tax on

Left: the Main Hall, and below, the Drawing Room, early twentieth century

JG JEFFREYS

I met JGJ on a prep school outing to the Dorset coast. Happy, outgoing, jolly, he joined in all the fun and swam in the sea with us. He had so impressed my prep school headmaster, Geoff Hoyland, that he now suggested we should go on to Bryanston.

We had been brought up to expect public schools to be places where young boys were licked into shape, being for a while slaves as they fagged for older prefects. We were told Bryanston was a new school with new ideas where each boy would be encouraged to develop his talents to the maximum of his ability and where he would learn to work on his own – the Dalton Plan. Added to these, here was a headmaster who was approachable.

We didn't need any further convincing. Bryanston was the school to go to. It fulfilled all my expectations.

John Gerrard (Shaftesbury '34)

the family estates. The 3rd Lord Portman, Henry, lived only till January 1923. Double death duties made it impossible for the childless Henry's brother, Claud, to hold on to Bryanston (and he lived only till 1929!) so that in 1926 the house and 450 acres of immediate grounds changed hands for £35,000.

The price and the immaculate condition of the property were noticed at once by JG Jeffreys, a young Australian schoolmaster (born 1893) whose ambition was to establish and run his own school. He had come to what most Australians saw as the Mother Country in 1921 to teach chemistry at Westminster School, where he created such a good impression that the headmaster encouraged him to go up to Christ Church, Oxford, to take a second degree. At the end of 'two years of bliss' he went to teach at Radley, but his vision of a school of his own remained uppermost in his mind. He set about seeking backing from the academic and business worlds as well as looking for a suitable property.

The Dorset choices were Brownsea Castle and Bryanston: fortunately Jeffreys chose Bryanston – the inconvenience of an island school in Poole Harbour would surely have doomed it in the Second World War. The Earl of Shaftesbury gave financial guarantees, as well as becoming Chairman of the Governors, and a mortgage of £50,000 was agreed with the Alliance Assurance Co.

The first term began in January 1928 with the Master, as Jeffreys was to be called, seven assistants and twenty-three boys of various ages from thirteen to sixteen. These included Michael Phillips, father of Nicholas Phillips, OB and Chairman of the Governors for a quarter of a century. The masters were all young men known to Jeffreys through Westminster, Oxford or Radley, and included Trevor James, vitally Second Master during and after Jeffreys' time, Harold Greenleaves and Wilfrid Cowley, who were on the staff until retirement, as was Ronnie King, a pupil of Jeffreys at Westminster.

Jeffreys chose for the school crest a rising sun and the motto, *et nova et vetera*, from Ormond College, Melbourne, where he had taken his chemistry degree in 1921. 'Both new and old' encapsulates Jeffreys' approach. He was a natural innovator but one who respected good traditions. His young staff had been chosen for their similar views, products of traditional public schools but eager, as a contemporary put it, 'to put right everything that was wrong with their own schools'. Jeffreys declared his aims in an article in the first printed edition of the school magazine, *Bryanston Saga*, which came out at Christmas 1928:

> It is the duty of the School to develop the individuality of each boy who comes into its midst, to give him a feeling that he is now a member of a community, the success of which is determined by the corporate endeavour to work for the good of the whole … to this end as much freedom as is compatible with the smooth running of the community should be allowed … let us have every kind of interest as fully developed as possible – literature, music (orchestral and vocal), arts and crafts, mechanical, electrical, natural history, athletic and a host of others. Let us be enthusiastic in everything we do and not frightened to show it … don't let ourselves be put into one particular mould largely determined by 'what's done'.

This may be a mainstream approach in the early twenty-first century but was controversial in the 1920s. Tradition, however, was respected in various ways. For example, the school uniform included blazer, tie and grey flannels (the shorts and sweater came later). The prefect system allowed boys as well as masters to use the cane. Clubs and societies included such universal activities as the Debating Society ('We disapprove of the Talkies' carried by thirty-three to thirty-two). Music-making, drama and the termly magazine, *Saga*, gave much emphasis to original contributions by the boys in prose, verse and art, as well as to the more usual documents of record – sports results *inter alia*.

Central to the life of any good school is its academic system, and here Jeffreys turned Bryanston into the first English school to embrace the Dalton Plan. An American teacher, Helen Parkhurst, had developed a scheme before the 1914–18 war that became known internationally when, in the 1920s, Dalton High School, Massachusetts, adopted it with great success. Its combination of the new and the old appealed to Jeffreys hugely. Its novelty was the flexibility offered by a combination of lessons in the classroom and time for assignment work in subject rooms, which gave boys the freedom to decide which pieces of academic work should have their attention. Jeffreys' Daltonisation had much common sense about it: juniors had a majority of classroom periods in their programme, but as they matured the emphasis moved towards assignment time. Boys were required to keep a daily record on a chart showing their use of working (and leisure) time. Their teachers then added weekly marks showing the standards attained and effort made, and of course the level of work set by teachers was adapted to the abilities of the boys in their care. With suitable inspiration from teachers some wonderful standards could be achieved, in arts and crafts as well as in academic subjects, and weekly tutorials ensured effective monitoring of each individual's progress.

Much later in life, Jeffreys was at the Royal Academy looking at his portrait which was newly on show when he heard another visitor say to his wife, 'I bet he was an old so-and-so.' He turned to the man and said 'I was – sometimes.' He was a difficult man to fathom. Clearly charismatic, he had drawn a body of able young men to join his staff, and OBs of his time speak of him with affection and respect. And yet when friction with the governors became intolerable and led to his resignation at the end of 1931, only one of his staff moved with him to his next foundation, Ottershaw College in Surrey. There has always been an undercurrent of mystery about the reasons for the break, but one result is certain: the appointment of Thorold Coade from Harrow as his successor ensured that Bryanston would surge ahead during the next quarter of a century.

***Bob Allan** was Housemaster, Second Master and Acting Headmaster and a member of staff from 1960 to 1989.*

Pioneers making a practice tennis court, 1933

THE NORMAN SHAW HOUSE

Although I was vaguely aware that the buildings were originally designed as a country house for the Portman family, I always felt it was ideally designed for a boarding school for over 300 boys: a large, solid, well-constructed building, tough enough to take the wear and tear of its occupants for generations. It is an interesting deposit of English taste at the end of the nineteenth century when people were tired with the Gothic Revival and returned for a short time to classicism before that whole era came to an abrupt halt in 1914.

Its architect Norman Shaw was highly regarded at the time – indeed, he was so highly regarded by Lutyens that he said: 'I believe Norman Shaw is a really great and capable designer, one of the first water. I put him with Wren – really.'

The building is indeed solidly constructed in Portland stone, clearly the right choice in its locality; and in an even, red brick, soft enough to rub around the window openings, and for insignificant adolescents to inscribe their names upon in perpetuity. It would probably have looked less Victorian if it were built entirely in stone. Shaw, in my view, was a competent architect with a good working knowledge of Gibbs and English Palladian detail. His handling of the entrance front with its large segmental pedimented wings shows that he was beginning to move in a Mannerist direction, as does his design of the entrance hall, main stairs and central dome.

The garden front has an interesting mix of scale with the gigantic sash windows and central door to the main

rooms on the piano nobile, the smaller first-floor windows above, the bold modillion cornice and Westmorland slate roof and dormer windows – all of which stand in contrast to the east and west wings either side, which have all of the same elements on a much smaller scale. The whole treatment of the steps, banks and ramparts down to the circular pond on the south side shows Shaw's consummate ability to handle space on a grand scale. But probably his greatest skill is the element of anticipation and surprise that he planned in the total layout, which starts at the Wyatt gates in Blandford, continues for nearly two miles and ends at the front door – a distance indelibly marked on the memories of generations of Bryanstonians who had to run this journey as a punishment on their free afternoons. The first-time visitor wonders when he will arrive, as the house is cleverly hidden throughout the journey. Towards the end one ascends a long and gradual slope which then turns left on a fairly sharp radius through a cutting, and then one is suddenly confronted with the entrance front and side wings less than fifty yards away.

This drama of anticipation and surprise is sadly marred by all the new buildings that have been erected over the last fifty years without any serious appreciation of Shaw's overall plan. Bryanston, like all public schools today, ever eager to provide new facilities at low cost, has not been able to continue in the architectural tradition or provide the quality of buildings worthy of the original foundation. However, we may console ourselves that Shaw's work will outlast all these petty exigencies of time and continue to be appreciated by future generations of Bryanstonians.

***Quinlan Terry** (Salisbury '55) is one of Britain's leading architects, renowned for his innovative use of the classical style in the Richmond Riverside development and many other projects.*

THE EARLY YEARS 1928–39

2

An American at Bryanston

I arrived at Bryanston in its third year. The first sight of the school was most impressive, as was the interior with its highly polished parquet floors, so smooth we soon discovered that we could run on them in stockinged feet and slide quite a distance. Everybody was very friendly. Benjy Hobhouse was head boy, notable for his curious habit of springing up on his toes when walking. I was assigned to Shaftesbury House with dorm windows looking out on the back lawn.

We ate in what became Harold Greenleaves's subject room (now Grosvenor). It had long tables and benches, one of which I upset, crushing my toe, which was the most painful experience of my young life. At noon each day we exercised on the Plateau with 'physical jerks' orchestrated by ex-Sergeant Major Howard. We swam naked in the river. I was allowed to bring a little flat-bottomed, 10ft × 6ft sailing dinghy to school, and spent a lot of time on the river with Bill Phelps, the Boatman.

Jeffreys was always much in evidence and not nearly as austere as his photos suggest. His room still had some of the original Portman furniture. Junior boys were not allowed to use the main staircase but had to use the back stairs, which were apparently renowned for their self-sustaining construction. As the School expanded, an outdoor dorm was built – a long shed-like building with two rows of beds facing the windows which hinged upwards and were seldom closed. When the rain came in, we put tarps on the bed. Every morning we had to take a cold dip in a bathtub, compensated for by soaking in a hot footbath in the locker room after sports.

For me this era ended with the unforgettable performance by Cowley and Bramall of 'Way back in 1931/When Bryanston had just begun/We used to have such bogus fun/In 1931'. If they did a performance in 1932 I was not there to see it as I was away, laid up with a back problem, for nearly two years.

On my return in 1933 what a change! A new headmaster with a new house where the outdoor dorm used to be. My house changed from Shaftesbury to Connaught. A new sanatorium (built in 1932) was now very much in evidence.

Coade was different from Jeffreys; quiet to the point of appearing diffident but always full of new ideas. He had a dry sense of humour and was a good host who sometimes entertained us at his house.

Some special incidents stand out. There was the mysterious package addressed to MacDuff left on the marble table where we got our mail. He was in hospital and could not pick it up. After a few days a terrible smell came from the parcel. It turned out to be a choice cut of venison sent by his father, the Duke of Connaught. *(The house named after him was founded in autumn 1931 during his son's schooldays. – Ed.)*

MacDuff, 1931. Forestry was a popular activity

Nude bathing in the river, summer 1935

Then there was the Jackdaw incident. A boy, Dawson, had an incredible rapport with animals. He had a German Shepherd, abandoned as too vicious to train, but after a few weeks with Dawson he was everybody's friend. He also tamed a wild fox which he kept in a box stall at the stables. But what impressed the rest of us particularly was his knack of calling jackdaws. We persuaded him to teach us his technique; soon we did not even have to call before they arrived looking for a treat. A new dining hall had recently been added to the School and one fine day all the windows were left open. Spotting us inside, our friendly jackdaws flew in hoping for a feast and soon the dining hall was filled with hungry birds. Needless to say, jackdaw-calling was immediately banned.*

Pioneering flourished. I learned axemanship, helping old-timers to fell, limb and split an old oak tree. Their cuts were as smooth as glass, an accomplishment that, in spite of much practice, I have never been able to emulate. I also took iron working from an old 'gaffer' who had a forge in the stables, and learned to appreciate the great craftsmanship that went into the wrought iron gates and railings that we too often ignored.

It has been written that caning was soon abolished, but I never saw any sign of physical punishment or fagging, which were standard in public schools at that time. There was never any lack of discipline, but punishment was even-handed and usually well-deserved, whether administered by a master or prefect!

Most commonly offenders were put on Early Morning Reporting which meant getting up before breakfast for one or more days to take a long early-morning run. For those of us who were prefects, this was a two-edged sword because we too had to get up to run or supervise from strategic spots. Sometimes we could make the punishment fit the crime, as we did for one boy who always cut obligatory physical training.

The History Room, 1933

I told him that we would go to the gym and I would teach him how to fence. He thought this a fine idea until he found out that the fencing position is like sitting down and then having someone take away the chair. Untrained, it can become extremely painful. He soon learned that PT was the lesser of two evils.

As prefects we had privileges such as our own studies with provisions for making coffee, toast, etc. We could go camping on the Downs in fine weather, which we did as often as possible, and for which we were given special rations. Also a group of us would walk over the Downs to the inn at Milton Abbas for Sunday lunch (sometimes accompanied by congenial members of staff). There, for 2/6 (12½p), they would put before you a roast of beef and a chicken to carve for yourself. I think a cider or a beer was sixpence extra.

Bryanston was then a very new and unique school. Its combination of personal freedom and discipline bred responsibility and character. Study was demanded but instead of a timetable involving hourly changes of lessons and classrooms, we were given time to reflect on what we were studying, which encouraged scholarship. I consider it a great privilege to have been there.

George Hanson (Connaught '34) was Professor of Geology at the University of Wisconsin and also State Geologist and Director of the Wisconsin Geological and Natural History Survey.

** Jackdaw calling is also remembered by Stanley Fisher, then Chaplain, who recorded going to visit a boy in the sick-room, and finding it full of birds which then flew out of the window. 'The boy called them back, uttering a variety of whistles, clacks and caws. Jackdaws, starlings, a thrush and a chaffinch returned. Then an owl was produced from under the bedclothes.' – Ed.*

A scientist remembers

I arrived at Bryanston shortly after TF Coade had taken over from JG Jeffreys as headmaster. Coade was something of a moderniser and had introduced a number of changes in the School. The most welcome (at least by me) was the abolition of beating by the prefects. Other changes, such as the replacement of long trousers by shorts, were received with mixed feelings. Like quite a few others at the time, I had previously been to the Down's School, Colwall, so had several friends and my elder brother, Theo, already at the School.

The Chemistry Laboratory, 1933

I much appreciated the new surroundings, especially the increased freedom in both work and play. I was not a great athlete, and gave up organised team games after a few years and concentrated on squash and fives. I 'distinguished' myself by becoming captain of fives – no great achievement, as there were only two of us.

I started off in set D and on the whole found the work fairly easy. Though not one of those geniuses who always came first in class, I was usually near the top. With the increased freedom in classes it was up to us to decide how hard we would work. Many took advantage of this and took things easy. When I was about to take School Certificate I decided to work really hard and managed seven credits, a rather unusual achievement in Bryanston at the time, and was given the title 'seven credit Fred'. More importantly, this qualified me for entrance to Cambridge, leaving me in my last term with time to concentrate on the subjects that interested me such as chemistry and biology.

My housemaster was HG Ordish, who also taught chemistry. I feel I owe him a great debt for introducing me to the joys of chemistry, which was to become my life's work. He used to do a little chemical research himself, making dyestuffs in his spare time, and allowed me to join him. I found it absolutely fascinating making, for instance, beautiful crystals, and spent much of my time up in the Chemical Lab.

Mr Ordish did not seem to me to be a typical school-master. Where others might be a bit hearty and patronising, he was quiet with a subtle sense of humour. The other masters used to call him 'Critters'. To us boys,

The Chemistry Laboratory in the 1950s

he was 'Uncle O'. Besides being Housemaster, he was also school detective. On one occasion some money disappeared from our changing room so Mr Ordish prepared a sticky green substance. This was stuck on to some coins that were put in the pocket of my trousers which I hung in my locker. After a few days, the coins were missing. The whole school was summoned. While waiting to be examined, I was alarmed to see a good friend of mine trying to rub some sticky green stuff off his fingers. That was the last I saw of him.

I spent the last half of my last term at Schule Schloss Salem, the school in South Germany with which exchanges were made. In retrospect, it seems a rather strange thing for me to have done. I was never very gregarious or adventurous. Perhaps it was the pioneering spirit nurtured at Bryanston. I was accompanied by David Forbes, who was younger than me and spoke less German.

It was at the height of the Nazi period. The founder and first headmaster was Jewish and had been replaced by an Aryan. At morning prayers he read a passage from the Bible or from *Mein Kampf*. Students had to give the Nazi salute at the beginning of every lesson. David and I decided not to do this which seemed to be accepted. The emphasis was all on sports and physical fitness, while the academic side lagged, especially in maths. Every morning we had to do the 'trainings plan', ticking off certain duties we were supposed to do. I remember particularly 'zweimal geduscht' (two showers).

Salem was near to the Bodensee (Lake of Constance) and we were able to borrow bicycles and go off for trips into the countryside at weekends. One Saturday I went off with two German boys and rather unwisely camped in a field near the lake which turned out to be in the grounds of another school (Spetzgart), the female equivalent of Salem, with whom they were having some sort of feud at the time. When we woke up in the morning we found ourselves surrounded by a ring of beefy schoolgirls. Alex and Ulrich made a dash for it, escaping on their bicycles, but I was captured and imprisoned in the girls' locker-room. There was an English girl at the school who came and chatted to me through the window. In the meantime, I was busy dismantling a 'Schuhspannung' (a sort of thing in a shoe to keep its shape) and preparing a piece of metal that would serve as a screwdriver. Fortunately the lock on the door was on the inside and I was able to take a few screws out and open the door. I made a quick dash for a nearby wood, found a road and hitch-hiked back to Salem, where I was hailed as 'Der Held des Tages' (hero of the day).

After the end of term, David and I decided to do a walking tour across Austria (we were already close to the border). The idea was to walk south across the mountains to reach Italy. It was a memorable experience. I remember particularly waking up one morning to see deer grazing quietly beside me, a day scrambling over a mountain pass, and ending up in a barn of straw belonging to a dear old lady who shared her supper with us. The whole trip was a great adventure, marred only by one thing. I was in charge of financial arrangements and made a complete cock-up of it, so that we ended up with not enough money to buy the food we needed. We were forced to live largely on bread. I think this was the only time in my life I have felt really hungry. I still remember walking along the mountain paths thinking of plates of bacon and eggs.

Fred Sanger *(Shaftesbury '36) is one of the world's most distinguished molecular biologists, having invented the techniques for sequencing both proteins and DNA, each of which achievements won him a Nobel Prize.*

AUTUMN 1935: A SUMMARY OF THE TERM'S EVENTS

12th December 1935

Above and below right: compulsory walks, unchanged in thirty years

In autumn 1935,
Returning, back along the drive,
So level, black and new, arrive
The old boys, new boys, schoolboys, we
Who, in this age of industry,
To cope with past assignments strive
In autumn 1935.

But hardly has the term begun,
When comes the hated Blandford run
For those who evil things have done;
And we bewail our cruel fate,
And get our tickets at the gate
And bear them homewards, one by one,
And swear our evil ways to shun.

Now ev'ry morning when we rise
We take our early exercise,
For this the Doctor does advise.
After a freezing cold ablution
Has petrified our constitution,
We hurry out, in various guise,
Beneath the bleak and bitter skies.

Corrections are begun anew;
Our charts assume a different hue
And tutors all are grimmer, too,
Till 'tis declared by T.F.C.
A marking system new to be:
'Don't worry if your chart looks blue,
Don't let your tutor frighten you.'

Along the main hall, to and fro,
Probationary prefects go
And thus in worldly wisdom grow.
Saved from the toll of our transgressions
By their repeated intercessions,
We bless the harmless creatures, though
They take the little boys in tow.

A haven for the smaller fry,
The Junior House was born, to try
With all the other ones to vie;
And for their master do they choose
Their dear old Uncle Reggie Hughes;
Then to the art-room daily fly,
Where stories pass the evening by.

And all around, along the drive
Our newly planted saplings thrive
And when of all and sundry things we talk,
While strolling round the morning walk,
We say: 'It's good to be alive
In autumn 1935.'

JL Putman *(Hardy '37)*

So read by his son nearly seventy years later…. I learn that it was in summer 1935 that the Drive was tarmacked; in that year too that the new plantations were established along the Drive; the chart system still operative when I was at the School in the early sixties was introduced, and the Junior House system (later Dorchester) was born. I discover that the afternoon punishment run of my time was preceded by an earlier Blandford run (and that my father got caught now and again…).

And cold baths and morning walks were the same in 1935 as in 1965…

Rory Putman *(Hardy '68)*

Rory Putman's grandfather, John William Putman, worked originally for Lord Portman and stayed with the house when it became a school, becoming Bryanston's first Clerk of Works.

1935: John Putman is on the left

SPECIMEN MENU

Actual Menu for Week Ending 28-1-34

	Monday	Tuesday	Wednesday	Thursday	Friday	Saturday	Sunday
BREAKFAST	Porridge Bacon and Tomatoes Marmalade	Shredded Wheat Poached Eggs on Fried Bread Marmalade	Porridge Fresh Herrings Marmalade	Porridge Eggs and Bacon Marmalade	Grape Fruit Sausages Marmalade	Porridge Liver and Bacon Marmalade	Shredded Wheat Boiled Eggs Marmalade
LUNCH	Boiled Beef Carrots Potatoes Semolina and Figs Lemonade	Irish Stew Greens Potatoes Jam Tart	Roast Beef Cabbage Potatoes Plums and Custard	Steamed Fish (Parsley Sauce) Butter Beans Mashed Potatoes Fruit Pudding Custard Sauce Lemonade	Roast Mutton Greens Potatoes Rice Pudding and Prunes	Rabbit Stew Savoys Potatoes Baked Apples and Custard	Roast Beef Cabbage Potatoes Gooseberries and Custard
HIGH TEA	Rissoles Watercress	Macaroni Cheese Oranges	Sausages Apples	Lancashire Hot Pot Watercress	Scrambled Eggs Cheese	Lentil Soup Cheese Oranges	Cold Ham Cheese Apples

Notes

1. FRESH FRUIT: Fresh Fruit is served every day (twice weekly in the form of lemonade).
2. MILK: Milk from Home Farm twice daily.
3. VEGETABLES: Green vegetables are served five days a week and watercress is given on the other two. Salads at least four times a week in summer. Green vegetables are from the School's own garden. Potatoes are baked and steamed *in their jackets* whenever possible. When served with fish they are mashed with milk and butter.
4. BREAD: Whole-meal bread is served at all meals.
5. BREAKFAST: Shredded Wheat and Grape Fruit are frequent substitutes for Porridge, except in cold weather. Tea, bread, butter and marmalade are always served in addition to the specified menu.
6. LUNCHEON: Meat is *never* twice cooked. Mutton is home-fed on Bryanston Farm and killed by the School's butcher. Beef is best chilled Argentine. English beef for stew.
7. 4 O'CLOCK TEA (not shewn on menu): Consists of tea, wheaten biscuits and cheese.
8. HIGH TEA: Bread, butter, jam and marmalade are always on the tables in addition to the specified menu.

Printed in England by Spottiswoode, Ballantyne & Co., Ltd., Colchester, London & Eton.

Tuck, trains and spotted dog

I arrived at the School in the autumn of 1938 with perhaps the lowest entrance scores in history – around four per cent as I recall. As a new boy I was placed in a dormitory on the top floor south side under the watchful eye of Mr Hughes, the art master, who wore a silk dressing gown at night. My friend Alfred Greaves somehow obtained a key to the wireless club on this same floor. So we would sneak down the corridor, enter the wizard space, lift the trap door, and drop down on to the linen room balcony, where it was warm. We could peak over the mattresses and see the prefect at his desk, guarding the door to the balcony of the main hall. Illicit excitement!

The next year my bed was in the central part looking out over the gardens. In the winter I'd wake up to find it covered with snow. Our routine was to jump out of bed, doff pyjamas, grab a towel and run to the bathroom, brush teeth, grab the sides of the bathtub, jump in, slide down rapidly into the cold water, which sloshed over the sloped end as we shot out shivering, towelled off on the way back into the dorm. We dressed rapidly in open-necked shirt, shorts, knee-length socks, and Norwegian elk-hide black shoes from Daniel Neal on Portman Square, London. Then it was rush downstairs, out by the Porter's Office, walk or run around the Plateau by the front of the School, making sure your house prefect saw you and checked your name off, and into breakfast.

Breakfast, as all meals, started with the sour smell of scrubbed wooden tables and benches. The meal was canned grapefruit, glutinous porridge floating in cold milk, bacon, eggs and fried bread, rancid butter, bread and jam. Lunch was hearty – meat, potatoes, cabbage or Brussels sprouts, and puddings – suet, spotted dog, Queen Charlotte, apple pudding, etc. and custard. We had our own pots of jam or honey, and high tea was sometimes shepherd's pie, usually a meat dish, bread and jam, and sometimes Bath or other buns: hearty fare supplemented with cheese. On those holidays that celebrated the birth of a master's child, we got bread and cheese from the kitchen and cooked out on the prehistoric hill forts of Hambledon or Hod.

One of the great things at Bryanston was that we were taught how to behave and survive anywhere in Dorset, including getting permission to camp in farmers' fields, eat raw mushrooms, etc. We could have bicycles and could leave early in the morning and only had to be back in the house common room by roll call in the evening. Two of us, railway fans, bicycled south one day, caught a train and spent the day number-spotting at Southampton. We had a great time and never got caught!

Other times we went to Templecombe where the up expresses thundered down through the station and over the Slow & Dirty, as we called the Somerset and Dorset. The latter was an interesting line. One of my era, Haywood, was crippled. He would go down to Blandford station and the engine driver would let him do the afternoon shunting with the LMSR Fowler 0-6-0. We envied him. The railway was part of my life day or night.

GV Morris giving out pocket money and signing charts, 1930s

I would awaken to the strained puffing of a night goods train climbing north up the grade to the summit above and across from the boathouse. In a way our love of trains was, though we did not know it then, very Victorian – a worship of machinery.

In those days of limited pocket money, we were great scavengers, especially of the detritus left from the kitchen – not food, but large coffee cans which were made of sheet tin which we could cut and fashion and then solder. My tuck box, an orange-yellow pine bound with black tin and lockable, was up in the Railway Club and filled with 'useful items' – a habit my wife of fifty-four years wishes I would break, but I still believe something may come in valuable some day.

Dotted around the school grounds were tree houses. I am not sure how Greaves and I came to have the one at the lower end of the formal gardens. But we did and repaired there on Wednesday and Saturday afternoons off.

One thing I learnt was to set snares for rabbits. I think the cook would skin them and cook them for us. The other sport engaged in caused a shortage of teaspoons in the Dining Room. The latter could easily be made into spinners by snapping off the handles and then drilling a hole at each end to take line and hook. Success was to land a fair-sized pike out of the river and have it for supper.

Normally we had gym or sports every day, usually under Mr Woodley, who was killed in the RAF early in the war. On rainy days we had a paper-chase cross-country run in minimum clothing, and then back into a forty-five-minute soak in a hot bathtub in the basement. After that we were free to go to the Railway Club in the attic or to the fug in the house common room – I was in Dorset.

On Sunday mornings we marched to the church, where occasionally the organ failed to function because someone managed to place carpet over the intake. A more enjoyable interlude was at the tuck shop. My allowance was only sixpence a week, so I concentrated on Fox's glacier mints. But others could afford chocolate bars and cream buns and the like. It was a place of joy and envy. Although we all wore the same uniforms with zipper jackets or/and sweaters, the differences in family finances were clearly evident at the tuck shop.

Money, of course, had to be kept in the pockets of our shorts. If a prefect caught you sauntering along the main corridor hands in pockets, you had to go to the matron, borrow needle and thread, and sew them

Outdoor PT, summer 1931

closed, usually for a week. As colds were common, what we did about blowing our noses I have forgotten – and probably just as well! While we were generally pretty healthy except for colds, I once had jaundice and ended up in the Sanatorium, then on the hill above the Headmaster's House. The place was run by a matron and nurses in blue or grey uniforms with starched headdresses that fell behind the shoulders.

The Physical Training movement began after the defeat of the French in 1870 and was taken up by Hitler as part of the revival of the German spirit of the superman. So at Bryanston, once a year as I recall, we had massed PT on the lawn at the back of the School. We performed in unison various standard 'gymnastic' routines, led by Mr Woodley, with music by the band led by Mr Rogers, the music master.

Between the Headmaster's House and the Sanatorium was a large sloping paddock in which on Parents' Day proficient boys demonstrated riding skills, especially putting a lance through a ring on a swivelling arm, rather like Don Quixote tilting at windmills.

Of course, we were really at Bryanston to learn, and that we did under the Dalton Plan. (Only in 2004 did I find out that the person behind Dalton was a woman.) We were given a very broad education so we could be aides to the gentlemen who would rule Great Britain and the Empire. This meant that we took geography, history, English, music, Latin, French, algebra, chemistry, physics and biology, as well as art, woodworking and metalworking.

Willi Soukop, an Austrian refugee who lived in the West Country, came as sculptor-in-residence for ten days a term. He was fun and I enjoyed the art. My first piece, a wild Grecian head, went to the School's art exhibition in London in 1939. My second was an alabaster squirrel which had a lovely warm colour after being rubbed with linseed oil and placed in the sun or with a lamp behind it. Soukop's studio was on the river side of the carpentry shop complex near the metalworking shop, where I attempted to build a working model of the then-new LMS diesel shunter. I don't recall who taught metalworking, but carpentry was my old Bembridgian teacher, Mr Muirhead. He showed us how to use hand tools, which I still have, and praised Joseph Marples's Sheffield steel chisels and the American Stanley company's hand-drills and planes. The more advanced classes got to build kayaks of wood and canvas for use on the Stour.

The rather austere Mr James taught geography and read either Hardy or Bulldog Drummond during our daily rest periods. We learnt all about the British Empire, well depicted in bright red on world maps – pretty impressive – and looked at the chart showing the location of all British merchant vessels on a certain day. Because trade was so important we had to learn all the British exports, to whom they went, and what those countries traded with us in return. We also learnt about the make-up of the populations, using labels that would be highly politically incorrect today!

Some mornings we had school assemblies with the masters in their academic robes where we heard various talks. There were several scholars of distinction on the staff: Aubrey de Selincourt, the noted translator, and Dr Brereton with his red, blue and ermine robe and fancy French doctoral hat. By the way, the exception to our shorts, also worn by some masters such as Tim Cobb, were the slacks allowed pupils from India. Other members of staff wore sports coats or suits.

The Hotchkiss School in Connecticut, to which I then went, was on a very different curriculum. By dint of trying and good teaching I left in June 1943 with a seventy per cent average; finally I was passing!

Bryanston gave me an excellent general education and has allowed me to be a generalist in history for the last sixty years.

From **Robin Higham***'s (Dorset '40) as yet untitled autobiography. Dr Higham was a pilot in the RAFVR. After obtaining his PhD, he taught military history at Kansas State University for thirty-five years, retiring in 1998.*

BGF Dodd, The Bearded Man *(alabaster), 1939*

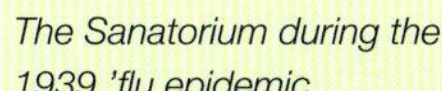

The Sanatorium during the 1939 'flu epidemic

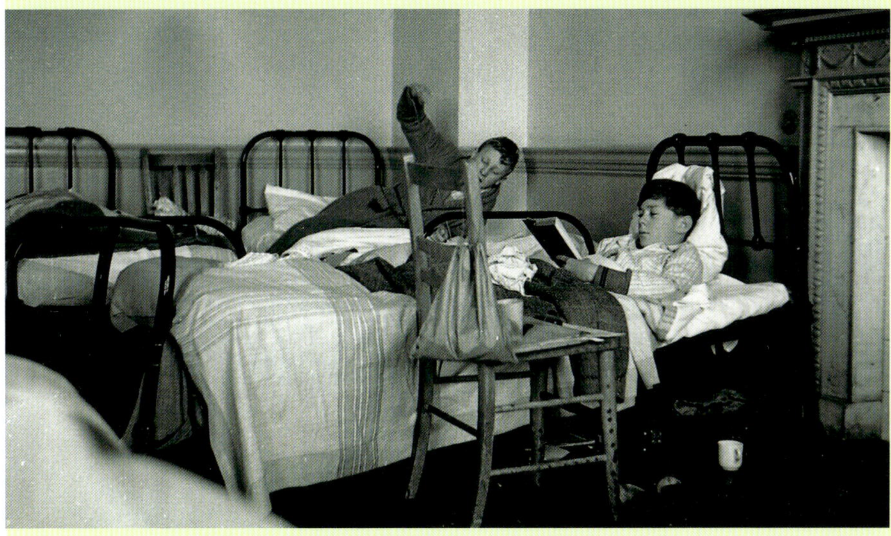

3

WARTIME 1939–45

At school in the Dorset countryside the long summer holidays were spent at work in harvest camps, a feature of the first few months of the war. The Autumn Term brought rationing, remembered for the small white coin-shaped butter pats, one per plate, which had apparently come as aid from our Polish allies. For seniors, including me, the School set up a platoon of the Local Defence Volunteer force, which reassured us that we could be part of the larger national effort. We only got five rifles of American design and four outside khaki battledresses. The idea was to keep watch for parachutists, and three boys spent each night on the hill behind the School and by morning looked distinctly dishevelled. Other boys on the school roof kept an all-round lookout for lights in the surrounding countryside which might indicate spies. On a fine summer night this was a most enjoyable duty, disturbed only now and then by the throbbing note of an enemy plane high up and heading north.

This was the period known as the 'phoney war', and we would eagerly mount our bikes and head off towards any reported aircraft crash. Three of us fooling about one day in the Hangings in a distant part of the grounds came across the crater where a Hurricane had plunged. All the brambles near it were hung with flecks of the pilot's flesh. Otherwise little seemed to have changed: mass air raids had not materialised and the Maginot Line was intact, and, as we all thought, impregnable. Living within twenty miles of the coast in a military zone, we soon had soldiers billeted on us, five in our games room plus two officers: first the Newfoundlanders, mainly Mic-Mac Indians, then the Reconnaissance Regiment and lastly the Norfolks. Their CO, a Major Colman of the mustard family, brought his wife, a Commandant in the WVS, and together they would inspect the troops drawn up in the village street. There was also a Captain Blood whose ancestor had stolen the Crown Jewels. Other images of the time were of joy-rides in Bren carriers careering down country lanes with old ladies clinging on to their hats. Also the ludicrous little anti-tank guns that appeared in the village, hardly capable of knocking over a Pomeranian Grenadier, far less a tank.

Nick Bartlett *(Connaught '40). Extracts from* Full Ahead Both, *an unpublished autobiography. Nick joined the navy in 1941, serving for nineteen years before retiring. He is now a painter.*

A master at LDV training

Right: The Old Coach House

LOCAL DEFENCE VOLUNTEERS

This is to certify that...F.N.O.BARTLETT...... has been a member of the Bryanston Section of D Platoon of this Company and has carried out his duties efficiently from May 31st to July 26th 1940.

[signature] Major

O.C. D Company Blandford (North),
Wimborne (Dorset) Battalion,
Local Defence Volunteers Force.

Blandford
July 1940.

A Fascist in the School

As the thirties ground to a close it was clear to anyone of 'progressive thinking' that the only hope for civilisation lay with Marxism and the Soviet Union. Opposing these were the dark forces of Fascism. This was certainly how most of us saw things at Bryanston, and when the Political Society invited a representative of the Communist Party to give a talk (an old Etonian, as I remember, who could nonetheless inveigh against Bond Street and other evils), he was greeted with cheers and clenched fists. When, by way of 'balance', a member of the British Union of Fascists was invited he was treated to so many boos and interruptions that Harry Greenleaves had to rise from his chair and point out that this was not the way we did things at Bryanston. All these feelings were crystallised in the Spanish Civil War then at its height: a classic example of 'Good fighting Evil'.

Dr Geoffrey Brereton took a sabbatical from French and Spanish lessons and went to Spain to see for himself, writing a book, *Inside Spain*, on his return, castigating Franco and the Insurgents. We were each urged to buy a tin of condensed milk with our pocket money (upper limit three shillings a week) and place it on the dado round the Centre Room. Soon there was a formidable display of tins, to be shipped, we understood, to Bilbao to succour the children of war-torn Republicans.

While this was going on we were becoming more and more aware of a resurgent Germany. Hitler's increasingly bellicose territorial demands went hand in hand with the Nazi persecution of the Jews culminating in the appalling *Kristallnacht* in 1938. Our dismay grew. Then suddenly Munich was upon us and we seemed to be staring into the barrel of a gun. Then all at once the tension crumbled. 'IT'S PEACE!' screamed the *Daily Mirror* in 2-inch headlines and we breathed again. But the shadow still hung over us. Air raid precautions became an increasingly important topic. Newly conscripted militiamen were seen marching through Blandford to the nearby army camp. When Hitler took over the whole of Czechoslovakia we felt the mantle of Lear about our shoulders. A jaunty sign appeared outside the Surgery. 'Gas Masks. Come in if you have a free period.' Inside, a self-important Mr Bramall sat you in a chair, selected a suitable gas mask, slipped it over your face, held a chart across the end and told you to breathe in. If the chart stuck fast you were now safe against chlorine, phosgene, tear gas, mustard gas and all the other agents of bronchial death we had been told about.

J 'Bobo' Lockhart (Connaught '40) believed passionately in the Nazi credo of Aryan supremacy

You might have imagined that in such times of heightened tension it would have been a brave soul who would champion Hitler, but we had such a boy in our midst. Lockhart was his name – 'Bobo' to all of us – and he believed passionately in the Nazi credo of Aryan supremacy. I was fond of Bobo. He was in my house and, even though I felt that everything he had to say about Fascism and Nazi ideology was rubbish, I never thought he was dangerous. It amused rather than infuriated us that he should send Hitler a greetings card on his birthday, the envelope dutifully and optimistically inscribed 'persönlich' in the top left-hand corner.

One summer's evening we enticed Bobo onto the steps outside the Centre Room. He needed little encouragement for we were urging him to make a speech. He stood on this platform while we grouped ourselves below expectantly. Then, with his face radiant, Bobo raised his right arm in a Nazi salute and declaimed: 'Members of the German Reichstag!' Which was as far as he got, for a cascade of water descended on him from an upper window. But Bobo didn't mind. He had had his moment – one glorious moment – when he had stood in the shining boots of the mighty German Reichskanzler.

I think Coade regarded the war, when it came, as an utterly tiresome nuisance. The entire school had to be blacked out, no mean feat when you think of the Main Hall. Fortunately many of the windows had shutters,

ATC training, 1941

which could be closed at dusk. Upstairs dormitories were converted into daytime classrooms. Ground-floor classrooms became dormitories – more building for the bombs to penetrate. Improvised shelters were made in the basement.

During the 'phoney war' Bobo continued to extol the Germans. I was put in charge of the telephone exchange in the Porter's Office when the porter was off duty. My job, and that of those under me, was to keep the exchange working so that any air raid warning could be received, acted upon where necessary, and passed on down the line to other posts. A side effect of this was that one could (quite illegally) listen in to conversations. It was thus, just after Dunkirk, one Sunday afternoon, when I put through a call from Ronald King to Paul (Peanut) Rogers, that I overheard these words: 'Paul, I've got bad news for you. All our aliens are going to be interned.'

It would have been too much to hope that Bobo would have escaped the net. He had made no secret of his membership of the British Union of Fascists and when Sir Oswald Mosley was swept up under Regulation 18B, so was Bobo. I wrote to him and got a letter back from him on prison notepaper. It was rather sad: 'I can't tell you how much your letter meant to me,' he wrote. He went on to say: 'While I've been here I've had many talks with the Leader [Mosley]. He makes it clear that in time of

Taking a rest in a slot trench, 1940

IN MEMORIAM

Donald Leven
Bryanston 1936—40

To the memory of Donald Leven, Pilot Officer, R.A.F.V.R., killed in a flying accident over the North Sea, June 14, 1943.

You left us not a month ago.
You looked an airman, fit and so
Young, yet undoubtedly a man.
We said: Well, write us when you can.
And as the car increased its pace,
I wondered why you turned your face.

On Saturday the letter came.
The words were blurred, I read your name.
Grangemouth . . . the morning's first patrol,
Two planes which touched and lost control.
And you, wing-forward of the sky,
Dived from the wheeling pack to die,
Eager as years ago in play
To be the first to break away.

There is a bleakness of the mind
Which cannot bear to be resigned.
There is a rigour of the heart
Which keeps the best of friends apart.
And silence, self-imposed would fain
Relive a fairer past again.

33

Saga, *Summer 1943*

war our duty to our country is to fight the enemy whoever he may be when he threatens our shores, and that is what I want to do.' Not long afterwards I was stopped by the headmaster in the Main Hall. 'John,' he said, 'I've just had a letter from the Governor of Wandsworth Gaol. He says Lockhart has been found writing a letter to you and wants to know if you have the same political views. I've told him that although you were friends with Lockhart you were opposed to everything he believed.' Evidently this satisfied the Governor, who had perhaps been wondering whether I should have joined Bobo in the next cell, but in those days of widespread febrile suspicion – had not SS men dressed as priests hiding sub-machine guns under their soutanes been parachuted behind the lines in Belgium? – I've no doubt that I went down on a list somewhere as a possible subversive.

Meanwhile air raid warnings were starting to come through. I slept in the Bursar's Office off the Outer Hall in a bunk bed. I enjoyed it there. I could read with the light on when all the other dormitories had lights out. All I had to do was answer the phone when it rang and then ring through to three other numbers. The messages were succinct. 'Air Raid Warning Yellow' meant an alert. 'Red' was the real thing, 'Green' the All Clear. The first time a 'Red' came through I sounded the bells and the whole school trooped down to the shelters. I manned the exchange and waited for the 'Green'. But no bombs fell and it was quickly decided that at the next 'Red' there should be no more disturbance of sleep unless a bomb actually fell – which might have been too late! Warnings continued to come through nearly every night, but never a bomb fell. Then, one night, as if to emphasise the perfidy of the Germans, an enemy aircraft jettisoned one on the playing fields when there *wasn't* a warning!

Eventually I was taken off telephone duty. Talking to Sister Benwell of the Sanatorium, a dragon of a woman, I proudly mentioned that I had been woken up three times the night before. This was unwise. 'I'm not having that!' she declared. 'It's bad for your health!' So the whole system was scrapped as far as Bryanston was concerned. Air raid warnings – false prophets that they were – counted for nothing by then. Shortly after that I left and went to fight for King and Country, and in the services I found the same casual attitude towards potential dangers reproduced and enhanced. But all that's another story.

John Temple-Smith *(Connaught '42) spent several years in the RAF and then spent his working life in the film industry.*

Two refugees' stories

My parents were liberal German Jews living in Berlin. My father had been a judge and, as he had not been in the army in the First World War, lost his job immediately after Hitler came to power in 1933. He devoted his time from then on to organisations helping victims of the Nazi regime in as many ways as possible. This included founding and setting up two schools for children who had to leave the state system – my brother and me included. One was roughly equivalent to a comprehensive and the other a grammar school.

After the *Kristallnacht* in November 1938 my parents tried to find a way for me to leave Germany. Arrangements were finally made with the aid of a German lady who, at great risk to herself and working together with an amazing lady called Mrs Atkinson in England, managed to arrange for about sixty people to emigrate. I was twelve years old and was the only member of my immediate family to get out (and, as a result, the only one to survive – all the others were 'deported to the east' and perished in Auschwitz as far as is known). Mrs Atkinson had had a son at Bryanston and she somehow arranged a place for me. This was initiated when I was still in Germany. Before coming to Bryanston, as I was still too young, she arranged for me to go to another school, so that between when I came over in August 1939 and my arrival at Bryanston a year later my English improved considerably.

The Refugee, *by D Barker*

Bryanston was for me a totally different world. Initially I went into Junior House where Mr Wigram was the housemaster and also my tutor. Whilst everyone was very helpful and could appreciate my language difficulties, I felt that they could not understand how I could have been born without knowing the rules of rugby and cricket!

After I transferred to Connaught Don Potter became my tutor. I believe I am the only Old Bryanstonian to have had this privilege. It was obviously arranged because of my special circumstances and turned out to be very good choice – his instinctive and practical approach was of great help to me. I also had the good fortune to be taught by many of the other great teachers who were at Bryanston during the war years.

Following the progress of the war, I was always willing the liberation of Europe to move faster, in the hope of stopping the Nazis from doing what they were doing. My emotion at the sight of the sky over Bryanston filled with aircraft from horizon to horizon and Blandford blocked by a continuous stream of military traffic on D-Day is something that I can never adequately describe or forget.

One, more personal, experience was my sixteenth birthday, when under the law, as a refugee from Germany, I became officially classified as an enemy alien. I had to be interviewed by the local police and the Inspector at Blandford police station took the opportunity to put on what I assume was his best dress uniform to interview me in what was at the time the Outer Hall. I have never seen another policeman in a similar grand uniform – not even at the Queen's coronation! Perhaps his father had been a policeman and the uniform belonged to him. I, of course, was in my Bryanston shorts.

King George VI pays a visit to the Harvest Camp in 1940

Bryanston proved unexpectedly useful when I applied for naturalisation. I was interviewed by a lady at the Home Office in Whitehall who, when she heard that I had been educated at an English public school, concluded that no further proof was required to decide that I was a suitable person to be given British nationality. This was before the Cambridge-educated spies were exposed.

After leaving Bryanston I had to 'fend for myself' – and my Bryanston education enabled me to continue studying in evening classes until I eventually became a chartered mechanical engineer.

***Ernst (Mic) Michaelis** (Connaught '45) worked for many years as a mechanical engineer and is still publishing articles and patenting new applications.*

It was 4 o'clock in the morning on the night of 9th/10th November 1938 that Nazi stormtroopers rampaged through our apartment in the Düsseldorf suburb of Oberkassel and left it in a sorry state. Valuable paintings were cut up with sabres and thrown out of the windows, a number of paintings stolen, old crockery and furniture wantonly destroyed. It was part of the pogrom known subsequently as the *Kristallnacht*. At that point it was clear there was no future for us in Germany and that we had to emigrate. I was lucky enough to find a place at the preparatory school, Durnford, in Langton Matravers in Dorset. I left Germany on 5th March 1939. My parents just made it, arriving in Harwich by night boat from the Hook of Holland on the morning of 1st September 1939, the day Hitler attacked Poland!

At Durnford I was started off immediately with two languages, namely French and Latin. This was a bit of a culture shock for I had only done one year's English and my knowledge of the language was, at best, scanty. In Germany I had been at the local elementary school where I was happy and had a good teacher who taught me the 'Three Rs'. Unfortunately, the discriminatory Nuremberg laws forced me to leave that school. I then spent one year in the local Jewish school which was so regulated by the Nazi authorities that I learned very little. In April 1937 I passed an examination to go direct from the third to the fifth class and obtained a place in the local Comenius Gymnasium which was allowed to take me as there were fewer than two per cent Jews in the school.

By the autumn of 1941 I had reached Common Entrance standard and after an interview with TF Coade, I came to Bryanston in the spring of 1942. JB Morris (JBM), my housemaster, made me feel at home straight away and I played hockey and boxed for the school in my first term.

My main problem, which my Latin master, Tim Cobb (THC), recognised straight away, was language. This would probably not have been so marked had I not been given both French and Latin from the start. As THC correctly put in my first report, 'he gives the impression that he is still grappling with two languages'.

My first English master was Mr Eric Bramall, from whom we learned early on that we could not know everything but who showed us where we could find what we were looking for, namely in reference books and encyclopaedias. History, my favourite subject, was taught by the impressive Teresa Hicks-Bolton who had a gift of making her lessons a fascinating experience. In

English we had Wilfrid Cowley (WSHC) to guide us through School Certificate. *Macbeth* was on the syllabus. I shall never forget when we came across the phase 'we have willing dames enough'. There was a chuckle and WSHC turned round to the person reading who blushed. WHSC, in his humorous manner, said, 'Come on, boy, what does it mean? You know perfectly well it means that there are plenty of ladies willing to pop into bed with him for a night.' Relieved laughter in the class!

No mention of my time in the School would be complete without GV Morris (GVM). He taught modern languages and I had him in French, German and Spanish (in 'A'). At the beginning of each lesson he would enter the classroom, pull up his shorts (which he normally wore the whole year round) and start the lesson in a businesslike manner with such words as, 'gentlemen, one job for today…'.

I well remember the night of 5th/6th June 1944. In the neighbouring Tarrant Rushton airport a fleet of Halifaxes and Stirlings with gliders took off and in the early morning the planes returned without the gliders. We then knew that the invasion of Europe had started. At breakfast the head boy, the unforgettable Richard (Bunty) Hunter, announced before the first 'SHAEF' communiqué was issued that the German wireless had confirmed that the invasion had started.

My last term in the summer of 1945 was memorable for a number of other events. It saw the end of the war in Europe. VE Day was, of course, celebrated quite wildly in the School. For me it was, naturally, an emotional event and to this day I am reminded of it whenever I hear Elgar's *Enigma Variations,* which were played on the BBC that night.

I was very sorry when my Bryanston days were over. The School had given me an excellent start in life which enabled me after graduation to become a chartered accountant.

***Hugh Markus** (Hardy '45) worked for many years as an accountant both here and in Germany. He wrote* The History of the German Public Accounting Profession*, which is published both in English and in German.*

A world apart

Behind the grand front entrance, which was scarcely ever used, the Main Hall always smelt of floor polish. Here the senior boys, the prefects and monitors, myself eventually among them, were posted at strategic corners to stare at the feet of the passing crowd, on watch to ticket anyone whose shoes were not properly polished. The grand rooms off the Main Hall served as library, assembly and headmaster's study. Round the corner in the wings, and upstairs, were dormitories and classrooms. In the warrens of the attic, the senior boys shared studies.

Bryanston was part traditional English public school and, with the Dalton Plan, part American progressive education. But there was also German influence through Kurt Hahn, who had founded the Schule Schloss Salem in 1920, dedicated to an ideal of strenuous, healthful, outdoor education. From here came our school uniform – blue-grey flannel shorts and open-necked shirts, summer and winter alike – and Pioneering. Kurt Hahn, I think, might have had something more in mind, but for us, Pioneering was repairing the footpath, which led from the School along the river to the gatekeeper's lodge, endlessly pounding chalk and cinders with a metal pole; clearing brush and chopping trees in the woods; building a hut for sports equipment; or bookbinding. I spent many Pioneering afternoons taking apart damaged books from the school library, sewing them back together again, trimming the edges and gluing them into fresh covers. It was not much, by way of exercise, but I loved the craft of remaking books:

Bookbinding was one of many Pioneering activities

During the average stay of a Bryanston boy some remarkable things occur.

The school bells, for instance, ring for six days.

One walks from Paris to Moscow, nearly two thousand miles, going to and from classes; one takes a month to do it.

A scientist walks from Blandford to Glasgow going up to the Labs., and everyone walks to Portsmouth on their way to the gym.

Apart from this one walks from El Alamein to Tripoli; for one goes two hundred and ten miles round the morning walk, seventy miles from one's dormitory to breakfast, a hundred and forty seven miles in the dining hall itself and four hundred and forty seven miles to games.

Six days are spent listening to notices. We are at church for five days and walk a hundred and forty miles in getting there. Prayers occupy a week and pioneer parade three days.

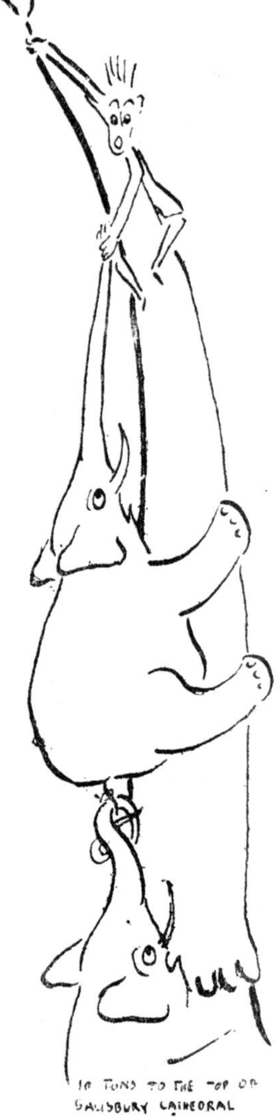

Climbing from the bottom of the school to the top only once a day, involves climbing twice the height of Mount Everest: and the same amount of work as taking a load of ten tons to the top of the spire of Salisbury cathedral.

However one also spends over a year in bed, dressing and undressing a total of seven thousand times.

G.T.S.

34

Saga, *Autumn 1943*

dissecting their anatomy, choosing patterned papers to match the cloth spine and corner pieces, pasting them all together, with the title neatly lettered on the spine, and so to hold in hand, finally, a trim, solid, elegantly dressed volume.

From Kurt Hahn, too, came cold baths and morning walks. Every day, before breakfast, you had to plunge into a cold bath. A prefect would sit beside the tub, ticking off names, as each boy, in turn, slunk down, sloshed the water up to his chin, and leapt out as fast as he could. Then you had to take a walk around the school driveway, running a stretch between two posts marked with red and green circles, and here too your name was ticked off by a prefect. We arrived at breakfast very wide awake, but by the time we were done with our powdered scrambled egg and porridge, I was sleepy again.

No one seems to have considered whether having fifteen or more boys share the same bath each morning might spread infection. And infection was rife – especially athlete's foot and jock itch. We were rigorously inspected for jock itch by the school nurse at the beginning of each term, lining up with our trousers down, while she peered at each crotch with a torch. We suffered from impetigo, too, which typically covered one's face with running sores and yellowish crusts. The only cure was to paint them with gentian violet, a lovely name for a deep purple dye, beautiful anywhere but in big blotches on cheeks, nose and forehead. I spent two weeks in the school sanatorium once with impetigo, filling the time with long walks through the countryside. Since it was easy to forget the vivid appearance of suppurating decay I presented to others, I was puzzled by the air of nervous constraint with which passers-by returned my greeting.

Bryanston's incongruous mixture of traditional public school and eclectic progressive ideas was reflected in the eccentricity of its headmaster, Thor Coade, who never seemed quite able to take it all seriously. He cultivated a disconcerting vagueness of manner – the result, some said, of shell shock in the First World War – by which he seemed to mock his own role. Once, for instance, after he had delivered to the assembled school a stern lecture on the wickedness of stealing, however small the amount, he sloped off the platform with a wave of the hand, saying 'I'm not talking *entirely* with my tongue in my cheek', puckishly undermining the whole performance. This self-deflation was, perhaps, an oblique defence against his wife's intensity. She encouraged prayer meetings on the terrace for selected

senior boys, urging them on their spiritual journey. Visiting the School once, on return from my military service, she asked me, over tea and biscuits, 'And was it an Enrichment, an Enhancement?'

The headmaster's passion was drama. He liked to act, and each year the staff would put on a play, such as JM Barrie's *The Admirable Crichton*, where he took the leading part. He liked to read aloud, too, in school assembly – the whole of Richard Llewellyn's novel, *How Green Was My Valley*, delivered in a rich Welsh accent. Most of all, he produced plays, gathering talent from every age group for Shakespeare or TS Eliot's *Murder in The Cathedral*. I disappointed him, as the young Macduff in *Macbeth.* 'As birds do, mother', the child says, when she asks him how he will live after his father's death. But try as I might, I could not get the emphasis to his satisfaction. We went over it again and again, as I posed on the rug in his study. He gave up, finally, grumbling 'you're not as good as I thought you were'. He might mock his role as headmaster, but he took acting very seriously; and he drew out some extraordinary performances.

The annual play became the theme for the skit on the school year, written and produced by Wilfrid Cowley, one of our English masters ('Omlet, or *Hamlet* in an eggshell', for instance), and they were very funny. Wifrid Cowley was our connection to the world of literary celebrity, a friend of WH Auden and Christopher Isherwood, of famous actors and actresses, who would visit the School, occasionally. His wit covered a bitterness, I believe, at the failure of his own literary ambitions. He had written an unpublished novel, he told me once, and wondered whether he should go back to try to revise it 'like a dog returning to its vomit'. There was a crispness to his delivery, a spring of coiled violence, in contrast to the mellow musicality of our other English teacher, Aubrey de Selincourt, whose novels – for children – *had* been published. Why was Prospero angry with Caliban? he asked us once, studying *The Tempest*. I muttered something about Caliban trying to interfere with Miranda. 'Why not use a stronger word?' he said: 'Rape,' rolling it off his tongue like gunshot.

As a progressive school, Bryanston did not countenance physical punishment. The standard punishment was to run from the School to the Porter's Lodge at the gates of the grounds and back again, a distance of two miles – timed at one end by a prefect and by the porter at the other. Serious offences were punished by a form of ostracism. The offender had to wear a white shirt, and was supposed to be shunned by the rest of us – to whom, of course, he was more often a hero. For drinking and sodomy you were liable to be expelled; and homosexuality was a constant, titillating undercurrent of gossip.

The School reproduced in miniature (and as much in rumour as in fact) the whole range of sexual relationships: faithful couples, passionate romances, orgies, coquettes, prostitutes. We knew, or thought we knew, which masters were inclined that way, and which were not – although none, I believe, ever abused a student. Some of the youngest boys, who had not yet reached puberty, had a feminine beauty that made them favourites of the seniors, seventeen- and eighteen-year-olds, cooped up for three quarters of the year in an almost exclusively male society. Isolated in its grounds, isolated, too, by the war, Bryanston was a sometimes morbidly introverted community. Trivial mishaps, like a blot on the Library register, could become blown up into major crimes; and the sexual experiments of frustrated teenagers became awful perversions, threatening expulsion.

The school employed a consulting psychologist, a Freudian refugee from Austria, who wrote nostalgically of the Vienna of the Hapsburg Empire, when young gentlemen learned about sex with the help of amiable hat shop girls. But there were no hat shops or hat shop girls in Blandford, the town outside our gates: the young women were all in the ATS, the WRAAF, the WRENS or the Land Army. Only once did I get to visit the nearest girls' boarding school, where the headmaster took his production of *Hamlet*. As the third player, I spent almost the whole afternoon in the lounge which served as the green room, entertained with cocoa and cookies by a succession of friendly young women, and for once I was glad that my acting career had not flourished.

It had begun well. In my first term at Bryanston, when I was turning thirteen, I played Androcles in our class production of Bernard Shaw's *Androcles and the Lion* – the performance that had misled the headmaster as to my talent. In that first term were some of the happiest months of my life. My class teacher, the producer of *Androcles*, became my hero, my ideal father – sophisticated, cultured, witty, and surely kind to me. He played us jazz records in his study, and talked to me as if I were grown up – about art, philosophy, life – opening everything to questions and possibilities in a flood of new ideas. His name was Michael Morgan. But at the end of the first term he was called up, to become an intelligence officer in some very secret code-breaking unit. So was the biology master, whom I especially liked. And the Austrian sculpture teacher, Willi Soukup, who delighted us with his autobiographical tales, delivered in a thick accent, was detained as an enemy alien and sent to work on the land. 'Ven I vas born,' he told us once, 'I vas covered vis long black hairs, and I vas dead.' Hard to beat, as the opening for an autobiography, even if it implies a very short one.

Despite the ration books we handed in at the beginning of each term, despite the household chores and the newspapers in the Library with their arrow-studded maps of contending armies, and aerial photographs of appalling destruction, the war intruded very little into our lives. We debated post-war reconstruction – social security and a national health service, an end to privilege. We were even ready to vote for the abolition of elite schools like our own. But we were conscious, I think, and made to be conscious, that we were to be leaders, by virtue of that privileged education, and the responsibility for the future of the country lay on our shoulders.

The war intruded directly only in odd, disconnected incidents. A boy came to sleep in our dormitory – a Polish refugee – and I was asked to befriend him. Somehow he had walked across Europe and found his way to England, so the rumour went. But he spoke too little English to allow us to find out much about him. He wet his bed, and kept a pistol under his pillow. With the callousness of children towards the strange and uncouth, we disliked him. Only the sky held the drama of conflict. Once, down by the river, I saw a dogfight overhead, the vapour trails swooping and twisting in the blue of a summer sky. We were supposed to take cover when there was aerial combat, but I lingered to watch, entranced by the beauty of it. The sky battles dropped their souvenirs, too: some of the boys collected pieces of bombs and wreckage from the woods. One had, as his prize possession, part of a German airman's boot, with a patch of skin still sticking to it.

Aubrey de Selincourt read Wordsworth as overhead planes flew to combat in France

On a summer morning in 1944, Aubrey de Selincourt took our English class out onto the lawn below the terrace, to enjoy the early June sunshine. As we sat on the grass, listening to him read Wordsworth in his beautiful voice, aircraft towing strings of gliders emerged over the school's grey roof – hundreds of them, rank after rank, filling the sky. We abandoned the lesson, and he began to tell us of his own experiences in the First World War. This slight, gentle, almost feminine man, who wrote stories for children about sailing, and essays on cricket, had been a fighter pilot, it turned out – surely one of the most dangerous and daring of all combat roles. He had never expected to come out of the war alive, he said. We see our teachers every day, I thought, we live with them, and we know so little about them. By the end of the lesson period, the sky was as empty and blue as a drowsy Dorset summer day could be.

Peter Marris *(Salisbury '45), after the RAF and university, spent two years in the Colonial Service in Kenya before taking up a career in social research and teaching in London, Africa and the United States. He has published many sociological studies and a novel.*

The Roll of Honour, in the centre of the Upper Terrace

War stories

The first thing to be understood about Bryanston 1939–45 is that to those of us who were there it was not a special phase. It was the norm. Of course some of us had brothers or fathers who were killed or were POWs, and Thor Coade would read out the Roll of Honour at Sunday services. But the School was our world and the only one that we knew.

I arrived at Port Regis Prep School in 1941. Port Regis was then housed in the wing of the School that had been Hardy House. We had no particular contact with the big school. Our world was that of the traditionally circumscribed prep school, but I remember one or two exciting occasions when we were all summoned out of bed by the alarm bells to go down to the school chapel in the basement which was our allotted air raid shelter. Much to our disappointment no air raids ensued.

Entry into Bryanston from Port Regis was eased of course by the fact that you knew the physical geography of the buildings, but I still felt the impersonal coldness of a great public school. I had left behind the comfortable world of the Port Regis matrons, the Misses Chetham and Heelas, for a broader world of boys and schoolmasters. The number of boys at Bryanston during the war was only between 200 and 300, and I found myself in an amalgamated house, Dorset and Portman, ably headed by Wilf Cowley. Apart from being housemaster he taught English and was the school librarian. He ran the Library with a remarkably liberal and catholic taste, but managed schoolboy behaviour with a rod of iron. If you were talking or in any way causing a disturbance he descended upon you with clipped and venomous tones, 'Get out of my Library!' And you did.

Another master, William Macnae (unfit for war service, owing to his chronic short sight), taught biology and took those of us who needed them for remedial exercises. I had a hollow back and fallen arches and so came into his remit. He always wore a kilt and as we conducted our exercises on the gym floor I can remember that we all tried to look under his kilt as he came our way since we were all curious as to what we might see. Possibly his greatest pragmatic influence on our lives was in biology classes. There came a point

Auxiliary fire drill, 1940

when he began to expound the mysteries of reproduction, and he began with male sperm and their swimming capacities for getting at and fertilising the female egg.

'Now Brown, go in there,' he said, indicating his office, 'go in there, take this test tube and get some sperm.' Brown disappeared into the office, but came back after a short while and said: 'Please, sir, where shall I find them?' 'Och! don't be a fool, laddie, ye know perfectly well. Go in there and make some, and we'll all see what ye are made of under the microscope!' It may be as a result of this pragmatic teaching that Macnae left Bryanston and took up a post as biology and nature conservancy officer on Tristan da Cunha.

The routine of work for School Certificate ran smoothly enough. Our schoolmasters were those who were unfit for military service, although we did not realise that at the time, and a number of lady teachers filled the gaps in the staff. I remember Miss Wilson for chemistry, whose corsets were hoisted to the flagpole on VE Day. And Miss Teresa Hicks-Bolton who took us for history. She was a devout Catholic and intensely emotional, five foot high with a mop of black hair and large dark-framed glasses.

Among games activities was the alternative of Pioneering. I learned how to handle an axe and fell unwanted timber, a skill which in retirement I have passed on to a young Scot on the Isle of Mull. But the greatest development in Pioneering was caused by the advent of Miss Procter as Estate Steward. Bryanston, like all well-run country houses, possessed a vast walled garden as well as a formidable array of greenhouses, all derelict. Miss Procter's lateral thinking married the potential of walled garden and greenhouses to a captive labour force of Pioneers.

The result was that in little over a year the School's diet was transformed from overcooked cabbage into a menu that included a variety of vegetables and salad. Miss Procter herself was a small but commanding presence built in the Victorian mould. When she lectured to the School on what she was trying to achieve, she appeared, as she was always dressed, in jodhpurs, shirt and tie. She was like others of the female staff, one of those grand Victorian ladies who came out of retirement to do their bit for the War Effort, and true to their ethic they gracefully withdrew when the men were demobbed and returned to school-mastering.

Once a term our turn came round for Kitchen Duty. You were wakened at about 4.30am to report at 5am in the kitchen to help get school breakfast on the table. The Dining Room was laid out by houses. Each house had about three long tables with wooden benches, and High Table for the masters was at one end of the room. We all stood when the head boy said grace (in Latin). Our duty consisted in the laying of tables; the carrying of as many bowls of porridge as you could manage, ladled out by the chef from a steaming cauldron; the collecting and returning of plates to the washing machine, which worked in perpetual movement; the stacking of clean, boiling hot plates, returning the half-washed plates to the beginning end of the machine; and so on. After your own breakfast, you serviced the spud-bashing machine. This was a large cylindrical affair into which we fed unwashed unpeeled potatoes as necessary. Apart from feeding the machine, it was our job to take out potatoes and remove the 'eyes' with a potato corer. Potatoes in those days were a happy field of food for a whole host of eager predators. There were no agro-chemicals to stop the pests. The potato machine was a monster which never stopped spinning. The sides of it were abrasive and in our efforts to grab a potato we almost always finished with abraded knuckles. It was not a popular part of Kitchen Day.

This cave by the river may have been used to store the magnesium flares

On Sundays we were allowed out for bicycle expeditions. We had the luxury that there was next to no traffic on the roads because private cars had no petrol ration. It was possible to do the return trip to Lulworth Cove, and have your sandwich lunch on the beach, and a swim. The swim was risky since bathing without supervision was, sensibly, not permitted, but if you had cycled twenty-two miles on a hot day, school rules seemed far away and remote in comparison to the immediate temptation of a dip in the cool blue waters of Lulworth.

For some there was an extra dimension to Sunday expeditions, from 1942–44. This was the increasing use of the countryside for mock assault courses and other military purposes. One regular challenge was to get to the butts on Crichel Down. The butts were a pair of earth ramparts about 20 feet high and about 20 to 30 yards long, and they were used as targets by Hawker Hurricanes. Crichel Down was guarded by a unit of the RAF whose job it was to raise red flags at practice time and monitor results. It also became their job to hunt down Bryanstonians in search of cartridge cases and warheads. You had to crawl and wriggle across the Down in order not to be seen. And I remember once the added pleasure of wriggling past a nest of skylark eggs.

On a cycling expedition towards Bulbarrow, a friend and I discovered a deserted army hut which still contained a cast-iron stove. It was at the end of a dirt track and made the ideal spot to shelter from the rain, and we could light the stove for toasting our spam sandwiches. Spam and peanut butter were welcome additions to our wartime diet, and we must have owed them to the advent of American aid. Peanut butter, which eked out our meagre jam ration, was rapidly re-christened 'peanus fucker' by a wit in an enthusiastic burst of cockney rhyming slang.

However, to return to our deserted hut, we found on a second or third visit that the hut was connected by a wiring system and fuses to two large circles of about 100 feet in diameter, each made up of little bags some 2 inches long by an inch. A lot of these bags were burnt out, but many others, probably as a result of rain, were still intact. We collected up as many as we could and cycled back, seeing six red deer on the way. We stored our loot in a tiny cave we knew of at water level in the Hangings. On a subsequent Sunday we built a fire in our cave and put two or three bags on the fire. Nothing happened, as no doubt the bags were too damp. I put in a thumb and forefinger to turn over a bag and the result was a spectacular magnesium flare and a blister of impressive proportions on my thumb. I put it in the river to cool the pain and reported to matron at surgery saying that I had burnt it making a bonfire. She appeared somewhat sceptical but treated the wound in routine fashion and made no special report to my housemaster. I don't think we understood at the time what our hut and magnesium flares were for, but with hindsight, I suppose we had found an abandoned practice dropping zone for agents and equipment destined for occupied Europe.

This was the first of many expeditions to assault-course sites in the year leading up to D-Day. The American ranges were much more productive than the British ones, where there must have been fatigue duty squads who went over the sites cleaning up anything that might be dangerous, although I did once find a PIAT (Projectile Infantry Anti-Tank) shell that had not exploded. The Americans by contrast were blissfully profligate in all their armaments. By the end of 1944, I had acquired several bazooka shells (the American Infantry anti-tank weapon), which I took to pieces and rendered safe; an American hand grenade, which had failed to explode and which I made safe, and quantities of abandoned small arms ammunition.

In retrospect I suppose that these extra-curricular activities with wartime munitions might be paralleled with drugs and alcohol. I do not remember that we ever had much to do with alcohol or smoking, and drugs were simply unknown. We occasionally bought a packet of Woodbines because it was grown up to smoke, and there were still Dorset cider pubs that would sell you a half pint of rough cider without remarking on your under-age Bryanston shorts! But we got our 'highs' by playing with munitions and explosives where later generations have taken to drugs.

All this fun ended just before D-Day when the skies were full of aircraft towing gliders away out of sight. The other great change was in the countryside. For the space of a year, 1943–44, every wood and coppice was full of camouflaged vehicles and tented troops. In two days in June 1944 the countryside emptied. I particularly remember a mobile US boot repair unit which was stationed in the stable buildings near the Portman Chapel. I often wondered how they fared in the invasion.

David Winfield *(Portman '48) divided his time between Byzantine studies and conservation and has published extensively in both these areas.*

4

POST-WAR YEARS 1945–63

44 Schooldays vignettes

The first thing that strikes me now, but which probably did not sink in until several years – perhaps even decades – after leaving, was what a civilised place Bryanston was compared with what came afterwards. 'Afterwards' in my case means from 1946 – rather a long stretch really.

Wearing shorts again after two or three years of 'long trousers' previously at a grammar school certainly felt very odd, almost regressive. This may be why I remember an often-told anecdote about Timothy Cobb, a senior master, who had been at the school since 1932 and always wore shorts and smoked a pipe (like Monsieur Hulot, I thought later). A very new boy (not me)

The Art Room, 1950s

is said to have approached a school prefect and asked quietly about Cobb: 'Please Sir, is that a boy?'

The grounds always seemed to me to be enormous, whether one was conscious of them during punishment runs from the big house to the front gates, or rowing the full course on the River Stour. The latter had a particularly sharp bend during the upper half of the course, sharp enough for bow side to have to paddle light for a few strokes while stroke side pulled the eight around. This was where we hoped our opponents would be unprepared and hit the bank. Both eights would then appear in line ahead for the second half of the race, where spectators could see them without risk of falling in.

Why should I remember games better than learning? In my later years at Bryanston the opportunity to write essays of unlimited length became enormously stimulating. It was amazing what we were able to get away with, provided we did it hard enough. Our outstanding English master was Aubrey de Selincourt, who used to read aloud to us very well. One of my essays for him began 'Chaucer is entirely new to me', of which he approved. I dropped far too many subjects in order to read what I liked, and while this certainly encouraged my imagination it left me somewhat short of variety in other areas of expertise, a point realised when I finally squeaked into Oxford by taking special papers at the college which admitted me. But Bryanston did teach me to find things out for myself, which later became enormously useful when I was in a position of having to teach fairly arcane subjects at short notice.

Then there was the Art Room. This was under the kindly and imaginative supervision of Elizabeth Muntz, an excellent sculptor who had studied with Frank Dobson, so there was a strong Bloomsbury influence. This was enhanced further by the best young painter in the School, my contemporary Anthony Fry (a much younger cousin of Roger Fry). There was also a close link with the art-orientated prep school, The Downs; we had several good painters from there, some of whom went on to Camberwell School of Art, which was at that time possibly the best art school in London.

The headmaster, Thorold Coade, known as 'Thor', was, of course, held in awe. He was in fact very kind, but he could not stand students who got bored – 'DON'T YAWN!' he once shouted at a student in his religion class, 'it interferes with your hearing.' I painted a mural of the Nativity for the Chapel. As I was finishing it, to my embarrassment, Mrs Coade came and sat beside me. She told me she saw auras of light round the three

The Famine Queue.

wise men and hadn't I noticed a similar phenomenon round the shoulders of Thor when his back was turned? I hadn't.

When Thor felt inspired with a new idea or ideal, the whole school had to fall in with it. Before the war the School had been strongly pacifist, but after Dunkirk many boys joined the ATC (Air Training Corps) unless they could declare themselves conscientious objectors.

In retrospect, it was probably a disaster that there were no girls at the School. The school dances were a nightmare (and I was subsequently told by a reliable source that the situation at Sherborne School for Girls, a near neighbour, was just as bad).

The School Train down from London will surely be missed. This consisted of two specially reserved and rather rowdy coaches from Waterloo at the beginning of each term, whence we transferred at Templecombe Junction to the Somerset and Dorset line (otherwise known as the 'Slow and Dirty') for Blandford. One late winter afternoon, when the London train stopped at an earlier station in pitch dark – it must have been Gillingham – an enterprising boy with a deep voice shouted 'Temple COOOMBE', and everybody started to get off, struggling with their luggage.

I suppose that what stayed clearest in the memories of a youth who was at Bryanston during his most impressionable years was not any conscious sense of character forming, but rather a series of visual vignettes, usually dormant but occasionally resurfacing at significant points of self-discovery, both of himself and of the outside world.

One thing I particularly remember learning from Bryanston, however odd or even trivial this may seem these days, was a sense of politeness – not in the sense of affected manners, but simply personal consideration, especially for strangers. And a sense of guilt if this is not exercised.

Bruce Laughton *(Dorset '45) is a writer and Professor Emeritus of Art History at Queen's University, Kingston, Ontario.*

Radio plays and spam fritters

During my first year at Bryanston, I was the cause of anxious letters to my parents from housemaster, Tim Cobb, and tutor, Joyce Wilson. I was horribly homesick – an experience made worse by not knowing where the upstairs lavatories were located and being frightened to ask. In the night, when called (and it was most nights) I had to make my way down to the known basement lavatories and back. Those floors were horribly cold in the middle of the night. On free afternoons, I would amble over Bryanston Hill and feel totally lost and miserable. One day, whilst I was so engaged, what can only be described as a warm flash of light surrounded

DR Wigram skiing, and Brian Falk's letters home

Today we have the art classes and today we had to draw the skull. I did it in two different positions. I also did a cartoon of Mr Bramall taking a photo of Mr Wigram on skies. Here is a reproduction. As a matter of fact it is a very bad reproduction

Thursday
Today the boiler bust or rather one of them did

Bryanston
Blandford
Dorset

Sunday

Dear Dad & Mum
I am so looking forward to half term. I will come down to the Crown after breakfast on Saturday and I will bring you a tin of, well wait & see! It is not sugar so don't get too excited.
Today I had to report to the housecaptain in games clothes then in pioneer clothes and then again in games clothes just for checking a moniter. We have now got

a new set of ~~rules of~~ punishments. If we leave a towel on the floor in the changing room or any garment we are fined 2d and if we are caught walking on places out of bounds we are then fined sixpence. If we get three untidinesses we have to scrub the floor of the changing room for an hour. The trouble is that they have not abolished runs yet. I did two yesterday and I am now completely tired out.
Yesterday we saw a film called "The Iron Duke". It was a purely historical film but it was very

and overcame me. All my homesick worry, misery and fear dropped away. I still do not know what produced this wave of wonderful freedom from my sense of desolation; it was the first and only religious-type fervour I ever experienced. From that moment on, slowly, I began to enjoy Bryanston life.

My sports were hockey and rugger, but increasingly poor eyesight made playing difficult, and drove me from the first teams into the second and on to the spectator line. I had no inkling which of the two balls speeding towards me was the one to hit, hesitated and lost both.

My main interest, despite being a chemistry, physics and maths student, was the Art Room and there I spent

Dorset Senior Houseroom, March 1948, by Alexander Plunket Greene

many, many hobby hours. Doyen of the Art Room was Charles Handley-Read, an artist in his own right, who was responsible for gently directing my interest into the possibility of studying architecture after I had failed to gain entry to Cambridge to study electrical engineering, my father's choice.

I wrote and Alexander Plunket Greene and I illustrated a children's book, *Gobi*, about a battle between green- and blue-faced creatures, he taking the green, I the blue. Entirely politically incorrect in today's climate, the book still vastly intrigues the grandchildren. An Art Room craze created endless theatrical scene designs and their transformations modelled in upended shoe boxes with a proscenium cut-out. Francis Capener (later ordained into the Roman church) and I wrote two radio plays, *The Fulmar's Egg* and *Lord Nithsdale's Escape.* I recollect our fierce arguments choosing appropriate accompanying music. The BBC rejected both in a curt letter accusing us of using what they called a 'clumsy mechanism' – having two commentators-announcers, ironically now their common method of programme presentation.

VE Day saw us celebrating and (then thought a great wheeze, now rather tame) carrying Wilf Cowley's car into the Main Hall and dumping it in the corridor outside the Staff Room.

It seems extraordinary, at a time when the fate of the country was being determined, to be shown, as part of a Pioneering course, how to plant daffodils in drifts. Miss Chrystabel Procter, dressed in jaunty jodhpurs, showed us how you throw the bulbs over your shoulder, planting them where they fall so as to avoid the aesthetic dangers of planting in a regular pattern.

There was the triumph, still remembered so many years on, of a rugby dummy pass so complete that it deceived two opponents who rushed away on a tangent leaving the try line clear; and the disaster of *Macbeth* where, in charge of the parade of ghosts (cardboard heads on strings rising from behind a rock) I dropped the lot, to the chagrin of the headmaster, himself a vague and distant figure who ambled the corridors, hands in pockets smiling gently. Ernest Sackville-West came as author of a play titled *The Rescue* (a rewrite of the *Odyssey*) to see Coade's production. I had designed the costumes, mainly flowing cloaks of scarlet. A bedraggled crow tumbled out of a dinner jug of soup; it was just put on one side, the remainder of the soup hungrily consumed. Lofty, the chef, was blamed. In spite of post-war rations, the food was acceptable, sometimes good; I still consider spam fritters a luxury. Seeking to interest boys in home economics the housekeeper, Mrs Daykin, taught how to bake queens' cakes. I cannot remember making them since.

But these are small flashes of memory, the terms, the years simply slipped by, and then it was time to leave.

Brian Falk (Connaught '49) qualified as an architect and city planner. He was a partner in a large practice working both in the UK and in Africa. He then became a planning consultant and has now retired.

No. 4 Hardy Roof studies

A trio in the Hardy Roof

When we came together at the start of the Spring Term 1947 in the Junior House, Tigger Hoare (or TGH) was housemaster – a grey-haired, bespectacled man, who padded along rather than walked, with round shoulders and a stoop. Tigger exuded kindliness through twinkling eyes that did much to calm nervous new boys and anxious parents.

Brian and Nigel were new boys in spring 1947. Bill had arrived a term earlier and remembers the first night in Junior House. Everybody was settling down amongst the chaos of unpacked trunks and overnight cases – and feeling a little apprehensive and somewhat homesick amidst new faces and surroundings. Just before 'lights out' Tigger came shuffling into the large ground-floor dormitory, sat down on the end of one boy's bed – and read everyone a story.

The start of Spring Term 1947 was exceptionally cold – the 'big freeze' – and all the games fields were frozen. Snow lay on the ground for what seemed like weeks. The problem for the staff was what to do with us during games afternoons. Pioneering was at a standstill and no outdoor games were possible. Someone had a bright idea – tobogganing on Walnut Avenue. So, every afternoon we would trudge over the Downs encased in as much warm clothing as we could muster. Some lucky people had proper toboggans; one person (probably a member of staff) even had a pair of skis. The rest of us made do with whatever we could find. Our favourite piece of equipment, a tin tray 'borrowed' from the Dining Room. Everybody joined in the fun – masters, prefects, boys young and old. Up and down, up and down we went day after day. Nobody was in any hurry for the snow to go and at the end of each afternoon we tramped back to warm, steamy changing rooms with red faces, frozen fingers, wet socks and soggy jumpers. If this was school life, then long may it last.

At this time there were over 320 boys plus housemasters, unmarried masters and domestic staff all living under one roof in the main building. There were Junior and Senior Houserooms, subject rooms, dormitories – everything and everybody together. Inevitably, life was somewhat cramped and personal space at a premium. The juniors had a locker for books, a space in the changing room for games clothes, a space in the tuck box room and, of course, the use of the Junior Houseroom with twenty to thirty others.

When we were given space in the Senior Houseroom it was a great step forward. The Dorset Senior Houseroom was on the top floor, overlooking the terrace and tennis courts. There were about eight to ten boys sharing the room. Each had a table covered with a personal rug or cloth which reached down to the floor.

After a year in the Senior Houseroom it was time to move on and we three inherited our first and last study – No. 4 Hardy Roof. The Hardy Roof studies were directly over the Hardy Wing. The roof space was divided up with a number of studies where the existing dormer windows would allow. Because the studies took up all the windows, the remaining roof space was always pitch black and lit by bare bulbs hanging at irregular intervals from the rafters. There were two staircases – one at either end of the roof. One was nearly vertical and had to

Nigel Hepburn and friends take an unauthorised river trip

be used with the help of two rope 'handrails' by which one hauled oneself up or slid down. The passageways were made up of narrow duck boards which rattled and clattered whenever anybody walked on them – an excellent early warning system of approaching visitors. And there was another thing. The smell: of dust, must and mice. The little devils got everywhere. We trapped as many as we could and threw them over the parapet. To get rid of the smell we burnt toast!

Nevertheless, we three, now at the venerable age of seventeen, were thrilled to have No. 4 – the premier site in the roof – and we made it as personal and cosy as possible. It was a corner position under the roof rafters with a dormer window overlooking the road up to the Science Labs and the Sanatorium. Having inherited it from the previous Dorset occupants we also took over various fittings and furnishings – a threadbare carpet, curtain materials covering the rafters, a derelict settee, an 'upholstered' window seat, a temperamental vacuum cleaner, a high-risk electric kettle with a flex with a plug at one end and bare wires at the other. The kettle worked by placing the wires very carefully on to the kettle terminals and plugging in and hoping nothing moved! Just as important to our creature comfort was our unique electric fire. With a bit of ingenuity, this doubled as a toaster. The fire was rectangular, measuring about 3 inches by 10 inches, and hung vertically on one of the timbers supporting the plywood walls. The top of the fire was attached to the wall by a hinge so that it could be raised to the horizontal position. A piece of string was fixed to the other end, then to a nail in the roof: hey presto – a toaster. And very efficient it was, until the string caught fire and the whole thing crashed down!

The study was L-shaped and formed from the plywood. Sound proofing was not supplied. Brian had a desk in the short arm and Nigel and Bill in the long arm. The remaining space was a 'sitting room'. Every surface was covered with rugs, blankets and curtain materials to provide as much 'hiding space' as possible. During class periods only one person was allowed in the study at a time. This was frequently inconvenient so it was necessary to have boltholes for when inspecting masters and prefects happened to come around. This became an increasingly risky business. They, of course, knew what was going on, and embarrassed people emerged from under desks and from behind curtains to be told to go elsewhere.

Sometimes it was necessary to use the boltholes for other reasons. The School was still undergoing the novelty of having a sister school at Cranborne Chase and Nigel had, somehow, met a girl but now wished to distance himself from her. Once when all three of us were in the study we heard voices, female voices, and feet clattering ever closer along the duck boarding. A look of alarm came over Nigel's face as he threw himself into the nearest bolthole. The door opened and in walked the girl plus companion asking for Nigel. Brian and Bill were left to cover as best they could, making all kinds of excuses, and providing coffee and toast, until fed up with waiting they left.

Most of the time we were three very fit and healthy seventeen-year-olds taken up with A-levels and tennis, hockey, squash, rugger, rowing and cross country. Because of rationing we were frequently hungry and school meals had to be supplemented. Food parcels were an important and eagerly awaited event. Brian's parents were living in Belgium at the time and frequently sent over a particular type of gooey cake about the size of a building brick and weighing the same, known affectionately by us as 'rubber cake'. We also had butter and jam so the eccentric toaster was in frequent use with whatever sliced bread we could squirrel away from the Dining Room under jumpers and shirts.

1951 gymnastics display commemorating the Festival of Britain

School drama productions took place in the wooden gym at the back of the Science Labs. As a member of the backstage crew, Nigel is certain the hair-raising antics of the lighting crew would have had the whole thing shut down by today's Health and Safety regulations. The lighting gallery was above the stage suspended from wooden beams on which the lighting controller stood. Freddy March, the lighting 'whiz kid', had devised a method of dimming the stage lights by a series of glazed drainpipes sealed at one end and filled with some solution. One pole of the electrical circuit was anchored at the bottom of the pipe and the opposite pole was lowered into the solution by a series of pulleys – a totally lethal arrangement. The solution was apt to boil, and during scenes requiring dimmed lights and absolute quiet the solution could be heard bubbling away. Fine for the Witches in *Macbeth* but not so good for quiet romantic scenes, when it gave the impression that a member of the cast had acute digestion.

During rehearsals for one play, so much light was needed that the fuse blew – and kept blowing. In the end somebody got fed up with it and solved the problem by sticking a screwdriver across the terminals. The only trouble was that the electricity sub-station blew and the electricity company was none too pleased to discover why.

Somewhere and at some time we must have done some work as well. For these and many other memories our parents were paying good money. A little while ago Bill came across a receipt sent to his father for one term's fees including 'extras' for £80. So for £240 for a thirty-six week year, Bryanston worked out at a fraction under £1 a day.

Fifty-three years on and we three have acquired wives, sons, daughters, and a small battalion of grandchildren. We see each other sufficiently often for it to feel as if the Bryanston we remember is like 'yesterday'. I can hear Harold Greenleaves, his hand gently resting on my shoulder, asking what I am doing and what do I think….

Brian Coulson *(Hardy '51) after spells in shipping and horticulture developed a company specialising in paperback books for schools and libraries. Since retirement he has dealt in antique prints.*

Nigel Hepburn *(Hardy '51) following a school ambition became a dentist in private practice. Since retirement he has become a painter in watercolour.*

Bill McWilliam *(Hardy '51) after a career in advertising took up furniture-making and design.*

A Barnardo boy at Bryanston

In the crowd of new boys jostling around the notice board in the Main Hall almost sixty years ago I was undoubtedly the odd one out. The others spoke in cultivated accents and were dressed in Bryanston Blue; I was inarticulate and wore ordinary grey. They searched the timetable with easy anticipation; I could hardly see it as I struggled to hold a bottle of ink in addition to my books. At that moment I found the whole business of being at Bryanston too much, and turned away from them to find myself facing my tutor, who lived at the top of the nearby stairway. I had met Joyce Wilson the day before and was more captivated by her well-dressed ample figure than by her account of the complex system. She had adjusted to my educational deficiencies by placing me in the lower sets of Block C with gentle charm. When I appeared at her door the following day in a tearful state, she reassured me with consummate skill, and lent me a fountain pen. I never hesitated again.

Boys like me who held bursaries at Bryanston some sixty years ago were a significant contingent. We came either from the surrounding counties or from further afield through arrangements that involved local education authorities, well-known business firms and specific organisations such as, in my case, Dr Barnardo's Homes. Judging from what I gleaned of my own bursary, governors of the School made the arrangements, including the financing of the places. Entrants were selected by the organisations, and sat a Bursary Entrance Examination at the School a month or two before their first Autumn Term. As their previous education lacked the Latin, French, and other aspects of that provided by traditional preparatory schools, the Common Entrance examination was clearly inappropriate. To the observant we were also distinguishable by our vocabulary, dress and social habits, having not been prepared for a conventional English public school, but the Bryanston of that time was in many ways not conventional, and its entrants came from a multitude of backgrounds other than the standard prep school.

My social progress was overseen by Bill Williams, my housemaster. Barnardo's had ensured my prowess in athletics, and I added to this sufficient achievement in ball games to contribute to both the School and Hardy House, with his approval; but I valued my contributions to the house music competitions more highly. By the time that the oddities of those who had come to Bryanston on bursaries were no longer noticeable

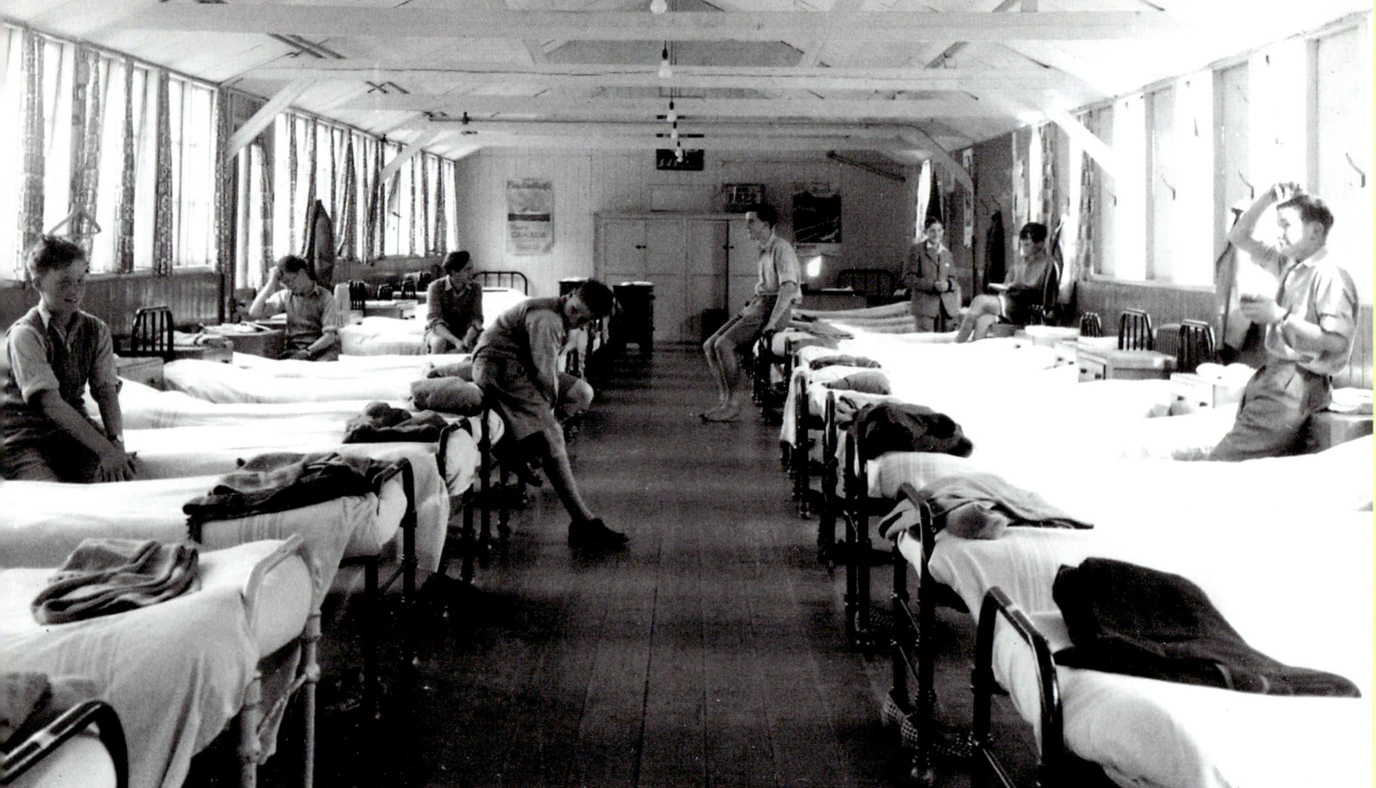

1956: the outdoor dormitory, left, and Senior Houseroom, above

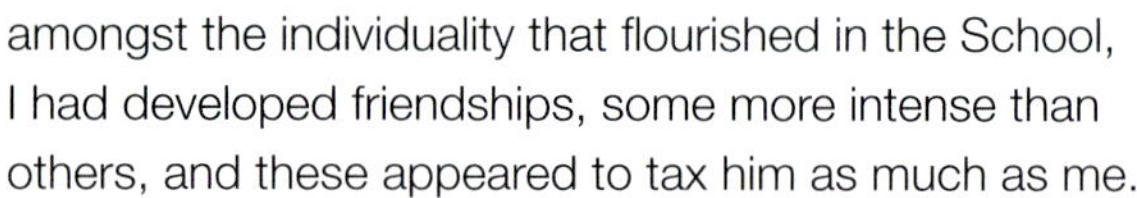

amongst the individuality that flourished in the School, I had developed friendships, some more intense than others, and these appeared to tax him as much as me.

Academic progress was guided by Joyce Wilson. She was an Oxford graduate who taught chemistry in a public pchool for boys, and I was from Barnardo's, but our assignment to each other as tutor and pupil was never discussed as in any way remarkable. I ascended the tall stairway weekly with my chart in hand, and her response to the appearance of red alphas on the front, and the honest account of my occupations on the back, was to ensure that I moved sufficiently upwards in academic status during those first two years to obtain a good School Certificate. I came to appreciate her coloured nails and perfume from across her comfortable room in a formal but personal relationship.

Joyce Wilson shrewdly matched the concurrence of my achievements as a scientist with my more thoughtful involvement in social relationships, art and music by suggesting that I might aim to study medicine in my last two years. There was a plan that I would exercise my athletics and German language ability by making an exchange with a student from Kurt Hahn's school at Salem the following term, but my acceptance at Cambridge to read medicine and a scholarship to see me through the five-year training took precedence.

The history of the English public schools dates back to the ancient religious and charitable foundations that had gradually opened their portals to a wider public than just the religious and paupers. It is only over time that fee-paying became a significant factor in determining the degree of affluence of that public, and the way they were selected. Bryanston, a newer school, ostensibly looking to combine the best of the new and the old – *et nova et vetera* – might have regarded the admission of bursary boys as enlarging its public status under either of those aspirations. The benefits to the boys themselves can be in little doubt, for most will have participated in the Bryanston experience sufficiently to reach worthwhile personal achievements, but what of their contribution? I venture to suggest that their presence, their background and their endeavours contributed to that ethos wherein each of us found our individuality.

***Gordon Brocklehurst** (Hardy '50) was a consultant neurosurgeon until his recent retirement.*

Bryanston childhood

To the children of staff at Bryanston, having all of the grounds to roam and explore was a natural, unquestioned part of our daily lives. We appreciated its beauty, but perhaps not so much the rarity of our circumstances.

In the 1950s and 60s the grounds were wild and the woods were spooky. Each spring we collected quantities of primroses from along the river path to decorate the church for Easter, and in the summer the field between the Bothy and Beechwood had such high grass that we could lie in it without being seen at all. We were brilliant at hiding, but hopeless at keeping quiet in

any of the hideouts that were 'top secret'. Climbing trees was a regular occupation, for the high, leafy branches provided perfect cover for dropping conkers on unsuspecting shorts-clad boys, and offered splendid views of teenage sportsmen walking down to the cricket pitch. For me, a seriously romantic moment was being rescued from the depths of a bed of nettles by Robin Pegna, having narrowly missed the iron fence on an unplanned, rapid descent from a chestnut tree, and then being escorted back to the Bothy, injured but thrilled.

Cycling across the front of the School during term time was considered quite daring, as was coming up to the School for events such as house music competitions, plays and evening concerts. Hiding in hedges to squirt 'the boys' in their Sunday suits with water from Sqeezy bottles (one known victim: John Eliot Gardiner) provided excellent entertainment, as did accompanying an older sister up to School with the intent of bumping accidentally into Ant Costley-White. Peter Simpson passed the Dealing with an Irritating Little Sister test with flying colours, as did many talented musical teenage visitors on coming to our house for tea and chamber music: Simon Standage, Martin Hughes, Antony Beaumont, Mark Elder, Robin Blech, Colin and Tony Hastings, Sebastian Tombs and many others gamely churned out Telemann, Mozart and more in the cramped sitting room at the Bothy.

Years of hearing my mother teaching at home have left my family with an in-depth knowledge of the flute repertoire, especially the difficult bits. Indeed, music and the arts, being an integral part of the fabric of the School, became a foundation stone for many of us, pupils or not. Despite my being a mere girl, at twelve it was a real thrill to be invited by Rodney Dingle to join the Bryanston Chamber Choir and sing in Benjamin Britten's *Hymn to St. Cecilia* for the opening of the Coade Hall, a momentous event at the time.

The Big Freeze in spring 1963 gave the whole Bryanston community a chance to skate on the river from the boathouse to the bathing place and on to the flooded, frozen fields for weeks on end. Surrounded by the crisp, beautiful landscape whilst the boys played ice hockey, we became adept at skating very fast, getting in the way and perfecting the art of doing a mobile 'teapot' at speed through the legs of willing adult enthusiasts.

For the wives of housemasters, throughout the term, every weekend represented cooking and baking not only for the family but for handfuls of boys as well. Coming to our house for Sunday lunch or tea might have been an ordeal for some, but for others perhaps it provided a welcome homely atmosphere that must have been sorely needed at times.

To this day, for many of us, growing up within the Bryanston grounds meant belonging to a large and benevolent family. From the talented tennis-playing WE Potter boys to the dottiness of John Tribe answering the phone with a cheerful, 'Hollywood I mean Beechwood', we were welcomed in every home, and greeted warmly by residents of all ages when on school territory. An abiding sound that remains strong within my memory is the richness and beauty of the birdsong at dawn, the eerie hooting and screeching of owls at night, and cuckoos in the distance on clear spring days.

Ours was an unusual childhood, enjoyed then, and much appreciated now.

Susie Carpenter-Jacobs's father, Bill Carpenter-Jacobs (WEWC-J), taught English at Bryanston from 1942 to 1975. Her mother, Margaret Morham, taught flute from 1942 to 1975 and was also a housemistress.

Frozen River Stour, 1963

5

WINDS OF CHANGE 1963–72

The revolting years

At morning assembly in the Coade Hall in mid-September 1970, a one-minute silence was observed by the whole school as a mark of respect to Mr James Hendrix, aka Jimi Hendrix, who had been found dead in his girlfriend's flat in London on the previous day from barbiturate intoxication.

Such a gesture for a guitar legend was symptomatic of the tolerant and appreciating approach of the Bryanston ethos even at a time when the stripe and prefect system was in disrepair, with frequent resignations or dismissals from office caused by various misdemeanours.

For my own part, I arrived into the homely embrace of Durweston House in September 1966, so ably run by Teddy Potter and Joan whose gooseberry jam was an all-time great. The physical separation of this junior house made for a real sense of family, with the added routine of the morning and evening cycle rides to and from School, come rain or shine.

Graduation into Forrester again gave a sense of 'otherness', and I recall the Forrester studies and Quiet Room atmosphere with affection.

Philip Chirgwin (housemaster) was once 'caught' looking for marijuana in the Senior Houseroom desk drawers after lights out on the headmaster's instructions

The Greek Theatre, 1963

and, taken unawares, admitted in his deep gravelly voice that he did not know what said substance actually looked like!

The story of the half-cooked pheasant being removed from the Baby Belling oven and thrown from the upstairs window of the study corridor to a boy in the courtyard below, then hidden in a Buffalo during a Sunday headmaster's inspection, was the stuff of legend.

Memories of the taxi arrivals as soon as the Sunday inspections were over to transport all occupants to The Saxon Arms in Child Okeford for protracted luncheons indicate a certain level of disposable income and sense of style. The real Scrumpy that we consumed made our ears ring, and strangely I have no memories of the journeys back to School. Perhaps it was forever thus: my father (William Kenneth Lowe, Dorset '34) used to tell the tale of his near-expulsion from Bry for 'driving a parent's car to Bournemouth during the night', only to be reprieved on appeal when my grandfather demanded a meeting with Mr Coade to explain that my father had not been the driver, but merely a passenger in the car.

Yes, we smoked 'enhanced' Old Holborn roll-your-owns anywhere and everywhere, in and out of school uniform; yes I ran a bar/tobacconist's shop from my tuck box in the Hardy Roof studies and was demoted from the rank of monitor for my troubles. But somehow that was all part of the revolting years of the late sixties. We did not rip up the pave and break windows like the Paris students. We were pacifist, tolerant, live-and-let-live, certainly dismissive of authority but somehow still respectful of and deferential towards our elders in a way that would be unthinkable today.

Forrester House prayers one evening even allowed an exposé of the musical and poetic merits of Bob Dylan vs The Doors. Secular certainly, but church attendance had become voluntary under the Rev. Paddy Magee and I recall escaping down the fire escape from our hostel accommodation in Salisbury on a pre-confirmation retreat weekend to see a late-night showing of 'Prudence and the Pill'.

No revolutionaries we, and when I reread my leaving school report of December 1970 where Mr. Chirgwin states, 'I was very sad that he behaved so foolishly and thoughtlessly in importing drink. He compromised himself for what?', I am left with the grateful memory of so many good times. Thank you Sir, and may you rest in peace.

***Anthony Lowe** (Forrester '70) has spent the last twenty-three years in engineering sales.*

Ice hockey on the Stour

Reflections of a staff son

Being a staff son was never a problem in my case. My father administered the language classes and was thus able to avoid having to teach me. I think he found it mildly amusing to supervise an Extra Work session to which I had been sent. Nobody took it out on me because they had been unfairly treated by EDHR and I never heard anything rude said about him. Parents can be embarrassing, however: sitting in the direct sun with other staff on the Greek Theatre stage during Speech Day orations, he opened the programme and put it on his head, continuing to wear it as an impromptu sun hat. This caused a ripple of mirth amongst the audience, but I wanted the ground to swallow me up.

One problem I did have was being a day boy. In some peculiar way I sensed an invasion of privacy. Not only were the woods where I ranged during the holidays now hideaways for smokers and drinkers, but our house was so close to the School that returning home felt like trying to hide in a goldfish bowl. Looking back, of course, this seems unjustified as the boarders had no privacy at all.

A more serious problem was that it was simply a bad era in which to be at the School. On meeting the headmaster years later he called it 'the lowest of the low'. As the swinging sixties lost confidence and fizzled out, it was a period of change and uncertainty in the School that possibly reflected the state of the country as a whole. The dawn of co-education was a mere glow on the horizon. The Sea Cadets were still going but only just; Pioneering, which had produced fine achievements in the past, now lacked focus and was considered a 'drag'. A look at the school photos shows what a dishevelled-looking rabble we were in comparison with earlier and later generations.

Newcomers to the teaching staff were fairly rare. Many of the Common Room had been there a long time and were facing retirement. Their position was justified by knowledge of their subjects and experience in the classroom, rather than the teaching qualifications that are required now. Although my father occasionally worked at foreign language schools during the holidays, it was unusual for staff to be actively engaged in work-related activities outside Bryanston. Hence, however academically accomplished they may have been, I think it was difficult for them to deal at a personal level with an increasingly sophisticated, rebellious bunch of youths, mostly from urban backgrounds, cut off for the duration of the term in this rural backwater.

How to exercise authority was evidently on the headmaster's mind as he organised a symposium on the subject, inviting other schools and guests to take part. In hindsight it would have been better to have changed the emphasis and developed the theme of 'leadership', which was not nurtured in us. I was eventually made a stripe but was not a good one and was given no direction on how to improve. It was noticeable that stripes in other school houses were not rigorous in, for example, supervising punishment runs yet gained promotion nonetheless. Towards the end of my time I asked to see the headmaster and attempted to join 'The Strike' by resigning my stripe. He said that this was not what was expected of me and 'the man carries on'.

One aspect of change away from old structures was that Sunday services gave way to more liberal school assemblies. On one such occasion we were packed into the Edwin Evans Music Room to hear an outside speaker attempt to deliver a message of optimism. On taking questions at the end he was stunned to be asked, 'How can you say everything is going to be all right when there are so many bloody people doing bloody things and fucking the world up?' The headmaster was present and said he hoped the speaker would forgive some sincerely held if unfortunately expressed views.

On a brighter note, I took sciences at A-level and have never regretted it, as what we did then has been at least as memorable and useful as my subsequent degree course. I was particularly pleased to have Dick Harthan as a biology teacher.

On retirement my father had to vacate his house in the grounds, so my parents moved to a house they had bought in Walnut Avenue, a track much used by cross-

The Headmaster's House on fire, 1973

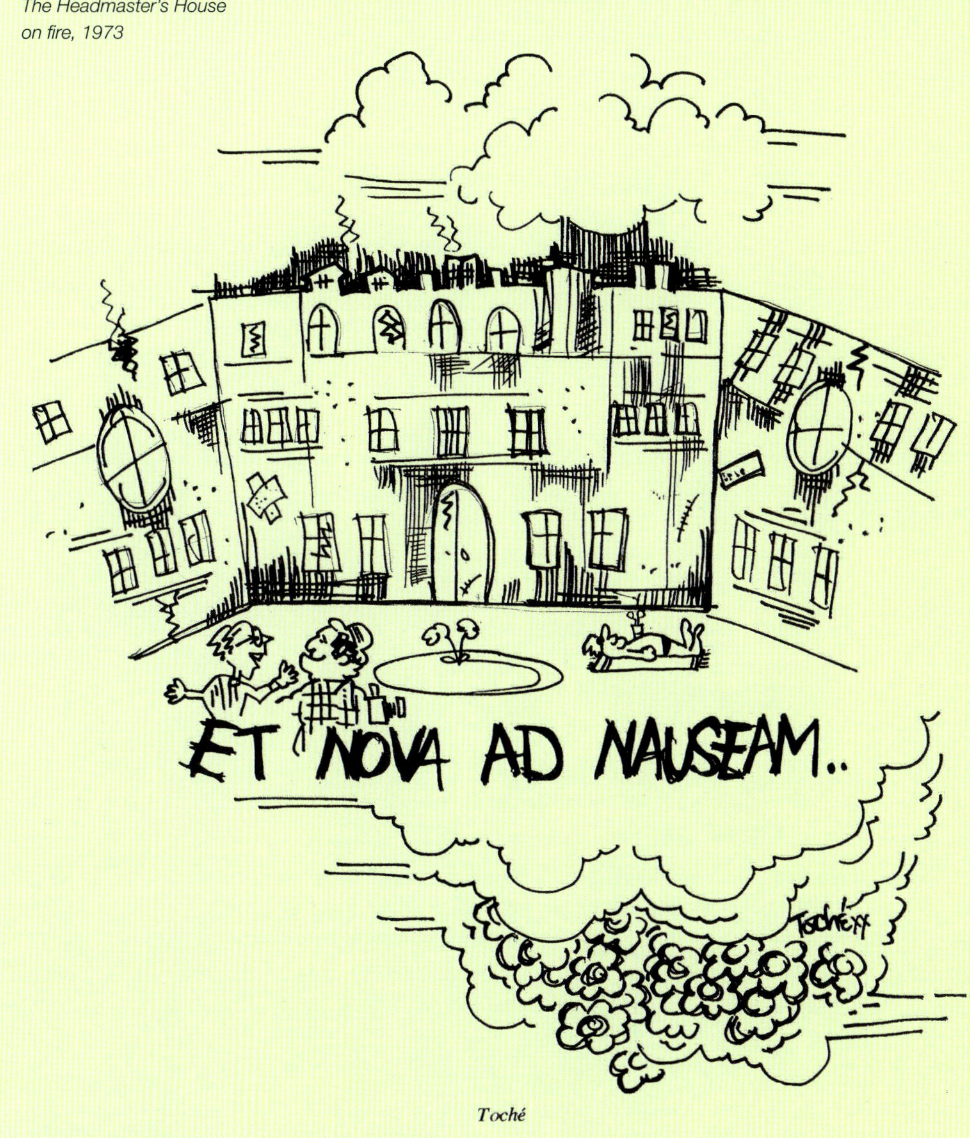

Toché

Saga, *Autumn 1974*

country runners. At lunchtime there one day in the late summer of 1973 we were alerted to a pall of smoke over the School. On walking across the intervening field we were amazed to see the Headmaster's House on fire. By then it was blazing furiously and all we could do was stand with some other onlookers and watch as the tile-hung façade crashed down. The Fishers had been away and were returning while we watched; there was no way of warning them and everyone felt deeply sorry for them.

My father, who liked the fresh air, looked fit and young for his years but contracted anaemia and died after a protracted illness. We buried his ashes in Durweston churchyard. John Tribe, an inveterate smoker, was beside me as I put the little box in the ground and kindly gave words of support. When, years later, my mother died she was buried also in Durweston churchyard, with a headstone commissioned from Don Potter.

I have kept the house in Walnut Avenue and rent it out to tenants with some connection to the School. This has meant frequent returns to the school estate which I have observed evolving over the years. Bizarre buildings have sprouted, pavements and outside lights have been installed. Whereas I used to walk home at night and see glow worms in the undergrowth, now the artificial lighting can be seen for miles from the surrounding hills. The Bathing Place on the river has gone and the playing fields have expanded into the adjacent meadows. Horses have arrived and displaced the Market Garden. Whilst the trees continue to grow, and occasionally blow down, the bushes and undergrowth beneath have been slashed.

Recently the grounds seem busier in the holidays than in the term time. The quiet holiday time enjoyed on the estate by staff families is a thing of the past now, as modern economic pressures force the facilities to be used. From a wider social point of view, as well as in economic terms, this is probably a good thing; however, the way the grounds have been managed in recent times raises concerns with a number of people. When so much of the countryside is intensively farmed and forested, the Bryanston estate has for a long time provided a haven of temperate jungle, a rare mixture of plants and habitats. This does need managing, but sympathetically. Excessive clearing at low level while allowing taller trees to take the light seems to be following commercial forestry practice at the expense of good conservation. Again, in the wider world there is a strong movement in favour of sustainability and volunteering for environmental work. The grounds provide an opportunity for the pupils to be introduced to this – a possibility that may not be being fully exploited, as most of the work appears to be done by professionals and their machinery. With the current emphasis on obtaining ever more expensive buildings and sophisticated equipment, it would be a shame if the School focused on materialism while overlooking, or even damaging, the unique nature of its surroundings.

Clive Renton *(Forrester '71) is a mechanical design and development engineer who is also involved in conservation projects.*

Above left: Clive Renton, 1956

Below and right: A new study, 1969. Under the floor a three-foot void provided a secret place popular with smokers

The School Union

If the Sixties arrived late at Bryanston, the Winter of Discontent arrived early.

The winter of 1970 and spring of 1971, if my memory serves me right, led to the formation of a School Union and a proposed school strike. I cannot precisely recall the origins. But like most revolutionary movements (and in the context of a well-governed public school I think one can call it thus), the spark came from a mix of petty grievances on the one hand and idealism on the other. Bryanston punishments were unusual: 'break runs' to the river and back for fairly minor offences, and 'afternoon runs' for more serious crimes – four times across the 'San Valley' and back (sadistic for the non-athletic). I think there was disquiet about how these punishments were being meted out. Some of the more intellectual pupils felt that pupils and not masters should be responsible for determining and managing punishment, and with this there was an implication that pupils could effectively self-govern.

In spring 1971 a School Union was mooted and formed. There was, I imagine, a good deal of discussion in the sixth form about what this would do and how. I recall a mass fifteen-minute silent sit-in in the Main Hall presumably to demonstrate solidarity and pupil power. There was talk of a school strike – I presume a boycotting of all organised school activities until demands were met. But a stand-off lasted until Easter. Then on return to school in the Summer Term pupil power collapsed. Robson Fisher decided he had to face down a potential rebellion. Allegedly he called the ringleaders into his study and threatened them with expulsion if they proceeded. The School Union was dissolved and things returned to normal and the leaders of the revolution settled down to A-levels. But I suspect that the episode did send out a message about the use of punishment and the importance of ensuring it was not felt to be arbitrary.

Paul Kelly *(Portman '74) has had his own radio show and has worked in the arts in various parts of the country. He has been Principal Arts Officer for Plymouth for the last twelve years.*

A new dawn

'Bliss was it in that dawn to be alive,
But to be young was very heaven!'

It was another Wordsworth, Andrew, descendant of the great poet, whose presence graced the corridors of Bryanston in those heady LSE/Sorbonne sit-in days of the late sixties and early seventies. In his Da Vinci Society you could hear an extraordinary range of revolutionary ideas whilst on Saturday mornings, in the Edwin Evans Room, you were as likely to meet Paul ('The Snowgoose') Gallico as you were Enoch Powell. Is it any wonder that the Vietcong flag was run up the flagpole on Speech Day or that the very nature of authority came under close scrutiny from some of the finest schoolboy minds of the time – Antony Appiah, Woody Caan, Jeremy Butterfield, David Barrie et al? All now in distinguished careers.

It was a time of joss sticks (and more) in the Hardy and Music Roof areas, a time for listening to The Doors and The Incredible String Band, a time when to be appointed a stripe was to invite comparison with SS guards at Treblinka and Sobibor. 'Riders on the storm …' you could walk through the hoovervillian Hardy or Music Roof areas and enter a twilight zone of student unrest. It was a world of coloured lights and interesting smells, of chocolate cakes and Penguin books … and in the years 1969–71 it was *the* place to be (at least before it was renovated and given the 'new study bedroom' treatment) if you wanted to debate the key issues of the day such as 'the nature of authority', 'the purpose of school uniform' and, above all, 'The Union'…

The 'Stripe Survey' of 1969 was an early sign that events in the outside world had not gone entirely unnoticed at Bryanston. The survey produced a variety of proposals including the idea of a 'Hall of Residence' for A1 and A2. 'Bunty' Hunter replied in *Saga* with a witty sideswipe at Lindsay Anderson's film, *If*: 'Perhaps

someone ought to make a film called *But*.' Then in February 1971 came the conference on 'Authority'. To say that a lively debate ensued would be an understatement…. In March a 'Challenge of Industry' conference was organised for A2 and the idea of a School Union was proposed. Within three weeks there was a sit-in demonstration in the Main Hall and the headmaster expressed the hope that there would soon be universal membership of the Union. At the start of the following term, however, it was said that 'the proposed Union cannot continue….' So why did it fail? Probably because the head believed that the Union would soon be challenging his authority in a variety of unacceptable ways and, as Bob Allan put it, 'a Union system would … have been a source of much more heat than light….'

By 1972 the winds of change had blown over, as the wise old heads had predicted, and the 'hoovervilles' had been demolished. It was going to be much harder now to discuss revolutionary philosophy in the 'new' Hardy Roof with its unaccustomed atmosphere of genteel civility. Now there were wardrobes and bedside tables, single bathrooms and daily cleaning ladies. This was no longer the world of Lindsay Anderson's single-sex public school. A new dawn was emerging in 1972 – and it was decidedly fragrant.

***Patrick Scanlan** (Dorset '72) has worked variously as international banker, educational publisher, writer and teacher.*

Summer 1975. Shorts were no longer compulsory but a surprising number of the more senior boys continued to wear them

6

FROM CRICHEL TO CO-EDUCATION

A Crichel romance

In 1949 my father, who lived and worked in Buenos Aires, decided to send my young brother Robin and me to England. Robin became a pupil at Bryanston, aged thirteen, and I, aged sixteen, was sent to Cranborne Chase School. The School had been founded about three years previously as a sister school to Bryanston, with Betty Galton, a one-time mathematics teacher at Bryanston, as headmistress. It occupied a very beautiful early Georgian mansion named Crichel House, near Wimborne, and was always known by the shorter name of Crichel.

In my first term I discovered that Bryanston's sixth formers were able to join what were then known as Bryanston–Crichel Activities – drama, Choral Society, tennis, country dancing and domestic science. These joint activities flourished in the late 1940s and early 1950s. I remember many visits to Bryanston. We went to film shows, plays and dances (both afternoon tea-dances and evening full-dress balls at the end of the Winter Term). Girls from Crichel took many of the female parts in plays and operettas.

I remember Crichelians Ann Mayo and Alison Marshall taking the lead female parts in *HMS Pinafore*. Twenty-nine senior girls were sent over to Bryanston to watch the performance one snowy night. Our bus got stuck in a snowdrift above Blandford, so we walked the rest of the way and arrived just in time for the last act.

In January 1950, another Crichelian, Janet Ferris, and I were sent over to Bryanston every Friday for a whole day of history lessons with the boys, under the tutelage of Mr Royds, as our own history tutor at Crichel was unable to teach that term since he was standing in the elections as a Liberal Parliamentary candidate. Some Crichelians were taken over to Bryanston for science lessons too, and it is said that TF Coade came into the labs during lessons one day, when showing some prospective parents round, and said, with an airy

Wendy Harwood (née Thomas)

Left: 1949, with her cousin on her first day at Crichel

Centre: 1949, dressed for the Bryanston–Crichel dance

Right: 1950, Wendy and Richard 'spent happy weekends illicitly contrived exploring Dorset in his bull-nosed Morris'

wave of his hands, 'I'm not sure what they are doing here, but I suppose they are prospective parents too!'

I joined the Country Dancing Society and soon decided that the most attractive boy was a certain Richard Harwood. He was eighteen years old and usually called Dickie. After a term and a half we became boy and girlfriend. Richard then left Bryanston and went up to Cambridge to read agricultural science. I stayed on at Crichel for a further year to take my A-levels. Richard came down to Crichel several times during his first year at university, and we spent happy weekends together exploring the Dorset countryside in his bull-nosed Morris. Most of these were illicitly contrived as neither the School nor my parents knew where we were staying.

There were several boy/girl relationships at Bryanston in the late forties and early fifties which presumably fizzled out as they generally tend to do. I only know of one, other than my own, which ended in marriage. Richard and I became engaged to each other in 1952 and we married in March 1953 before he came down from Cambridge. We have been married for fifty-one years and have five children (and nine grandchildren). Three of our own children have attended either Bryanston or Knighton House, Durweston, and Cranborne Chase when it had moved to Wardour Castle.

Our own experience of Bryanston–Crichel activities has been a very happy and life-transforming one!

Wendy Harwood (*née Thomas*)

Schoolgirls and schoolboys

Old brown Bere Regis buses were a familiar sight at both Bryanston and Cranborne Chase in the 1950s. Betty Galton, headmistress of Cranborne Chase, and Thorold Coade had agreed various joint activities and the buses took pupils to and fro. Crichel girls came over for plays

Left: Crichel girls in The Mikado

Below: Tim Roberton (right)

PUBLIC OPINION POLL

A representative selection of Bryanstonians were questioned on their activities at Crichel. 27·3% last went " last week or the week before," 1·4% went earlier this term, 25·6% went " sometime last term," 45·7% went " ages ago." Those who had gone were 12·2% of the population, the rest (mainly juniors) had never been.

Of those who had been 77·6% enjoyed it last time, 14·5% did not, the rest could not remember. 39·1% shaved before going, 53·9% definitely did not. 87·4% sang on the bus back, 9·2% (mainly seniors) did not: the rest did not know (fancy that!) 82·5% did not like the cocoa, 3·7% did, the rest wisely refused it.

Questioned on their motives, 63·3% went for the " entertainment," 21·9% went for the girls, 11·1% to escape Bryanston, 3·7% went for the sake of the cocoa (drug addicts?). Only 13·0% (unlucky?) could honestly claim to have spoken to a girl—of these 42·3% found her " nice," 35·8% said " not nice," the rest somehow did not know.

68·4% wanted to go again, 26·3% " Never," and 5·3% just grinned sheepishly.

P.J.S.

Saga, *Spring 1956*

* * *

which were put on in the Greek Theatre or the Old Gym (*Chester Miracle Cycle* and *The Mikado* in my time), or for Choral Society rehearsals whipped into shape by Peanut Rogers, or even ballroom dancing on hot Saturday afternoons (tortured tangos on a gramophone).

Bryanston boys used to travel in the other direction for Scottish country dancing or take part in play readings (*Phèdre*) or chamber music. As a side issue, I learned all the verses of a number of rude songs as the bus toiled up the hill past the aerodrome at Tarrant Rushton, on the way to Crichel on cold winter evenings

At this time, the atmosphere at Bryanston was still slightly puritanical, with just the beginnings of signs of relaxation. The headmaster agreed that jazz might be played on the gramophone on Sunday afternoons only, but it would be another year before Tony and Julian and Graham got a band together and made music for real.

During the time I was at Bryanston, I had a sister at Crichel. I took part in everything involving the School, but not only to see her. At various times I also had a fondness for Rosemary and Willy and Pia, all of whom, I am bound to admit, had other suitors too, such as Porridge or Keith or Martyn. Sometimes one or two from Bryanston would cycle over to Crichel (we never called it Cranborne Chase) on a Sunday. But it was an age of tortured teenage anguish and uncertainty. The Crichel girls were so much more sophisticated than us Bryanston boys at this age. They were practically women. We were still boys.

I can still remember (God was it really fifty years ago?) the heart-thumping moment of going down the bank and playing tennis with my Crichel partner in mixed doubles on the front lawn (shades of Joan Hunter Dunn), or dancing the Eightsome to a gramophone on the grass beneath the staff room and touching hands and swinging a girl around. And that is as far as it went. There was no 'hanky-panky' in those days. Even the school dance was chaste and slightly terrifying. In this respect, Crichel were 'family'.

I recall we once had a dance with Talbot Heath near Bournemouth. Most of us lived in high hopes that 'something might happen' because the girls there were not 'family' – in fact they did not know us at all. Alas, it turned out that they were no more racy than Crichel girls.

Tim Roberton *(Connaught '58) qualified as a chartered surveyor and spent almost his entire career in the City. Now retired, he still acts as a trustee and sits on several charitable boards.*

Brief thoughts from a Crichel old girl

I was a Crichel girl. We never called it Cranborne Chase.

The school was in a big drab grey house in a village called Crichel in the middle of the Dorset nowhere. I never did find out why my parents chose to send me there. My mother banged on a bit about Coade and his principles and this being the sister school to Bryanston, but I didn't care to listen and my father just nodded and went on trying to finish the *Telegraph* crossword before she did. I think she had a notion that it would suit me better than somewhere like Cheltenham Ladies College where she had actually enjoyed herself. Or maybe it was just the cheapest decent girls' school they could get me into. My brother went to Marlborough. I went to Cranborne Chase. My parents went to Africa.

It was a pretty alien place for a little girl who had been very happy at Hanford Prep School with her Welsh mountain pony to keep her company. I didn't care for Betty Galton, the headmistress. I didn't like the food, the grey uniform, the cold or being forced to darn socks. I thought I might run away and become a missionary. I thought I might run away and climb to Machu Picchu. I couldn't run away home because the army was renting our house.

I did, of course, find solace – leaving me with three abiding memories: Taffy, Lindsay and Jointactivities. Taffy was the Welshman who ran the nearby stables. The place was out of bounds, of course, but it was closer than Machu Picchu and much more comfortable. Taffy gave me strong tea and racing tips, which I passed on to my mother when she was in England. She made a profit out of my illegal relationship. I was frequently caught and constantly gated. Betty Galton can't have cared for me either.

Lindsay was my best friend. The stables weren't exactly her cup of tea and she was more law-abiding than I. She would have made a good missionary but not a great explorer. She was everything that was needed in a friend – constant, supportive, forgiving, fun. I don't know what happened to her when she left school but I hope it was all good.

Jointactivities was Bliss. Jointactivities was Bryanston. Jointactivities gave us the opportunity to get on the School Bus and trundle across the countryside to spend a few hours at Mr Coade's splendid (but very very cold in winter) red brick institution in the company of Boys. You had to manipulate the system to get there. Lindsay and I joined the Choral Society; we signed on for ballroom dancing; we would even have taken up rowing had it been a thing girls could do. Jointactivities meant that the Bryanston School Play, performed in the Greek Theatre in high summer, had Crichel girls playing the female roles. It meant that we had crushes on boys instead of our own prefects. I never learned to waltz, let alone foxtrot. I never learned to sing in tune either. But I did learn how to sneak out at tea break and find my way up to the Portman Roof studies, where I listened to the Great Thoughts of various youths before scampering back to join the virtuous choristers on the bus.

Jointactivities also enabled me to meet Toby, who became my lifelong friend. Indeed, from time to time I still have to listen to his Great Thoughts. One of which is that the Bryanston of today is almost unrecognisable owing to the presence of female Bryanstonians whose civilising presence has made dyed-in-the-wool old male teachers polish up their act.

Of course the presence of girls at Bryanston has done much more than that. They compete with the boys on a level playing field and I envy them their resulting academic confidence. I envy the opportunity co-education gives them to accept boys as equals in and out of the classroom. I'm even envious of the fact that girls now row on that formerly all-male river.

I would never have sent my daughter to Cranborne Chase, whether at Crichel or at Wardour Castle. I didn't have to. I sent her to Bryanston.

Katherine Lee (née Newton, Cranborne Chase '60) has been a model and a journalist, worked briefly at Bryanston as registrar and is now a writer.

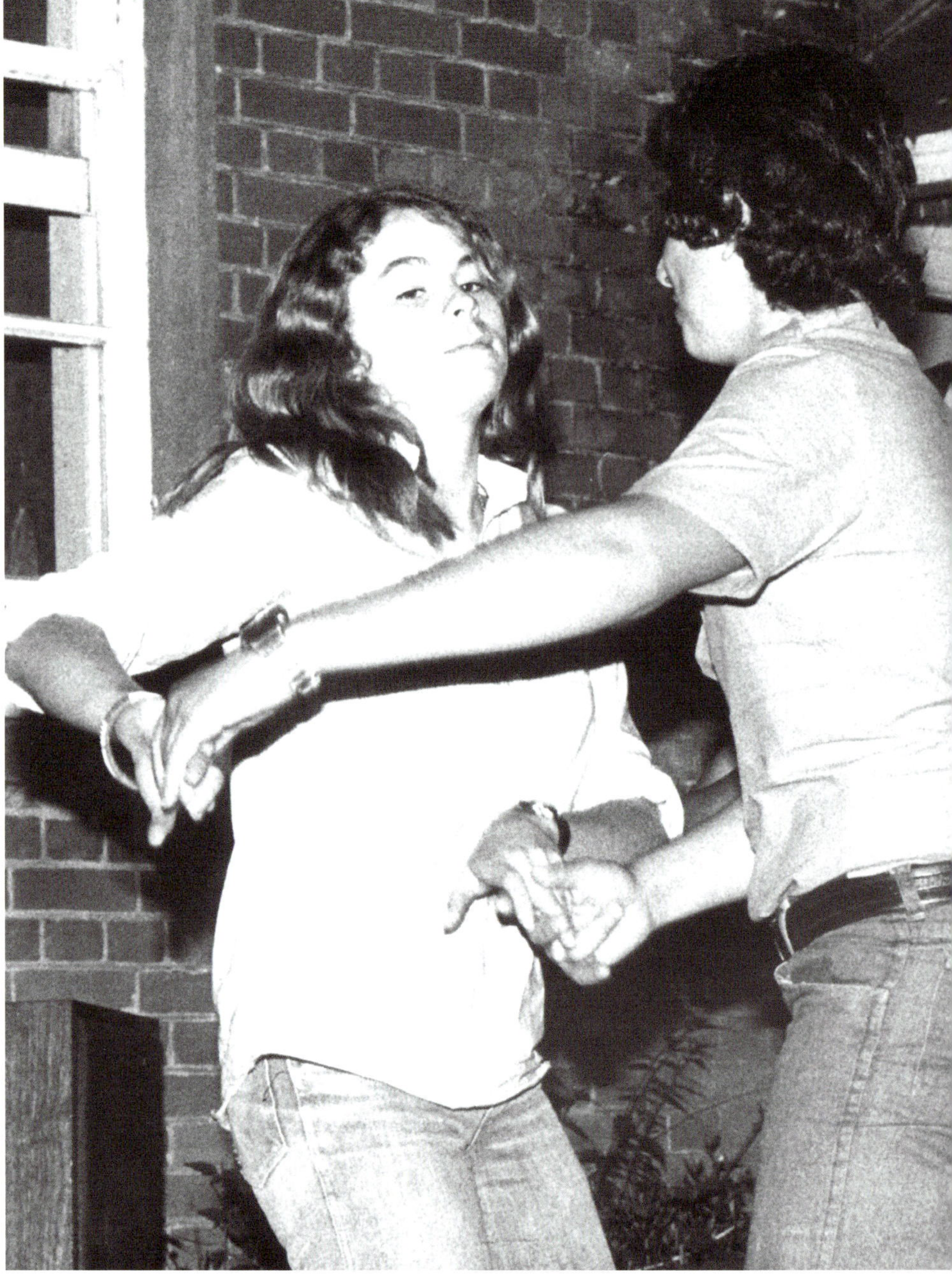

Co-education comes to Bryanston

Co-education came to a large number of 'traditional' all-boys schools rather like an epidemic of some challenging but not life-threatening adolescent disease. It posed the same questions: is it better to have it now and get it over with, or should we try to avoid it, knowing that it might be more painful if we get it later on? Put in a less metaphorical way, the question asked in most schools was 'Do we need to do this?', and, if the answer was 'Yes', then the secondary question was 'Why? Do we need to do it for financial or for educational reasons?' At Bryanston, we prided ourselves on being liberal and forward-looking, and we felt that we came within the second category – probably!

Within the Common Room, some members (and not just the young ones) warmly welcomed the prospect; some (and not just the older ones) displayed considerable insecurity and were truly worried. I don't think anyone left the staff because they would be expected to teach girls, but I do remember agonised debates about how girls should be addressed, and in particular how they should be reprimanded or even, just possibly, actually *punished*. And what would they wear (this seemed to boil down to 'How long should their skirts be?')? What should we do if, God forbid, they actually *cried*? There were also some questions that related to the education of the girls themselves rather than to the reactions of the staff. Should we be introducing 'feminine' subjects, like, um, home economics or, um, um…? Do we have anyone who is qualified to give university or careers advice to girls/women? Should girls have male tutors, given that they will meet regularly, *à deux*, and often rather privately? I don't think I was without my worries, but from my lofty position as 'Master in charge of Relations with Cranborne Chase' (and what an outrageous job description that was!), at least my worries were based on a certain amount of reality rather than phobia.

Now that girls are a fully integrated part of a majority of independent schools, the discoveries we made in those early years of co-education at Bryanston seem 'old hat' – but, I am sure, still true. At all levels, they worked more conscientiously, though usually not daring to pose that penetrating question, from the front desks where they sat, which some languid male would cheerfully produce from the back of the room largely because he was getting bored. They contributed hugely to choral and instrumental music, and their presence on the Coade Hall stage or in the Edwin Evans Music Room emancipated, and enriched what was possible. (I write as one who, in boys-only prep schools, started his acting career at the age of ten as the Virgin Mary and ended it at thirteen as Lady Macbeth. I am still not sure how to interpret this 'progress'.) The sheer normality of seeing girls around the School all day every day was socially educational in itself. Although the girls thus had a 'civilising' effect on many of the boys, it was a shock to discover amongst the younger ones that their language amongst themselves was frequently more 'earthy' than that of the boys. Age for age, the girls were usually more mature than the boys in their understanding and their attitudes, but this was one aspect of 'maturity' that was disappointing.

It was a shock to discover after a year or two that the sixteen-year-olds to whom we had become accustomed were not the same as those who entered at the age of thirteen. Amongst the older girls, storms tended to build up gradually, insistently, until they broke in fury and then ebbed away gradually, leaving a lingering and slightly threatening swell on the surface. Amongst the younger ones, squalls and waterspouts could rise up without warning from the placid seas of routine living, only to fall away with equally mysterious suddenness.

Academically, the girls' interests in matters historical were different from those of the boys, as was their sense of humour. This necessitated the loss of some stories and even some whole topics in history classes, though it meant also the inclusion of much more 'social' interest. As pupils in a potentially punitive situation, they were much harder to cope with, and seemed to have a far wider range of defensive mechanisms, ranging from real or 'crocodile' tears to the unspoken but clear intention to stick pins in a wax model of their persecutor for ever. Paradoxically, in a tutorial or pastoral situation, the girls were generally much more prepared to share their deeper thoughts, and more open, engaging and emotionally honest than their male peers.

I never had any serious doubts that for a majority of boys and girls, co-education was the best approach for many reasons. There was mutual benefit in the combining of different approaches. There was stimulus and solace in working and playing in the company of the opposite sex. There was a more 'family' approach to everything and everyone, and that made it easier to keep pace with the changes in society at large. I remain immensely grateful that I had the good fortune to be at Bryanston in those early years of co-education. Not only were they very enjoyable times, but I am sure that I owe the progression of the rest of my career to them.

Dick Poulton *was a member of staff from 1966 to 1980. He went on to be Headmaster of Wycliffe and then Christ's Hospital. He is now development director for Round Square.*

The first girls

Co-education in public schools is now so commonplace we tend to forget that it ever had a beginning and that it has only comparatively recently become the norm rather than the exception. As ever, Bryanston was one of the innovators. In the autumn of 1972 I was one of the first ten girls to arrive in the sixth form. Nine went into A3 and I went straight into A2 having already done one year of the sixth form elsewhere.

It wasn't all perfect – although with thirty years' hindsight I remember it as such. The first term certainly had its problems. In practical terms the school wasn't yet ready for us. We lived in small groups with members of staff while the original San was converted into a girls' house to be ready for the second year. It would probably have been better if we had all been living under one roof from the outset (though a number of us made lasting friendships with these families). More importantly neither the boys nor many of the staff knew quite how to react to us so it could be lonely. The boys were initially wary of us and many felt safer with their own, long-established friends whilst some of the staff, also unsure how to cope with us, resorted to treating us as honorary boys and addressing us by our surnames.

These difficulties, however, were far outweighed by the new opportunities and experiences. Academically, the teaching at Bryanston was an eye-opener for most of us. Many of the non-curricular areas of life enabled us to turn our small numbers into an advantage and join in alongside the boys in a number of sports (rowing, tennis, squash, even some rugby) rather than being confined to 'girls' games'. Similarly we were able to play prominent roles in music and drama and enjoyed all that the Arts Centre had to offer.

By the spring and summer of 1973 many of the initial uncertainties had been overcome and I have many happy memories of that time – sculling on the Stour, swimming in the river early in the morning, watching the cricket, playing lots of tennis and going for long walks along the Dorset coastline. I even took a few A-levels. We became part of the school rather than outsiders and I hope that we were able to lay some foundations for future generations of girls.

A year or two was not long enough. My only regret is that for me there was neither the time, nor the opportunity, to make lasting friends with either the boys or the girls, and few of the first girls have maintained contact with the School or each other. In those days we were very much categorised as 'boys' and 'girls' and neither side was practised in establishing long-term friendships rather than more intense and short-term relationships. Now that my own children have been to a mixed public school I have seen how it might have been: the relaxed familiarity which develops over a period of five years, the mutual appreciation of the differences and abilities of others and the fun that co-education provides. These are attributes that now characterise life at Bryanston but that we, in the first intake, were only able to glimpse.

The people who worked so hard to introduce and integrate the first girls have left a lasting legacy, and Robson and Sheila Fisher will always deserve our gratitude. It was a privilege to be one of the few, something that will remain special to me all my life, and it was a wonderful place to spend a year or so. It was the first time that I had lived anywhere that touched my soul – and that valley in Dorset will always have a special place in my heart.

Sue Laing ('73) did her PhD in medicine specialising in vascular disease. She has worked at Charing Cross Hospital and the London School of Hygiene and Tropical Medicine, and is now at the Institute of Cancer Research.

Early co-ed years

I arrived at Bryanston in 1974, joining A3 as one of the third intake of girls. There were only thirty girls in the School at the time and right from the outset we were scrutinised keenly – a bit like exotic creatures from another planet. The boys still wore their distinctive grey uniform – at seventeen or eighteen some bizarrely even wore knee-length shorts – so the overriding memory of my first few days was being confronted by a sea of grey wherever I looked. *(Shorts had become voluntary about this time, but while juniors all jumped into long trousers, seniors tended to stick with shorts. – Ed.)*

The balance of the School changed completely the following year when Bryanston took the momentous decision to go fully co-ed – one of the first public schools in the country to do so. Harthan House was built, connected to the main school building by a narrow corridor, and five of us – Anne-Marie and Jane Backes, Angela Fiddes, Jane McGill and I – duly moved down from Greenleaves to welcome the new young arrivals. Dr John Baker (JB), head of English at the time, was appointed housemaster of the new girls' house and he and his family took up residence in the far end of the building.

Lucy Graham, Speech Day, 1977

Jane Rose, George Sharp, Denise Beckett, Kate Burton, Sue Barlow, Sally Breverton and Gaba Lauterpacht outside Harthan House, 1977

Sarah Baldwin, Liz Mead and Phil Scott, Harthan House 1977

Harthan was modern and new – and miraculously equipped with hairdryers and fridges – but it didn't have nearly so much character as Greenleaves. We felt much more in the thick of things, though, and even better, we no longer had to brave the wind and rain to walk back to Greenleaves after lessons and games. We spent hours drinking coffee, baking chocolate biscuits and listening to Jim Capaldi songs on an old-fashioned record player. Harthan's ultra-sensitive smoke detector caused lots of problems early on. We were making toast one day and accidentally set the fire alarm off during exams. The whole school had to be evacuated. We were treated as heroines by the boys but the teachers weren't quite so impressed.

The first intake of thirteen-year-old girls settled in remarkably quickly. There's no doubt they were an impressive bunch. They seemed impossibly young when they arrived, with ankle socks, hair in pony tails and teddy bears peeping out from their pillows. But they were also remarkably confident and sped about the School in an energetic posse, charming everyone from older masters who'd been dubious about going fully co-ed to some of the younger boys who'd previously denounced girls as soppy and irritating. They all fell madly in love with head boy Rick Lamb, who sweetly humoured them by inviting them en masse to his attic study for coffee on a regular basis. On Valentine's Day he received a shoal of cards from his gang of young admirers.

Lucy Graham was the smallest girl in the School but took the place by storm with her big character and merry nature. The only battleground I remember with Lucy and her pals was the afternoon rest period after lunch. The younger girls were supposed to lie on their beds and read quietly – but they far preferred to listen to Radio 1 and gossip at the tops of their voices.

As stripes, Anne-Marie, Angela, the two Janes and I were in charge of everything from making sure everyone was up on time in the morning to checking that everyone's clothes were named. I came a cropper when I became head of house and found that Mrs Allan had confiscated most of my clothes for not having any nametapes. The young D girls thought it was hilarious.

Looking back on Bryanston's transition from a school that took a few girls in the sixth form to going fully co-ed, it seems remarkable how seamless it all was. From the age of thirteen, girls and boys mixed happily, forming friendships that lasted for years afterwards. Once there were girls in every year group, the whole school seemed more relaxed and at ease with itself. The arguments over girls' clothes – 'no cords' and 'trousers must have a crease in them' were the edicts in the early days – and the extent of physical contact were resolved and boys and girls co-existed in harmony. And after a few years, no one batted an eyelid when a girl walked past....

***Emma Lee-Potter** (Harthan '76). After graduating from York University, Emma trained as a journalist and later worked for the* Evening Standard, Sunday Express *and* Today. *Emma is now a freelance journalist and novelist.*

7

THE LAST THIRTY YEARS

A to Z of life at Bryanston (1976)

ART Nude life-drawing classes run by Mike Suffield – quite a waiting list for these!

BOYS Boys are rather like ladders – you climb the rungs and before you know it you are over the top and beyond the point of no return (or so John Baker told us in 1975).

CHARTS Forging one's tutor's signature and being threatened with punners.

DRINKING Blaming the Bry food for a dormitory-wide episode of alcohol poisoning.

ELEGANCE The loose and creative interpretation of the prescribed clothing list – cowboy boots and three-tiered skirts anyone?

FIREDOORS Sticking drawing pins into the alarm on the Greenleaves fire doors to ensure a silent escape at night.

GAMES Jumping on a coal truck to the front gates one bitterly cold morning in January 1976 in order to avoid a cross-country run (they caught us and sent us back again).

HANGINGS Endlessly falling into the river from 'The Rope'….

ILLNESS Eating toothpaste and putting blotting paper in shoes in order to get admitted to Sister Clarke's ruthless (but happily lessons-free) regime in the Sanatorium.

JUKE BOX John Peel, Peter Powell and Radio Luxembourg – hours spent fiddling with the radio under the duvet after lights out.

KICKERS The shoe 'du jour' for any fashionable D or C girl.

LOVE Who wasn't in love with the 1st XV rugby team (those legs)?

MUSIC Endless houseroom battles between Supertramp, Santana, and Saturday Night Fever.

NOONERS Bribing the prefects to tick us off the list, thereby avoiding a run to the barn.

O For the dunces (one of us) – between 'B' and 'A3'.

PORTERS Befriending the porter ('Flash') in order to intercept a letter informing my parents that I had been caught smoking. Again.

QUENTIN CRADDOCK Hiding behind a tree whilst he undertook his searchlight patrol in the Hangings.

ROMANCE 'Always keep four feet on the ground' (The Baker advice to new girls).

SHEETS Stealing Harthan sheets and transforming them into frilly petticoats during Mrs Sayer's sewing classes.

TEACHERS Falling in love with Nobby Boulton on day one and pursuing him relentlessly for the next five years. Never forgetting the powerful influences of Bunty Hunter and Ray Herbert.

UNDERWEAR An anonymous bra catching fire in the Harthan drying room and setting off the school fire alarms.

VICARS Being picked up by the Rev. Jones at 5am in the Police Station after a nightime stroll and party in Blandford.

WATERLOO STATION The start and end point for every holiday and half-term.

X Xtra study nights in the sixth form from 7.30 to 10pm. Agghhh….

Y Yellow and blue. Rugby shirts, socks and scarves (some of us still wear them today!).

ZEBRAS If the boys' houserooms had 'buffaloes' then perhaps the girls could have 'zebras'?

Anonymous *(Two 'D' girls in January '76)*

The Don Potter Art School, opened 1997

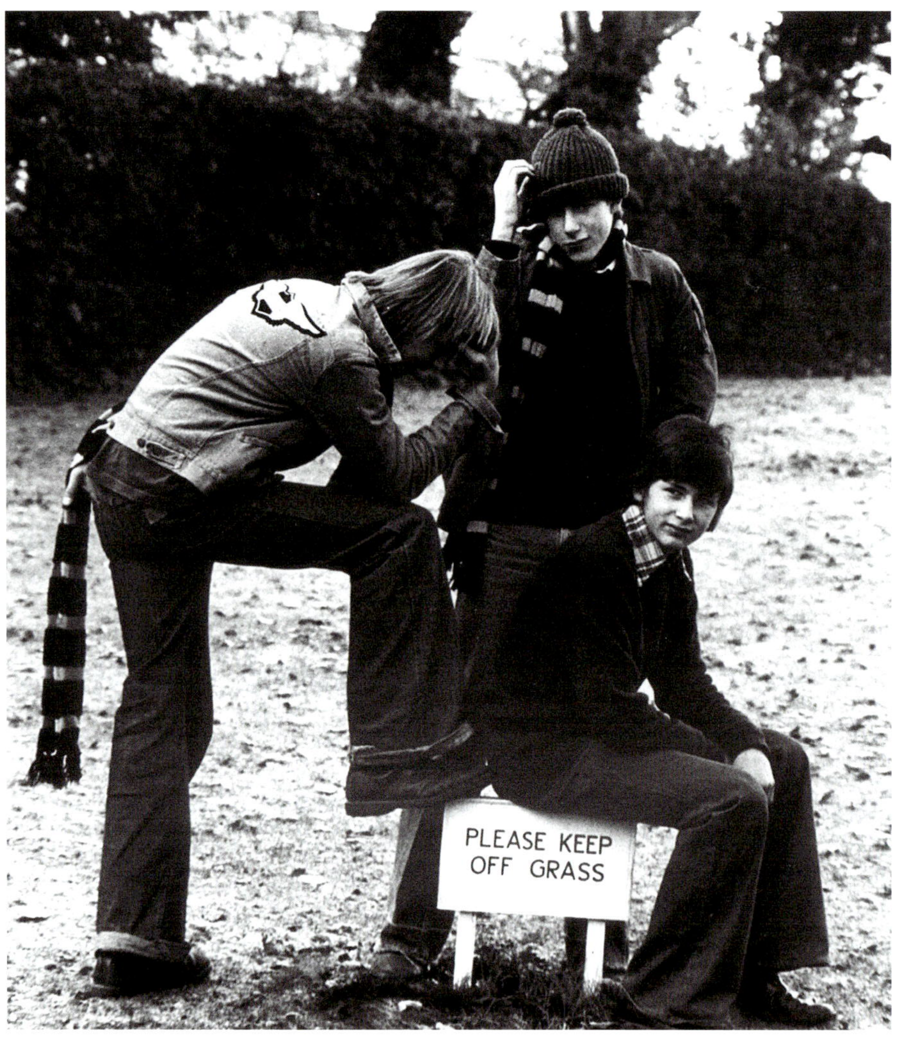

The cusp of change

I remember my first arrival at Bryanston School back in the depths of 1982: first I was faced with the archway then the long, long drive past soaring plane trees and over speed bumps, which were, inexplicably, painted red, yellow and green. The mysterious painters had left their monikers and the odd expletive. The lump of anxiety rose in my throat as the car neared the end. The last sharp turn brought me face to face with that huge red façade, stolid and theatrical at the same time. This was shock and awe – the size, the splendour, the isolation.

My year was chosen by the past headmaster, David Jones, and by the acting headmaster, Bob Allan. The Common Entrance pass mark (if, indeed, there was one) for Bryanston back then was 50%. Clearly they had a policy to select whom they liked rather than the academically brilliant. Intellectual rigour didn't matter much in 1982.

We were Jones' and Allan's intake but we came to a Bryanston that was on the cusp of change. The successful building programme had not yet made it to the drawing board. In 1982 Dorchester, the junior boys' house, was still a one-room 1930s pre-fab. Thirty-five reeking boys all stank in one big mildewy room together. The only thing that stopped the Dickensian bathroom from flooding was when the pipes froze in the winter.

What Jones and Allan did do was choose an incredibly nice year, in an extremely nice school. Bryanston had a wonderful atmosphere. It was its marketing point before schools considered such things. That was why I assume many of us chose to go there rather than the chillier atmospheres of academically aggressive institutions like Westminster and Winchester. Bryanston was unhurried and unpressured. It was draughty, baggy like an old pair of corduroys.

Best of all Bryanston had girls. They were sequestered in separate buildings with alarms switched on at night to keep the boys out. The alarms didn't cover the windows. It was a perilous business shinning across Purbeck roof at 2am, with a roast chicken tucked under your arm and ardour in your heart. Prospective parents should understand that none of this was encouraged but it was part of the fun.

Back then Bryanston had an antiquated punishment system lifted straight from *Decline and Fall*. The most minor was the blacklist. Prefects were charged with making sure that the blacklist was completed. When I became a prefect I was also allowed to dream them up. One evening I noticed a surprise in the lavatories. Someone somehow had managed to place a turd on the edge of the cistern some seven feet above the bowl of the lavatory. It was a mystery worthy of Arthur Conan Doyle. Who had put it there? And why? More to the point, how? I offered a particularly badly behaved kid the opportunity to erase four blacklists if he would dispose of it. I suggested he use the end of the mop to dislodge it into the bowl. To his credit, he refused.

The best punishment was the 'nooner'. The 'nooner' was an afternoon run. Boys had to do three laps, girls only two. If you were really lucky you would find yourself doing your laps with a favourite girl. This was no punishment. It was a social event. The authorities wised up to this self-evident fact and discontinued the 'nooner'; a Saturday evening detention was implemented instead. These were no fun. The demise of the 'nooner' was the first sign that Bryanston was changing, that the eccentricities that had flourished in the past might be out of vogue.

The last vestige of old Bryanston was the Stourpaine Steam Fair. The steam fair was a get-together for steamroller enthusiasts. It was held in late summer on the first weekend of the Autumn Term. We did not go for the rollers but the fabled beer tent. Hours later emboldened on snakebite the boys and the girls would roll around in the endless bales of hay that the steam fair generated. Bliss it was to be alive at the steam fair. A few years into my time at Bryanston the steam fair changed its date to earlier in the summer. We all suspected a plot to deprive us of our jolly.

What did not change were our eccentricities. My study mate got in terrible trouble for trying to make explosives. He was a computer whiz and his plan was to build a missile that would bring down a friend's remote-controlled aeroplane. This was Bryanston at its best: imaginative, slightly mad, yet grounded on perfectly achievable principles. I am sure he now works in the bowels of GCHQ. Just the man they were looking for.

What did not change either was the enduring patience of many of our teachers. They let us off time and time again. They engaged us and indulged us. There is a long list but particular mention must go to Mike Wagstaffe, Peter Hardy, Garry Sayer and Chris Poole. We did not deserve them.

By the time we left in 1987 the changes were well under way. The ambitious building project had begun. The academic scores improved, though not ours. The new students seemed a bit sleeker, the food a bit better. These changes were not bad. When I first arrived the top female student position was 'Senior Girl', which had all the glamour of a milk monitor. By the time I left a girl rightly got to be the joint head of school with a boy.

We did not go quietly. The Leavers' Ball was on the last day of our time at school. It was the Stourpaine Steam Fair in black tie. The party, our last hurrah, went on all night. In the morning the survivors went to breakfast. George Butler and Simon Vincent, who was incapable of obeying or even remembering any rule, and is now a teacher at Bryanston, spontaneously shouted: 'Food Fight!' The place erupted. Mess was made. The powers that be were 'disappointed'. The Leavers' Ball was duly moved to a date after term had finished, where no doubt it has stayed. We went down but we went down fighting.

Alex McBride *(Salisbury '87) is a barrister specialising in criminal law.*

A family at Bryanston

Bryanston has been my family home for twenty-four years. It's where I learnt to walk, talk, read and ride a bike. Jo (my older brother), Rach (my younger sister) and I saw the School grounds as an extension of our garden – our very own adventure playground. We knew the best trees to climb, the most hidden dens, the shortest short-cuts and the longest detours.

The students were our friends, babysitters and role models. We watched them in hockey matches, concerts and plays, hoping that one day we might be students too. In the meantime, we did our research. Next door was a boarding house full of fascinating teenagers. Rach and I would drape a cloak over our heads and sneak through the upstairs link door. We were under the mistaken impression that we were invisible. Luckily, the girls chose to humour us and continued their cryptic chatter about boys, periods and assignments, while we whispered and giggled.

When our grandfather was dying of lung cancer, Jo and I formed the Smoke Busters. Our mission: to stop student smokers. Our tactics: stroll towards the notorious smoking dens, chattering loudly. 'I think our camp's this way,' we would say. And, as if by magic, a huddle of students would slope out of the bushes, furtively checking if our Dad was with us.

During term, Bryanston buzzed with energy and excitement, but secretly we longed for the holidays. Once the students had gone home, the School was ours again. The first Sunday after each term, Mum allowed us to 'glean'. This meant scouring the girls' dormitories for goodies. A broken alarm clock, the end of a lipstick, a

THE BRYANSTON STEREOTYPE

The Bryanston Girl's hair is either feathered, layered, or streaked and always worn in such a way that it may be flicked from side to side at regular intervals. The make-up is minimal yet effective – enough to make a difference but not so much as to draw the boys' attention. Iridescent eyes, neutral lips and a reassuring amount of cover-up consitutes her daily look.

Her walk is easily identified – shoulders back, hips, tits and legs thrust out, stomach painfully in. Her sense of humour is adaptable and can generally survive the boys' crude jokes. Despite protests concerning her insecurities her ego is surprisingly resilient. Her diet consists of salad, bread and more salad, but her plate is often piled high so as to give the illusion of a healthy, happy appetite, but do not fear, the lollipops make up her daily calorie quota. The Bryanston Girl's life is never complete without a member of the opposite sex to pursue and a member of the same sex to bitch about.

Now for the male species at Bryanston: surfie, grunger and the smart outdoors look are firmly within the criteria. Layers upon layers of clothing allow them to keep warm but 'cool', whilst enabling them to remove a layer to give to a chilly girl (who, although it is the middle of winter, is goose-pimpled by the impracticality of her thin and flimsy amount of clothing). Chinos, combat trousers and cords (is there something dreadfully wrong with trousers beginning with any other letter?) are incorporated into the individual look – be it British preppy boy or the hippie, grungy and generally baggy bloke (these two types will be guaranteed to walk with their hands in their pockets, head down and scuffing their feet), or the smart, smooth but pretty hip and with-it guy (this one is obviously a victim subscriber to *GQ* magazine).

The sporty, preppy boy wears chinos, checked shirts, V-neck jumpers and Timberland shoes. He is a reasonably intelligent, sweet and uncomplex person. His tastes, such as in music and pastimes, are quite mainstream.

The hippie, grungy and generally baggy bloke models worn-out, old school trainers, hoodies, jumpers, hats and gloves that are stripy and woolly, along with combat trousers

extract from ...

Katie Birks (née Daynes) married in Bryanston Church, 2004

that are ten sizes too big, accompanied by many faded T-shirts. His hair is gelled, waxed or soaped into subtle spikes and generally stuck together by any half-suitable material. He composes and listens to meaningful, moody music or the new and most bizarre sound of the week. 'Retro' sums up his interests and attitude.

The smooth, smart and trendy teenage male wears the newest fleece of the warmest and most advanced technical fabric which is as soft and cuddly as possible for the girls to enjoy whilst hugging them. Obviously at the height of today's fashion is the sleeveless puffa jacket. Thus, if they don't have one yet, it is at the top of their list for Christmas. Underneath this is worn some kind of highly labelled sporty jumper or plain shirt – preferably Ralph Lauren or Nike. Trousers are pretty basic, but smart – be they any of the three Cs – whilst footwear is of the hiking trainer type or something with a gigantic air-bubble in the bottom for an extra trendy bounce. Their hair is quite short and inevitably covered in gel, and the sports watch must not be forgotten. Their music tastes tend generally towards the hip-hop, R&B, drum and bass side but still retain the acoustic guitar 60s sounds. Sport, girls and future London work are all important

Kinna Dyson and Katie Elliot

lidless eyeshadow, maybe even a baggy T-shirt – the girls' unwanted items were treasure in our eyes. Imagine my delight when I unwrapped my first tampon and realised it made the perfect pop-out mouse.

One Easter holiday, we started a guide to Bryanston birdlife. We climbed trees, found nests, counted eggs and took meticulous notes – until a squirrel ate the blackbird's eggs and we quickly lost heart. That summer, Mum and Dad left us at the bottom of the games pitches with a trailer full of camping equipment. We assured them we'd catch our own fish for supper and patiently held our rods over the River Stour. Two hours later, we were very grateful for the emergency supply of baked beans and chocolate.

Eventually our time as Bryanston students came. Friends thought it must be awkward having parents as teachers, but we'd never known anything different.

'My French teacher's mad,' said Suzy, a girl in my houseroom. It was our first week in 'D' and we were all trying to get to know each other. 'First he pretended his toy crocodile could speak French, then he jumped on the table and started singing a song!'

'Sounds like my Dad,' I murmured.

'He can't be,' she assured me. 'This man was a vicar.'

'So's my Dad!' I said, with a grin.

Suzy turned white and ran to phone her Mum. Before long, we were best friends.

My happy-go-lucky childhood continued right up until the lower sixth, when we received the ghastly news of my brother's death. He was killed in a road accident on his Gap Year in Zimbabwe. Those awful months of grieving were made bearable by Bryanston. I wanted to be inconsolable, angry and irrational… and the School let me.

One night, my housemistress caught me coming in through a window after midnight.

'I've been sitting in a field,' I explained, barefoot and shivering.

'Well warn me next time,' she answered, 'and I'll come and sit with you.'

Jo's funeral was the first time Dad stood down from the altar at St Martin's and sat with us in the congregation. The second time was this summer when he became father of the bride and gave me away to my husband, Malcolm. The two occasions touched the extremes of sadness and joy and will stay with me for ever.

After our wedding service, Malcolm and I led our guests up Beechwood lawn, past the Round Pond and on to the terrace for drinks. We wanted to make the most of the glorious setting, so lunch was followed by tennis, croquet, jazz and a cream tea. As the sun began to set, we climbed into a hot air balloon on Beechwood lawn and took off for destinations unknown. Looking down on our family and friends, the School and its rambling grounds, I was powerfully aware of how lucky I've been.

Katie Birks *(Hunter '95) is a writer of children's books for Usborne. Her father, Andrew Daynes, has been School Chaplain since 1980. Her mother teaches geography and is Senior Mistress.*

Reflections from 2004

Bryanston? Marlborough? Downe House? Sherborne? How to choose? Each school has its merits, but in the end you have to rely on your instincts as to whether a school is going to be right for you, or you for it.

My first insight into Bryanston was revealed in Mr Wheare's study, where he described education as merely a 'taxi ride'; the destination was the same, it was just a question of the route that your driver took. I decided that Bryanston was my taxi of choice.

Coming up the seemingly endless drive on the first day I did not really take in the stunning surroundings of Bryanston. However five years on, I appreciate how special the Bryanston grounds are – everywhere from the imposing school building to the beautiful church, where I was confirmed.

My house, Greenleaves, has been a major focal point for me, where my experience of boarding has varied from a sleepless 'D' nine-dorm to my last year, where I have had the retreat of my own room, allowing me to get more sleep and concentrate better on my work. My housemistress has created the perfect balance of fairness, respect and fun; and how she manages sixty teenage girls still leaves me in awe. The friends I have made in Greenleaves are ones I will never forget. I feel sure that meeting a wide range of people has set me up for life after Bryanston as I have learnt to

Greenleaves House

live and compromise with others despite any differences.

As my year group has developed, we have all grown closer and become one. We started as nervous thirteen-year-olds, slowly forming groups, and now enjoy a broad friendship having matured and developed an understanding of each other. With numerous balls and dances along the way, we have reached our final year and the A2 Social Club. This has its own fond memories, particularly the theme nights when a few people always go over the top! For reasons slightly lost in the mists of time, I managed to escape the joys and tribulations of HMC (Headmaster's Chart) until my second year, where the EMRs (Early Morning Reporting) and breakers in the pouring rain left me vowing that I wouldn't do it again… it did not quite go to plan!

The notorious 'D' exams made people panic over their marks, but having reached A-levels, I have realised that those petty worries were soon forgotten. The main aspect of the academic life that I have really appreciated has been building relationships with the staff. Meeting my tutor on a weekly basis has been fantastic, either just to touch base, or to delve into lengthy conversations about anything from boyfriends and break-ups to serious chats about where I should be applying to university. My tutor has backed me all the way, encouraging me to do things that perhaps I might have brushed off initially.

Throughout my time at Bryanston, I have tried a range of different things. Some worked out better than others. Duke of Edinburgh, with its 5am starts on our training weekend, a crow waking me up and minus temperatures outside, was not for me. However, there have been other things such as pottery, directing a play and music that have gripped and inspired me. Our 'C' trip to Skern Lodge was memorable in different ways, from the freezing weather and bridge jump in the middle of the night to wild hysteria at the top of the ropes course. It was most certainly Outward Bound at its best and a lot of 'bonding' besides.

Now, at the end of my taxi ride, with five years well 'spent', I have ended up with a fantastic group of friends and many memories. I suspect that I made the right decision!

***Agi Heale** (Greenleaves), Head Girl 2004–5.*

Three generations at Bryanston

1934–39

What do I remember of Bryanston? Not very much about the actual life I lived there from 1934 until 1939. Perhaps the strongest memory is the smell of wax-polished floors, which I note is still there today. I do remember that dreadful feeling in the pit of the stomach as one rounded the drive and saw that building in front on the first day of term; a building my wife was to name Blood and Bandages on being asked her views many years later.

However, if memories of the daily life have grown dim with time or have been eclipsed by the stronger memories of the war that followed all too rapidly, other memories do remain. An awesome respect for Thorold Coade; I was not one who got to know him well but he has been a figure alongside me for all the rest of my life. Encounters with him at Bryanston were more for disciplinary reasons than an opening of the mind, but looking back the mind was opened. What headmaster in the 1930s would summon a young boy he saw in need of help and get him into the study on some pretext and then teach him how to relax by making him lie flat on the floor and think of each muscle from the toe upwards?

The waxed floors, as shiny now as they were in the thirties

JG Jeffreys and the 1st VIII, 1931

I remember, too, days spent on the river; the friendship of Bill Phelps; the rowing with Ronnie King, who coached us in the 1st VIII and the early morning fast walk round the grounds (part of our training) with a united very loud 'Good Morning Mr King' as we passed his house and made track back to school. Then the delights of the Boat Club team table with its extra food, a perk for the team believed to be in need of extra calories. The heady days of pre-war Henley Royal Regattas and the entry of an eight stiffened by Dick Harthan in what must have been the final Thames Regatta at Kingston before war broke out.

Other memories: struggling with history under Harold Greenleaves, and even now remembering how he could strike terror into one's heart, and then later appreciating his friendliness on a walking trip to the Lakes. The Portman Passage, cold baths in

Pioneering in the thirties, left, and in the sixties, below, building the Hawker Pavilion

the morning and the wretched prefectorial task of ensuring no one skipped them. Pioneering under Tim Cobb, equipped with pickaxes, spades, shovels and saws, and building the Causeway down to the boathouse. I cannot remember particularly enjoying the job but there was a certain satisfaction in walking over it when completed.

When I visit the School now as the first of three generations of Bryanstonians I note in particular how it has adapted so successfully to the differing demands of each generation. I suppose the 1930s were heady times both in and out of school but I am eternally grateful to those I met there for their ability to reveal a little of the vision which they had. Surely Thorold Coade's genius lay in his ability to pick staff. What a Common Room it was: each member an individual, and allowed full scope to go his own way, yet a powerful body devoted to the aims Thorold Coade set forth. Other memories lurk in the mind but not substantial enough to write about: Wilf Cowley's pantomimes, Eric Bramall's plane landing on the grass above the San, bicycle rides in the summer to taste the local beer, the sight of Thor walking down the main passage, one hand always in his coat pocket and a wry smile of acknowledgement as he passed. It was a cloistered existence, and yet for my generation how lucky we were, for shortly afterwards we were all engulfed in the war and more than a few of our contemporaries were killed.

John Bowes (Portman '39) after reading history at Cambridge and a spell in the RAF, taught at Cheltenham College where he became Housemaster and subsequently Second Master.

1965–69

At my first maths lesson John Tribe enquired whether I was the son of John Bowes whom he had taught at Bryanston in the thirties. When I confirmed this was the case, he diplomatically suggested it would be better if I moved to the front row….

I arrived at Bryanston on the day of the 1965 Cup Final which my father and I listened to in the car as I tried to dispel all thoughts of homesickness. We arrived at school early, for father had to return to Cheltenham where he, himself, was a housemaster. I remember standing alone in this vast building with a sinking heart seeing his car disappear round the bend in the drive. How different it was thirty-three years later when taking Oliver to Beechwood House for the first time to see the warm welcome from Housemaster and stripes.

The three Bowes were all in Portman. For my father and me there were the same draughty dormitories of iron bedsteads and wooden floors in the wing of the main building and a study in the hazardous Hardy Roof. For Oli – a purpose-built, warm house with excellent facilities including spacious study bedrooms.

In addition to John Tribe, a number of stalwarts from my

Dining arrangements in the fifties, and in the present day

Opposite: The Rope in the nineties

father's day were still there including Harold Greenleaves, Dick Harthan, Bill Williams and Ronnie King. It was still a boys-only school, we proudly wore shorts, swam in the river, went for early morning walks and jealously viewed the 1st VIII's special table. Pioneering was still a major activity that took place one afternoon a week, and helping in the construction of the Hawker Pavilion was one of our tasks. The only visible changes since 1939 were the Bramall Block, Science Building and the Coade Hall, which I remember the Duke of Edinburgh opening in 1966.

It was certainly not the warmest of schools and to start with I found life a struggle, but I was extremely lucky to have Bunty Hunter as a housemaster, and it was mainly due to his encouragement and extraordinary support that I was able to make the most of my time at Bryanston. Whilst my academic record may have left a lot to be desired – and indeed the Dalton Plan may not have suited me at that time – the Bryanston education offered a wide range of benefits including the art of communication which I found a tremendous asset as I had to embark on a career immediately after leaving school. For my father it was Cambridge and the war and for Oli it is university after a wonderful gap year.

The cafeteria system, introduced in my time, allowed us a choice which we all found to be a marvellous step forward, and it did away with boys having to wait on tables. Having had the opportunity of eating at Bryanston frequently in recent years, I am staggered at its quality and choice – a huge tribute to Mike Thorne and his team.

Hockey was a sport I enjoyed and played to a reasonable standard, but how we would have wished for today's Astroturf pitches as matches succumbed to frost and flood.

One of the nicest changes in recent years is the way the Bryanston family has developed, enabling all members and especially parents to share in what is an extraordinary environment: an environment the like of which I have never witnessed at the many schools Ros and I visited when watching Oli play in away matches. Bryanston remains unique.

Simon Bowes (Portman '69) went into the tea trade and is currently Managing Director of Keith Spicer in Dorset.

1998–2004

September 1998 saw the third member of the Bowes family enter the Bryanston arena. A lot had changed since my father left all those years ago. Most notable was the introduction of girls throughout all the year groups and the general warmth of the School itself.

My earliest memory of Bryanston was being dropped off at Beechwood House and being met by Duncan Fowler-Watt and his army of stripes, who made me feel very welcome and really put me at ease – which helped a huge amount, especially as I had gone to Bryanston not knowing anyone.

The next thing I remember was waving goodbye to my parents. Immediately after they had gone all the new boys from Beechwood were whisked away and drafted into a football match. This really helped break the ice and it soon brushed away homesickness and the uneasy feeling of not knowing a single person. As soon as the match was over, we went off to meet the tutors. I walked down the main corridor towards the Cowley Room feeling tiny among the high panelled walls, with the shiny wooden floors resounding with the boisterous noise of the senior years coming from Connaught, Salisbury and Shaftesbury. As I opened the massive doors of Cowley, I scanned the room nervously and found the name I was looking for, scrawled on an odd piece of paper – 'Jonathan Fisher'. I went over and introduced myself and he jumped up beaming, shaking my hand vigorously. Within a minute we were out of Cowley and I was being given the tour of Bryanston in fast forward mode – Jonathan, a giant of a man, striding forth, and little me having trouble keeping up. I think we had the whole tour done in less than fifteen minutes. It must be some kind of record, but exactly what I needed; Jonathan was fantastic and remained that way throughout my career at Bry, playing a large part in my life there.

Another great memory was the food, which had improved 100 per cent since my father ate there thirty-odd years before. Now it is brilliant, with a fantastic selection to choose from, including one hot bar, a salad bar and an omelette/theme bar.

I played rugby in the autumn, hockey in the spring and cricket in the summer. I enjoyed all of them and everyone always played in good heart. Cricket was my best sport and in my last year we went to Barbados to take part in a tournament. In my father's time, it would have been a tour round the British Isles. Now teams go much further afield; from Barbados for cricket to Australia and New Zealand for rugby. I suspect that sport gets much more backing than in my father's and grandfather's days. It certainly played a large part in my life as well as my friends'. Most days I played some game, timetabled or not, with football in free time. We were lucky to have fantastic facilities in beautiful surroundings.

Unlike my grandfather, I never took to rowing. I fell in once and kept away from boats ever after. But I enjoyed mucking around down by the river swing (The Rope), which sadly was taken down because of Health and Safety Regs, and I always got pleasure from the long sweeping lawns and lower games fields in summer, which were transformed into a large lake when flooded in winter.

I loved every minute of my time at Bryanston, mainly, I think, because of the welcoming and friendly atmosphere of the School and the friends that I made there.

Oliver Bowes (Portman '03) is at De Montfort University, Leicester, reading design and technology.

part two : at school

LESSONS FOR LIFE

8

Working with Dalton

The Dalton Plan allowed pupils to organise their own work. Stimulating the creative imagination was as important as academic study. Lessons seemed but a small part of overall school life. Each week an amount of school work was set for each subject, and assignment time allowed during each day to complete it. Progressing through to the senior years involved fewer lessons and more assignment time. Having 'free time' with deadlines made establishing one's own timetable second nature.

Every week a chart was signed in each subject by each teacher awarding a mark for the standard of work completed, with a second mark for the personal endeavour involved; it was possible to get a low mark for work content but high for the effort. Red markings would show diligence and achievement, blue showed lack of care and performance below potential. *(There was also the possibility of getting a pencil mark (black) for showing absolutely pathetic effort. One OB, taught Latin by Coade in the 1940s, remembers getting a green (worse than black) delta. – Ed.)*

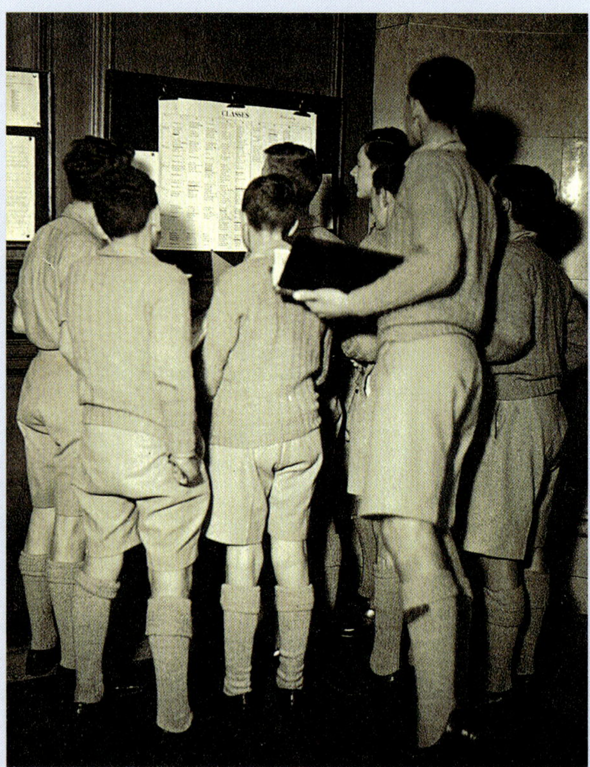

My term assignment in the first year of English was to produce a medieval commonplace book. Each week I would write and illustrate an entry detailing some aspect of life and customs of the time. Cheekily I wrote about Squire Cowley offering fealty to Sir Bryan. Cowley's laconic comment at the end of the commonplace book is: (in red) *Good work* (and in blue) *except for the mistakes*. The Dalton Plan was excellent for teaching how to carry out, programme and correct work on one's own. I remain an enormous fan of the Dalton system. I believe it greatly aided my later education and career as it taught self-help and self-organisation of time and skills.

Brian Falk *(Connaught '49) qualified as an architect and city planner. He was a partner in a large practice working both in the UK and in Africa. He then became a planning consultant and has now retired.*

The tutorial system

When I arrived in 1953 there were still many of the old stalwarts who had contributed to the ethos of the School as I found it. I was attached (in more ways than one) to Dick Harthan as assistant housemaster. Ronnie King was a hero whose unflagging enthusiasm and good cheer had created the successful Boat Club which I took over in '54. Bill Williams became a close friend. By the early fifties we had weathered the trials of early growth in the thirties and wartime hardships in the forties. We had no background of solid investments, legacies and wealthy Old Boys. The School finally paid

off the original debt during my first year and we could begin to take our first hesitant steps in expansion. Thus I was on a cusp (as they say). The School's history and traditions stretched back a mere couple of decades, while I was involved in the next two decades of growth. I have watched the recent achievements of creation and financial security with wonder.

We prided ourselves on being different from the ordinary run-of-the-mill public schools. Uniform shorts, rest periods after lunch, no fagging or capital punishment (as new boys sometimes listed in their 'advantages'), a relaxed attitude to relationships. All this is due largely to the benign philosophy of Thor Coade and the early members of staff. But I am convinced that one of the major contributing factors was the tutorial system coupled with the attendant set-up of correction periods. The chart was fundamental, and although it is possible to disparage its efficacy and it was easy to 'cook', the fact remains that it was the cement which bound together all the bricks (we have to say 'building blocks' nowadays) of academic subjects, hobby activities, games, private study, relations with subject teachers, and of course the overall control and care of the tutor. To lose one's chart was to be temporarily without an anchor.

I am further convinced that as a direct consequence of our Modified Dalton Plan, boys soon came to realise imperceptibly that these men (most of them, anyway) were on their side and keen to help. Even if you didn't like a subject and didn't much care for the subject master, you saw him for five minutes or so each week so that he could explain where you had gone wrong, and the steady drip-drip of these interviews with ten or a dozen masters must have dispelled much of the inborn hostility between teacher and taught. Added to that, you had one adult, generally not your housemaster, whom you saw weekly and who again was clearly concerned for your welfare. The relationship between tutor and tutorial pupil was often rewarding for both sides. Of course, relations were not always rosy, and we all used to sing Wilf's cynical chorus in the pantomime ending '… and then go and tutor a far nicer boy'. It was less easy for the boy to go and find a far nicer tutor, but it was possible. Thirty-plus years after leaving, I am still in touch with as many tutorial pupils as members of my house and of the rowing crews I coached or boys in my classes.

Now that most boarding schools operate on understanding and consent rather than stern tradition and discipline, it is easy to forget how much Bryanston was a pioneer, particularly in the thirties. Where we led, the rest of the academic world has caught up, so we are no more considered to be 'progressive' (dangerous word) and have moved gently into the 'liberal' category. Consider: in the decade before the Second World War, public schoolboys were beaten, sometimes savagely (my housemaster used to take a run), chapel was compulsory – daily and twice on Sundays – very few boys knew the masters as people and likewise masters took little trouble to get to know boys before the sixth form, youngsters fagged for seniors, Latin was often compulsory, maids made beds and sometimes waited at table, 'the Corps' was compulsory, there were few organised hobby activities, and so one can go on. We were years ahead of the times, and so we suffered from ill-informed criticism and the establishment's well-known distrust of the new. If there was any occasion for mention in the press, we were all too often 'the do-as-you-please school in Dorset where the *boys swim naked in the river!!*'.

Thor Coade must be ranked as one of the great headmasters. If in his later years he was viewed with perplexity by boys and younger staff, there is no doubt that he inspired genuine love and respect among the Old Guard, and was certainly an acknowledged force in the independent educational world.

***Rodney Dingle** was a Housemaster and member of staff from 1953 to 1970. He was later Head of Modern Languages at Exmouth Comprehensive and is author of the biography of Roger Altounyan.*

Charting the way

If you have been brought up in it as a student, or have been required to perform as a teacher within it, you will have an understanding of the phrase 'Modified Dalton Plan'. Clear definition, however, is elusive. The different perspectives produce diverse responses as to what it actually amounts to.

There are a number of key characteristics, though, and these are familiar enough to the practitioners, irrespective of their position within the system.

First is the emphasis on self-direction. A task is set and there is a deadline. Ideally that is met. The routes towards it are suggested. You struggle with the problems and deliver a response. In reality, you have competing problems to handle and finite time constraints. To offset this, rather more leisure is available to be used to meet the challenges set than would be expected in a conventional school environment. The founding fathers rather hoped that the training provided would serve as an effective preparation for study at university as it was conceived in the inter-war years. Although expectations are rather different seventy-five years later, there is still a good deal to be said in favour of developing autonomous methods of learning.

Internet search engines are now the preferred method of approach, but you are still better placed if you possess some method of checking whether the knowledge that has been acquired is applicable and fit for the purpose. The real secret of the Modified Dalton system rests in the relationship it fosters between the teacher and the student. In modern circumstances this

Latin Reports: Peter Greenhill (Shaftsbury '60)

BRYANSTON SCHOOL

Subject	Name	House
Latin	Greenhill	Durweston

…RT—

Better than last term. He has swum into the higher reaches of a rather stagnant set.

WDK

BRYANSTON SCHOOL

Subject	Name	House
Latin	Greenhill	Durweston

REPORT—

On paper he sometimes shows a little knowledge of Latin but in class it generally appears to be Greek to him.

WDK

can be obscured: payment by results, teaching for testing, knowing with some precision what pleases assessors, all appear to take serendipity out of the equation.

So the second element of the approach is the fostering of a teaching style that tries to limit didacticism and enhances individual approaches. Teachers spend less time in formal classes, often a pleasing prospect. But you are expected to see individual students to discuss progress, in a correction period. Teachers are advisors, a source for guidance, may be opinionated, but are expected to encourage, perhaps inspire if things go really well.

Third as a key element in the Modified Dalton system is the reduction to the acceptable minimum of the tyranny of the system. There are no forms. There are no forbidden subject combinations, as such. There are no areas of learning that are confined to particular élites. External demands may have circumscribed things over time, but there is still plenty of latitude.

Finally the system places a premium on self-assessment and awareness, to try to prevent latitude from becoming indolence. The chart was used from the outset as the tool for that purpose. It remains a key element in underpinning the system. Freedom without accountability was never to be regarded as part of the approach. Charts need the tutor to interpret what is going on, and thus teachers have a dual role in this system.

Thus, in essence, to make the system work effectively, individual approaches have to be adopted. As a teacher, you have to try to attend to individual needs, rather than operate only with groups. As a student, you need to learn to take individual responsibility and not shelter behind the protection of a class. The system has to be responsive to the needs of disparate and competing claims for attention. This turns out to be quite enlivening for everyone involved, though not entirely straightforward or easy to execute.

A system that can respond to disparate and competing needs is by definition flexible. This flexibility has, in recent times, allowed Bryanston to accommodate the seemingly constant state of flux in educational thinking. For all that has been said of changing standards, the demands placed on students nowadays are considerable. Interpretation rather than regurgitation is the name of the game, discernment a vital skill in a world in which a deluge of information is released from the internet at the click of a button. Learning how to learn, fundamental to the Dalton philosophy, prepares the student well for such challenges. Breadth, that longtime cornerstone of a Bryanston education, is now valued by all, as is manifest in the introduction of both the old and the new AS-levels. Where Bryanston charted the way, others are following.

Neil Boulton *has been Director of Studies since 1989.*

Reflections of a junior teacher

I joined the staff at Bryanston in 1966 as a newly qualified teacher of physical education and assistant to the person I came to know as the legendary Harold Tarraway. I had no experience of boarding but I found myself as the assistant housemaster of Dorset House which was run by Bob Allan (an awesome figure). I was asked if I had any connection with the military (a very non-Bryanstonian thing I was to discover) and suddenly found myself as the Officer Commanding the Royal Marine Detachment of the Sea Cadets Corps.

In addition to teaching PE, I was expected to teach an 'academic' subject. The one available was geography which I had given up in my third year at school in favour of biology. Robin Scoones came to the rescue and gave me a pile of books to mug up before the start of the Autumn Term.

I was given a room in Dorset right amongst the boys, with a shared staff bathroom some distance down a corridor where I first met 'Bill Will' as he surfaced from a bath. The idea of inviting a girl to one's room would have been greeted with disbelief.

As a shy, callow youth, what did I make of Bry? I learnt how to drink sherry and say 'decent'. I learnt that Bryanstonians were regarded as some sort of alternative creatures by teachers from other schools (long hair, shorts, etc.) and I learnt the most valuable lessons of my entire working life. The senior staff set the example to the youngsters. They were innovative; they had skills and talents outside their subject areas. They worked immensely hard and expected me to do the same. They tried to bring the most out of individuals. One size did not fit all. They tolerated (and encouraged) the misfit. There was an all-round nature to the education given to the boys, not just the narrow prescribed offering that most children now have to endure. There was a belief in Christian values and of what was right and what was wrong. There was little 'stuffiness'.

And then there was the introduction of girls just as I left!

As I have moved through my teaching career I have taken with me the lessons and memories of my mates Ray Herbert (sadly deceased), Richard D'Silva (who introduced me to choral and organ music), Garry Sayer (star), Alan Shrimpton (mystic) and John Sutherland-Smith (mushrooms on toast). And I have often asked myself what would Bob Allan, Bunty Hunter, John Griffin, Dick Harthan, Harold Greenleaves, Robin Scoones, Peter Brewin or Rodney Dingle have done when it came to making a tough decision. But my biggest mentor was Harold Tarraway without whom I would never have learnt how to get the best out of children, and how to duck and dive, bob and weave.

Schools are about people, and it is has always been the people that have made Bryanston the unique place that it is.

***David Crawford** taught at Bryanston from 1966 to 1973 and was later Headmaster of Cokethorpe School and Colston's School, Bristol.*

An abundant education

Having compared notes with my immediate contemporaries at other schools, I'm firmly convinced that Bryanston in the early 1960s offered what was then the best available education in the world. If we interpret the word 'educate' in its broadest sense, its literal meaning of 'leading out', then there was nothing to rival the richness of cultural experience offered by the School, and I'm doubtful if this abundance has ever been reproduced. I look back with wonder and delight at a place in which the Anonymous Society rubbed shoulders with Hakkabod, Bryanston Poetry, *Saga*, the Chamber Music Society, the Cercle Français, the Jazz Band and the Lulworth Cenacle. I recall with amazement a series of House Drama Festivals which included offerings as eclectic as Brecht's *The Trial Of Lucullus*, Frisch's *Andorra*, Arrabal's *On The Battlefield* and Middleton's *A Trick To Catch The Old One*. Where else could I have played a bride with three noses and green hair in *Ionesco* one term, and a Tsarist secret police chief the next, in a performance of Camus' *Les Justes* in its original French? Even Bryanstonian cultural stamina boggled a little at this one. As we pushed earnestly onwards with the densely undramatic discussion of revolutionary values that occupies most of the play, the audience, through the darkness beyond the footlights, could be seen voting with its feet.

Lessons complemented rather than diminished our extraordinary absorption with such activities. We were largely, I believe, well taught, and I can't recall any of us feeling that we were being sold short academically. What strikes me, on looking back at my first two years (in 'C' and 'B') was the singular patience and friendliness of my teachers in those subjects for which I had neither aptitude nor interest. Maths was a write-off from the outset. I had not even sat the paper for the scholarship exam and was given a correspondingly reduced award. Yet Tusker Tribe valiantly continued the struggle until deciding that it was time, as his report put it, 'to draw the curtain and close the chapter', removing from me the ultimate humiliation of abject failure at O-level. The sciences were made bearable by Gulp Greenwood and Froggy Harthan, both of whom had the human touch and sense of fun that are essential qualities of good teaching. I even managed to scrape a pass in biology after a second go, the first having been botched by my insistence on cutting my specimen apple vertically rather than horizontally in the all-important practical section.

In the humanities the level of instruction was exceptional. As a teacher myself, I've frequently set the example of my Latin master John Griffin before me as somebody whose fairness, clarity and even temper matched his commitment to the subject. For modern languages we enjoyed an unbeatable double act from Jerry Renton and Ken Gillett, the former pin-striped and anecdotal like a brigadier in a club bar, the latter the nearest most of us had so far got to a Rive Gauche intellectual. Was he, as some supposed, working for MI6? Certainly his interpretations of Voltaire, Gide and Musset made us feel that we were being given privileged access to classified material.

The greatest good fortune lay in being promoted, after only a few weeks of my first term, to WEW Carpenter-Jacobs' C1 English and history set. Yellow-faced and atrabilious, Car-J was not easily lovable. If I managed to hit it off with him, this was because of our shared enthusiasm for the seventeenth century, which he encouraged us to explore in a hands-on fashion that anticipated today's empathetic history lessons. We got Milton sonnets and Cavalier lyrics by heart, we drew maps of Dutch War sea-fights, wrote eyewitness accounts of the Great Fire and turned the Glorious Revolution into a play. Best of all were those visits to Dorset churches and country houses, to draw the strapwork screen at Shroton, the staircase at Kingston Lacy or the façade of Stepleton.

I only returned to Carpenter-Jacobs for the intensive Oxford entrance coaching that took place during my final term. In the intervening three years Wilfrid Cowley taught me English, a figure whose air of sleepy urbanity (his bald head gave him the look of a worldly Chaucerian monk) belied his shrewdness when commenting on our weekly essays. I don't recall ever having worked very

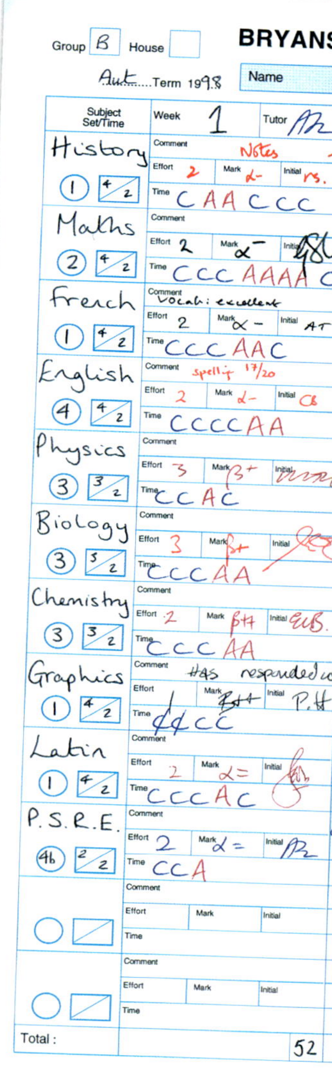
Group B House

BRYANS

Aut.....Term 1998 Name

Subject Set/Time	Week 1		Tutor
History ① 4/2	Comment: Notes		
	Effort 2	Mark α-	Initial rs.
	Time CAACCC		
Maths ② 4/2	Comment		
	Effort 2	Mark α-	Initial
	Time CCCAAAAC		
French ① 4/2	Comment: vocab: excellent		
	Effort 2	Mark α-	Initial AT
	Time CCCAAC		
English ④ 4/2	Comment: spelling 17/20		
	Effort 2	Mark α-	Initial CB
	Time CCCCAA		
Physics ③ 3/2	Comment		
	Effort 3	Mark β+	Initial
	Time CCAC		
Biology ③ 3/2	Comment		
	Effort 3	Mark β+	Initial
	Time CCCAA		
Chemistry ③ 3/2	Comment		
	Effort 2	Mark β++	Initial EuB.
	Time CCCAA		
Graphics ① 4/2	Comment: Has responded w		
	Effort	Mark β++	Initial P.H
	Time CC		
Latin ① 4/2	Comment		
	Effort 2	Mark α=	Initial
	Time CCCAC		
P.S.R.E. 4b 2/2	Comment		
	Effort 2	Mark α=	Initial
	Time CCA		
	Comment		
	Effort	Mark	Initial
	Time		
	Comment		
	Effort	Mark	Initial
	Time		
Total :			52

hard for him, but his has become one of those inherited inner voices in which, as a schoolmaster now nearly his age when he taught me, I find myself expounding a text to my pupils.

Most of us were excellently supported by our tutors, who played a key role in the Dalton system. Andy Wordsworth, instinctively knowing who I was as an individual and what sort of stimulus I needed, embodied that essentially Bryanstonian spirit of unorthodoxy which I very much fear may have been killed off since by the awful pressure to conform dictated by today's league tables and market forces.

I've never revisited the school, for the simple reasons that I don't drive, am never in Dorset and am certainly not famous enough to be invited back. But I hope, goodness how I hope, that somehow, amid all the timorous, creep-mouse mediocrity of modern education, a little of the sparkle, verve and singularity of '60s Bryanston has managed to endure.

Jonathan Keates (Portman '64) has had parallel careers as a teacher of English at City of London Boys' School and as a writer, journalist and critic.

Winning the 'Young Engineer for Britain' competition

I used to enter as many projects as I could, knowing how good it is for young people to stand by their work and explain it to knowledgeable people (usually professors). It was an interesting day away from school, great fun, and made a nice addition for the CV. There was always the hope of a prize. In fact if Bryanston did not win at least a third of all the prizes going at the regional West of England finals, I thought we were not up to standard. Later I began to expect at least one a year to be chosen for the national finals in London (best thirty-six in the country).

It was while several projects were being prepared in the Physics Labs that I came across 'Tom's'. It was a complete muddle. 'Oh "Tom",' I moaned, and tried to think of the simplest way out. Then I said in resignation, 'Make three columns, and label them "What it is for", "What it is" and "How to use it" and then tell them that.' So he began. After about an hour a recent school leaver from Blandford, who worked as the lab assistant, saw 'Tom's' efforts and said 'Your spelling's awful.... Here let me show you.' So they rewrote it together.

We arrived on competition day at Bath University and set up our exhibits. There was to be a special prize for the best-presented exhibit. 'I know who won't get it,' I thought to myself.

At tea we sat around tables for speeches and prize giving. A distinguished professor from London described how he had assessed the presentation. 'I thought I'd do something different,' he said. 'So instead of interviewing you with your work I looked at it carefully in your absence while you were all at lunch. It was really quite difficult to find out from some of your displays what was done and why. All I really wanted to know was: what it is, what it is for and how to use it.' Then he then added almost as an afterthought. 'And I like a chap who can spell.' He called up 'Tom' for the substantial award.

The rest of us sat goggle-eyed in amazed silence until someone said, 'He's just getting it. We'd better start clapping'. We did so furiously and delightedly. 'Tom' returned with the biggest smile I'd ever seen. I swear it went from ear to ear. The prize was probably the first commendation he'd ever got in anything. On reflection, perhaps he made better use of it than any other contestant, because it opened an horizon of possible achievement which he might otherwise have thought denied him. From this I learnt again how a 'failure' can kick-start a fresh approach to life.

Patrick Rolleston was a member of staff from 1973 to 1984, and after leaving he continued teaching. He organised the exhibition at the Royal Society in 1991 commemorating Robert Boyle (of Boyle's law fame).

OOL CHART Tutor Tutorial Week

TFC

THOROLD F COADE 1932–59
Headmaster

When I was being interviewed for a job by a headmaster I was asked how Thorold Coade influenced Bryanston. The word that came to mind was 'permeate'. In my mind's eye I saw him shambling, if that is the right word, down the Main Hall corridor en route from his office at one end to the Common Room at the other. Dressed in grey flannels and a green sports jacket, one hand in his coat pocket, he looked anything but an authoritarian figure. Next I saw him reviewing the events of the term at assembly, with typical self-deprecating humour. The 1st VIII had 'rowed quite well', when they had reached the final of the Ladies Plate at Henley. This was counterbalanced by the seriousness of his sermons in Bryanston Church which were always thought-provoking, original and deeply felt. I also remember prefects' meetings when we discussed not the latest changes in the school rules but the problems raised by John Macmurray's *Freedom in the Modern World,* a work by a contemporary philosopher, which we were all given to read.

On reflection, what I gained from Coade was the conviction that the purpose of education was to encourage a sense of enquiry into what really mattered. In his own case, Christianity provided the bedrock, but his concern was not so much to spread that particular faith, though that was part of it, as to encourage each of us to find a true sense of values. It was this, I think, which explained his emphasis on the arts. In one of his sermons he said, 'When we want to see things more clearly we do well to go to the artist whose spiritual senses are sharper than ours.' For it was here that illumination was to be found. He relished success on the games field, and in the winning of scholarships to Oxford and Cambridge, but they mattered less than the performing of a good play or the successful rendering of great music.

For Coade himself, it was drama that provided the best key to understanding our humanity. Throughout his time as headmaster he regularly produced plays, and in my time at the school I remember plays by Shakespeare, Shaw and Oscar Wilde. I was never more than a humble spear-carrier in one of his Shakespearean plays; I recall being one of a group of soldiers in *Anthony and Cleopatra.* We changed uniforms, depending on whether we were in Caesar's or Anthony's army. One of our number with a congenital limp always brought up the rear as we trooped on to the stage. Our successive appearances were greeted with increasing mirth, but fortunately did not detract from the quality of the performance as a whole. It was a bold choice of play for a boys' public school, and it came off triumphantly.

The seeds planted at Bryanston bore fruit. Mainly because of what I learned there I became a schoolmaster. The search for what really matters goes on.

William Simpson (Dorset '50) taught at various schools, was Head of History at Cheltenham College and has written several history books for A-level students and undergraduates.

My first year at Bryanston coincided with Mr Coade's last year as headmaster.

There are numerous anecdotes about him, but mostly before my time. I was, however, present at his valedictory speech to the School, all assembled in the Centre Room. If I remember correctly it drew heavily on 'Jerusalem' and when he reached the part about the 'bow of burning gold', Coade, who was a toxophilite, shot an arrow down the length of the Centre Room over the heads of the boys to hit a suspended target.

In today's dull world he would no doubt have been severely reprimanded by a Health and Safety Officer!

WJ Champion (Forrester '62)

WSHC

WILFRID COWLEY 1928–64

Housemaster, Head of English, actor, drama producer and chief author of legendary pantomimes

He was the perfect housemaster: warm, lenient, instructive, wise and totally uncondescending. He was the perfect teacher: inspiring, enthusiastic, informal, with a passionate knowledge of his subject that you could catch and begin to share the instant a lesson began. He was a fierce games master; so much so that I was almost glad my tennis was so incompetent I never had the chance to lose to Canford, with his disappointed fury quivering from the sidelines. His acting was brilliant. His writing and in particular that art form he made peculiarly his own, the pantomime, was so sparkling that I remember year after year travelling home after the Autumn Term in a glow of satisfaction and joy at living in such a clever, witty, irreverent and friendly community as Bryanston.

He had 'presence'. A quality of authoritative stillness more effective than any actor could create. His great scene was so often some anarchic, violent, confused dormitory fracas, overwhelmed with tumbling small boys. Suddenly the silence would ripple out from a central spot, jumping from appalled boy to appalled boy. And in that spot was Wilfrid, standing very still. A pause, and then a few well-chosen, devastating words.

He was equally brilliant with the acting techniques of high camp. Once in a cross-talk act with Eric Bramall he unexpectedly found himself with a half-eaten banana in his right hand. Violent two-handed action was imminent. For a second he was perplexed. Then he leant across the table at which he sat and stubbed it out in an ashtray, little finger elegantly outstretched. – *Saga*, 1964

Nick Tomalin (Portman '49) was a journalist tragically killed in the Yom Kippur War in 1973.

Thorold Coade giving his valedictory address – crook in hand

HAROLD GREENLEAVES 1928–70

Housemaster, Second Master and twice Acting Headmaster, Master i/c Pioneering

I don't think I ever exchanged more than a few words with Harold. And yet he was still a great figure in my life; in the background maybe, but a doughty pillar nevertheless, a man to note and a man to follow. What did we absorb from him? Reliability, loyalty, kindness, service, doing the job well, an abhorrence of sloppiness, and no doubt much more in that line of unobtrusive qualities which keep ships on even keels, creating and supporting a stage on which showier talents can perform.

OBs would frequently say, 'No one else could have taught me maths as Harold did' and other remarks of the same ilk. He had no 'show' about him; you just gradually discovered what he did, quietly, as teacher, tutor, master in charge of Pioneering at its very beginning in 1933, housemaster (Hardy, from its foundation in 1930 to 1939), an energetic part of Bryanston's pre-war left-of-centre political team – an active supporter of the Liberal Party, and Thor's trusty support during the difficult post-war years.

From his retirement in 1970 right up to his death in 2003, Harold and Betty lived in their Durweston cottage, editing the *OB Yearbook*, supporting the OBA and the School, watching rugby matches, entertaining the steady flow of Old Bryanstonians returning to pay homage to this pair who had done so much to help them in their teenage years.

Anon

ERIC BRAMALL 1930–58

Housemaster, Bursar, OC Air Training Corps,

EJNB had a precision of manner about him, a fastidiousness that lent him a true air of distinction, as if he had descended from a higher plane. I never knew him well, but he impressed me as one who set high standards as to what he expected of you.

He was a businessman – though I didn't know it at the time – and he had a well-developed and eclectic interest in music, which he indulged by means of the best hi-fi equipment available. My father was also a businessman, with an enthusiasm for new technology and an interest in music, who had taught himself to play the organ. Perhaps that is why I related more to Eric Bramall than to any other member of staff.

These were the early days of the long-play vinyl record, and EJNB would affix record covers to the house notice-board, announcing a soirée in his study just before bedtime. His eclecticism came to the fore at these events in surprising ways: he once introduced Shostakovich's *Tenth Symphony* and *Foghorn Boogie* during the same soirée.

Inevitably, and sadly, my most vivid recollection of him is of the heart attack that killed him. We were gathered – an English Lit. class – in his study, listening to a Shakespeare play (I forget which) reproduced on his incomparable equipment. Part-way through the proceedings I chanced to lose my concentration and look up. Eric Bramall was sitting bolt upright on the edge of his armchair, gripped by what appeared to be a violent epileptic fit. I watched in silent horror for some minutes. I had no idea what to do: looking about me, I realised that I was the only one in the class who had seen what was going on. Worried

GDH

about embarrassing him, I hesitated to draw anyone else's attention to his distress, so I looked down again at the text of the play.

When I raised my eyes a few moments later I saw that he had managed, by means of what I now realise must have been a tremendous effort, to recover himself – sufficiently, in fact, for him to be able to tell us he was not feeling well, and we should leave. He asked me to stay behind to turn the record off and telephone the Sanatorium for help.

Then I asked him if he was all right and if there was anything more he wanted me to do. He thanked me and said I could leave.

The following day we were told that he was dead.

Peter Greenhill (Shaftesbury '60) studied printing management and technology, worked in the US in computer applications research and now runs his own business in Toronto.

DICK HARTHAN 1937–73

Housemaster, Head of Science and Biology, Second Master, Master i/c Pioneering

When I was a boy doing A-level biology, I suppose the thing we noticed most about GDH was that he seemed to do twice as much work as two ordinary masters. He was housemaster of Salisbury, tutor to about thirty boys, 1st XV rugby coach, Colts VIII coach, i/c Crichel (Wardour) relations, president of both the Agricultural Association and the Natural History Society, senior science master, not to mention running biology with virtually no technical assistance.

Of course, we also noticed the sheer niceness of the man. To be with him for long was to discover his ability to continue teaching and radiating magnanimity when in pain or fatigue. Always his voice carried that special warmth and sympathy; not only a reverence for life, but a love for it – whether the life was in his pupil, in a flower nodding quietly in the breeze, in some invisible part of a cell, or in the unfortunate animal on the dissecting board – and one knew that, like many biologists, he inwardly loathed the necessity for this part of the job.

Was he never angry? Occasionally, *very* angry. Usually at some piece of utter selfishness, some thoughtless abuse of the privilege of being at a place like this. To hear GDH angry was to feel a worm, for his anger was totally fair and devoid of hostility. Even in his anger, friendship flowed. *'Well,'* he might have said, *'the humble worm is man's best friend.'* Whenever he felt that relations were clouded with anger or embarrassment, this twentieth-century Merlin would flick his wand, and some delightful thought would clear the air. – *Saga*, 1973

Alan Shrimpton (Hardy '55 and member of staff since 1964)

The Nitrogen Cycle

Our O-level biology set in 1961 was taught by 'Froggy' Harthan, a very kind man and experienced teacher. In our last lesson before the final exam, he gave us his predictions for questions he thought would be included in the exam paper. There was one topic that was most overdue and he felt sure would be included this time: the Nitrogen Cycle. He was so confident he said he would eat his hat if the topic was not included.

Lo and behold, we sat the O-level exam and there were no questions about the Nitrogen Cycle. So it was that I landed up contacting his wife and discussing how her husband could escape from his predicament. A plan was hatched and she swore she would not divulge it to her husband.

For the first biology lesson after the end of exams, we placed a knife and fork on the master's desk together with a straw boater between. When Froggy came in and took in the reminder of his promise to eat his hat, he looked quite nonplussed. He left the classroom to fetch a copy of the exam paper and no doubt ponder what he was going to do or say.

AEJW

On his return a couple of minutes later, he saw a beautiful iced cake had replaced the inedible boater! He beamed; problem solved. The class cheered and eagerly helped him eat the cake there and then.

Robin Goodman (Portman '63) is a bridge engineer.

JOYCE WILSON 1942–71
Head of Chemistry, Careers Advisor

'Dear Careers Advisor, We are worrying about our Jimmy: he doesn't seem to have any idea …' You can fill in the rest. Maybe it was written about you; maybe you've written it. But what was the response? From most schools, I dare say, Standard Soothing Waffle-Letter no.1. From most good schools, an invitation to drop in for a talk next time the proud parents are visiting. And from ours?

The careers mistress in my time was Joyce Wilson, who brought back from one conference the immortal words of a seasoned employer: 'Oh yes, we always recognise Bryanstonians. They try so charmingly to put the interviewer at his ease.' Returning from such a meeting, with her den on the Dorset floor calling her back, I don't doubt, quite as enticingly as Mole End to Mole, AEJW drove twenty miles out of her way on a cold, black, wet winter's night to call on my parents beyond Poole and talk, not just reassuringly, but very much to the point. As she didn't teach me, she had consulted those who did. They never forgot this, and nor did I. When Joyce Wilson did something, it got done better than well.

She was also our safety officer, a thankless job when dealing with irreverent adolescents certain of their own invulnerability. But if I'm ever run over, I'll be where I should be, walking on the right to face oncoming traffic … which is why I'm still alive to say so.

We called her 'the Bitch', and she knew, and minded. For nearly thirty years bitches (four-footed variety) have been my daily companions: loyal, intelligent, loving and loved. Even so, I wish we hadn't. We thought of her with deep appreciation, affection and gratitude. I hope some of us told her so. I wish I had.

Theodor Ross (Portman '57)

'TEDDY' POTTER 1947–83
Housemaster, Head of Science and Physics, Secretary and Treasurer of the OBA

I knew Teddy from 1951, when he became my tutor, and we both worked in the Science Department for some twenty years, but the range of his influence upon Bryanston life was so great, and it has been so admirably and lovingly praised in the *OB Yearbook* for 1997–98, that I shall touch on only one area. This is the Old Bryanstonian Association, where we really did work together, and from which I absorbed some of his warm affection for all OBs. From the moment when he was elected the OBA's Secretary and Treasurer in 1953, Teddy increasingly *became* the OBA. He loved many things in life but perhaps above all he loved fellowship. You did not have to work with him for long to discover how much he loved gatherings of OBs, for sport or for purely social reasons. And did he make those gatherings 'go'. He gave heart to all OBA dinners, and to the Bryanston Butterflies in particular. A real family man, he probably did more than anyone else to create a family feeling among all Bryanstonians; without his devoted work, the new Bryanston Society would not have a fraction of the foundation that it enjoys today.

I cannot resist recalling one episode from some time before I knew him. Teddy's war service involved checking ships sailing out of the Thames Estuary to make sure they were 'de-gaussed', a process which neutralised their magnetic field so that magnetic mines posed a lesser threat. His unit received an urgent signal that

one particular ship must not be delayed on any account; the ship was packed with children being taken to greater safety in Canada. As she passed the monitoring station, it was obvious that, not only was she not de-gaussed, but the de-gaussing equipment was connected the wrong way round and she was doubly at risk. Contrary to orders from the top, Teddy ordered her to stop. All hell broke loose, but Teddy's order held. A few years later, on arriving at Bryanston, he recounted this story to Joyce Wilson. 'Oh! So it was you who stopped that ship! It was I who loaded all those children on board and, because of you, I had to take them all off again!'

Alan Shrimpton (Hardy '55) has been a member of staff since 1964.

ANDREW WORDSWORTH 1947–71

Taught English and Classics, President of the Da Vinci Society

Andy Wordsworth was a gentle man, who was loved by his pupils for his sincerity, compassion and human fallibility.

In a class in the 1950s he realised that the houseroom radio had been left on very quietly and there were a few smirking faces in that corner of the classroom (classrooms doubled up as houserooms in evenings and weekends). Enraged, he pulled the radio from its power socket. It slipped through his fingers and crashed to the floor. 'Look what you've made me do,' he said, 'now I'll have to buy a new one.'

Towards the end of the lesson he intercepted a note being passed covertly from one boy to the next. 'No, sir, you mustn't see that', said a boy as he grasped it. Too late. On the note each boy had pledged his pocket money to replace the radio.

On another occasion he took a party of us sailing in the old Bristol pilot cutler, 'Erne'. We had moored for the night near Brownsea Island. At dawn he quietly left his bunk and slipped over the side for a swim. Some interesting foliage on the island caught his eye so he duly went off to collect it to show us. He walked back along the beach with his trophy. By this time we crew in the main cabin had woken and looked out to see our revered skipper returning apparently carrying a posy and quite unabashedly naked.

Jeremy Houghton Brown (Dorset '59) is a Fellow of the Royal Agricultural Society, hippologist and author.

Latin with AW

AW having great difficulty in getting over the difference (in Latin) between 'in' and 'inside'. Large cupboard in corner of room – AW rushes over, wrenches open the door, jumps in and slams door. Voice from inside cupboard, 'Now I …' At that moment door to classroom opens and in comes Thor Coade plus a Mum and Dad and offspring. Thor does not seem to hear noises from cupboard until shouts of 'Can't get the door open. Somebody let me out. GET ME OUT.' Thor ambles over to cupboard and, after much tugging, door opens and out tumbles AW, who gets up off floor with words, 'Just demonstrating the difference between "in" and "inside",' and goes on with the lesson as if nothing unusual had occurred. Thor looks a little perplexed, prospective parents somewhat worried, and with 'now let's see what else is going on,' Thor ushers visitors out.

I often wondered if the child ever came to Bryanston.

Roger Baker (Salisbury '57)

JOHN N GRIFFIN 1947–49 and 1952–87
Housemaster, Head of Classics

There were other masters' desks in Dorchester as well as John Griffin's, but his was the one you approached with trepidation when the time came to have your work assessed and discussed.

I speak of trepidation, but not because he was fierce. He was *exacting* – a very different thing. You have to get your scansion right, and the endings. Endings are what all those declensions and conjugations in Greek and Latin are about. They are what make the languages work. John took delight in getting such things right, and his delight was infectious. If you had got them right, or most of them, you felt pleased because you had achieved something that really mattered. I do not mean that it mattered to him, but that it mattered. Full stop. Period. If you did not get them mostly right, you went off to try harder next time.

My other picture is of John pacing round the edge of a cricket pitch or rugger field. Round and round he goes, on and on, completely caught up in the progress of the match. When you think about it, winning, or at least playing well, is itself about getting the endings right. Cricket, John's special love, is an art of exactitude. The art of placing the ball in just the right spot when bowling or batting is not unlike the art of writing Latin verses, into which John initiated me. For that requires an apt placing of each word where its quantities fit the metre.

Myles Burnyeat (Hardy '56) is Senior Research Fellow in Philosophy at All Souls and was formerly Laurence Professor of Ancient Philosophy at Cambridge.

RICHARD 'BUNTY' HUNTER
Salisbury '45 and staff 1956–77. Housemaster, Second Master, Acting Headmaster

On the first day of school in September 1956 a couple of hands were needed to shift furniture for a new master. A kindly fate made me one of them and gave me one of my most cherished Bryanston memories.

The 'newcomer', in fact (as he was presently to tell us) no such thing, was Bunty Hunter. He had come to Bryanston originally as a boy, when his prep school was evacuated early in the war. He'd liked what he found and (no matter where else he'd been put down for) said firmly that ours was the school he wanted. He came … rose to head boy … and in time, as we all must, went out into the world. Years passed, and then Mr Coade wrote to say there was a vacancy on the staff.

The room he was moving into (trust TFC to add such a perfect touch) was Tree, on the Portman corridor: the old head boy's study, the very room from which, eleven long years before, Bunty had left, as he imagined, for ever. He was standing there, quite still, looking round, with an expression I've only seen one other time in my life: the dazed, incredulous happiness of someone who against all hope has come back to the one place on earth where he wants to be, and this time will not have to leave it.

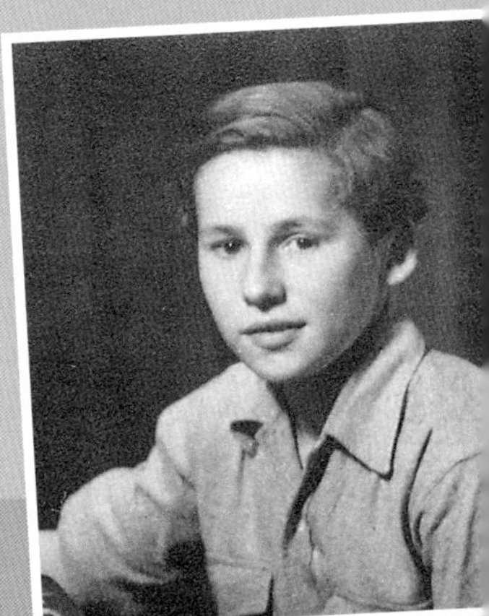

As we know, he never did. He rose again – to housemaster, to second master, briefly to acting head – and then, far too young, he died; but not before enriching generations of Bryanstonians. They will remember him as a teacher, housemaster, tutor, colleague, friend and guide – but I have something none of them has, I saw Bunty come home.

Theodor Ross (Portman '57) worked in academic libraries and tourist information and is now retired.

Bunty Hunter was a remarkable teacher. He never actually taught me – in the classroom, that is. But he did have a rare gift – the ability to look beyond his immediate circle of friends and pupils and to inspire others who had, until then, hardly crossed his path. It seemed that he wanted to involve *everyone* at Bryanston in his vision of all-round education whether he knew them or not.

It was March 1971 and A-levels were fast approaching…. Did I want to join his 'reading trip' to North Wales? It didn't matter that I wasn't in his house, or that he had never even taught me – 'if you can get yourself to Wales we'd love to see you …' 'Oh, and by the way, we'll probably be climbing Snowdon'. So a lift was duly arranged (in a tiny Fiat driven by Geoff McLardy) and I seem to recall that about ten of us spent the mornings revising and the afternoons walking in Snowdonia – including the infamous Crib Goch trek up Snowdon – before completing the horseshoe descent. Was it Matt Ristuccia with whom I chatted on the way down? Did we drink gallons of beer in the pub at the bottom? Was there an amazing meal (prepared by his sister) and a log fire awaiting us in the stone cottage?

It was Bunty's firm conviction that learning and activity go hand in hand and this was just one of many occasions which proved that he was a 'doer' rather than a philosopher. For me he personified the true 'pioneer' spirit of Bryanston. And he certainly made some of the Hardy Roof regulars ('abandon hope all ye who enter here…') reconsider, if not necessarily change, their ideas about revolutionary politics in the early seventies. This was the point about Bunty, at least from a student's perspective. He didn't force his ideas upon you – he just quietly impressed you with the wisdom and logic of his approach to life. He was a remarkable teacher.

Patrick Scanlan (Dorset '72) has worked variously as an international banker, educational publisher, writer and teacher.

PJB

PETER BREWIN 1950–85

Housemaster, Head of History, Master i/c Junior Dramatic Society

With Peter, of course, the History Department came absolutely first. He was head of the department and I had the greatest admiration for his scholarship, his thoroughness, and his intellectual honesty. Not for him any pretences! There are so many of us who teach and have taught history at Bryanston who, when we are in a tight corner about our knowledge, are liable to take the line of the notice that appears at the far end of the chemist's shop in Blandford, where it reads 'We dispense with accuracy'. A terrible confession, but not one that Peter himself ever had to make. He was a man who managed to communicate, extraordinarily well, his delight in this, our favourite subject. If you look up the Book of Proverbs you find the bit where it says 'A merry heart doeth good like a medicine', and Peter came beautifully into this category. There have been many merry moments, and I will give you just one. A boy had written something in an essay about Nazi Germany and concluded, 'Adolf Hitler was sentenced to five years' imprisonment but served only nine months because of his good conducting.' So Peter, characteristically, wrote in the margin, 'Wagner, I presume?'

Bob Allan was a member of staff from 1960 until 1989.

SPIRITUAL DIMENSIONS

9

The Church

Many prospective parents visiting Bryanston for the first time ask where the Chapel is. They have in mind something perpendicular and central, a visible, stone-built manifestation of the School's membership of the Church of England and New Labour at prayer. But it isn't like that here! Asked where the Chapel is, a Bryanstonian would conduct the visitor to the Basement Corridor and show the quiet place at the heart of the School. The headmaster, more experienced in these requests and knowing the mental picture that lies behind the question, will talk about the school church.

Lord Portman made good provision for the spiritual needs of the villagers on his estate and Bryanston is a fine example of a traditional country parish church. Rescued from redundancy by the inspiration of David Jones, St Martin's served as the school church for many years, but its present layout and ambience owes much to the relocation of the organ. The pattern is now 'in the round', and that brings choir and congregation together around and over the central altar. This has created a unique atmosphere, shared by staff, parents, pupils and friends in equal measure. Sometimes full, sometimes thinly populated, the Church witnesses a family communion thirty-six Sundays in the year. A rhythm of prayer and worship has been established which is greatly valued by the regular 'parishioners'. The fact that pupil attendance is voluntary is fundamental to the experience of church at Bryanston. It is immensely moving to see the altar surrounded by confirmed and unconfirmed alike and to know that our pupils leave Bryanston 'churched'.

Memories of chapel are a common ingredient in the recollections of former independent school pupils, perhaps because church has now become nothing but a memory. I hope and believe that Bryanstonians will have such memories but that they will be part of a continuing relationship with the spiritual. St Martin's has many physical examples of this stream of continuity. Memorials recall the village's war dead and the service of Arthur George Courtney, for forty-one years verger of the Church. Here are the names of that other Bryanston – Bryánston – as well as the names of great figures in the School's history, David Jones and Geoff Udall. Of David Jones it can be said as it was of Christopher Wren, *si monumentum requiris, circumspice*. For a tribute to Geoff Udall you must climb (as did the Bishop of Salisbury when he came to consecrate our newcomers) to the belfry where *Geoff* and *Ellie* were hung to expand the ring to eight and to recall two much loved members of the Bryanston family. The organ bears witness to the work of Peter Lattimer, for thirty years director of music, and in windows and inscriptions the Portmans are there as well.

Religious observance at Bryanston has not been 'an ever-rolling stream'. Although two headmasters were ordained and all five have been practising communicant members of the Church of England, the School has reflected the ups and downs (rather more of the latter it is fair to say) of Christian observance and worship in this country in the second half of the twentieth century.

St Anthony's Chapel was and is a second centre to the school, hidden away but, almost literally, fundamental. Variations in our public worship were inevitable. Compulsion came … and went. 'Assemblies' were more and less religious in their character. Humanities flourished and mutated under John Mott and John Rose. Pat Magee was an ideal chaplain when the demand for change and relevance was at its height. Somewhat like a recusant priest he kept the flame of faith alive whilst satisfying all political parties with a sufficiency of respect for tradition and a flow of new ideas for the forward-looking, however short-sighted. In the end it comes down to a story of two organs – an electronic installation in Coade Hall, epitome of the state of the art and soul of the time, and a tracker action neo-classical organ built in St Martin's when David Jones and Peter Lattimer led the school to a leap of faith.

So there it stands – St Martin's in the fields – offering to share with all who pass by *et nova et vetera,* welcoming and sustaining each new generation of Bryanstonians, reassuring and reinspiring those whose time has passed but whose hearts have been caught by this house of God.

Tom Wheare, Headmaster 1983–2005.

Bothersome questions

Existentialism and Zen Buddhism were some of the baffling concepts to test teenage minds like mine, before heading off into the big bad world of 1963. I never really did understand such things.

But if Bryanston did anything for me, it made me think and it made me question.

Being 'into Zen' was a bit fashionable at the time. In French, more seriously, there were studies on Camus and Sartre. The whole existentialist idea that living for the moment is the essence of life was strangely appealing.

One of my Zen friends became a class hero when he stood up to the chaplain in a scripture lesson, as a result of which several of us were invited round to tea, where the debate continued. In the general mix of Bryanston, free thinking was encouraged and even if it wasn't, it still happened. There were robust challenges to the status quos of Society, the Establishment, the Church and Politics.

I always thought it a great pity that Bryanston's own general election – held at the same time as the national one – was cancelled during Fisher's first year as headmaster.

It all started with the Tory party writing 'Vote Conservative' in conkers on the grass plot in front of the School in time for the early morning four-minute walk. As the whole school paraded past, others of different persuasions, such as myself – an Independent – thought the conkers would make good ammo, which they did. Into the fray came the hand-pushed fire-engine and great fun was had by all. This was deemed a riot and in assembly we were soundly told off, so no general election forthwith. There was free speech – but only up to a point!

However it was the encouragement of the arts generally that for me provoked deeper questions about life and meaning. I was never any good at maths or science, so art and English became my main A-level options. For me the studies in literature, poetry, theatre and art were licence to explore a whole new stratosphere of ideas. Despite not being particularly academic, I loved it. Here was a heady mix of the philosophical, metaphysical and spiritual.

There was *Paradise Lost*, Chaucer and *King Lear*; there was Wordsworth and Keats; there were the Impressionists and the challenges of Expressionism and Cubism. There were the wonderful school plays in the Greek Theatre and the singing in *The Messiah*. And yes, the attraction of 'Joint Activities' with Crichel was all part of it!

But there were also deep and surprising moments of the numinous. I remember in particular being transfixed during a concert listening to an extraordinarily beautiful deep female alto voice. She was singing: 'Be careful for nothing, but in everything by prayer and supplication let your requests be made known unto God; and the peace of God which passeth all understanding shall keep your heart and mind through Jesus Christ our Lord.'

They were words that rang bells in every part of my being and I never forgot them or the beauty of the moment. Years later I discovered they came from the New Testament in Paul's letter to the Phillippians chapter 4, verses 6–7. It was the first time I remember being so profoundly touched by Bible verses.

There were other similar moments. I remember on two separate occasions, sitting on those incredibly squeaky chairs in the Centre Room, being enthralled by the speakers. One was a missionary from the North-west Frontier in Pakistan; the other was one of the 'Brown Brothers' from the Franciscan Friary at Cerne Abbas. There was a third time too in the chapel at Glastonbury Abbey during my confirmation retreat – again with a Brown Brother.

There was lots of fun and fooling around and many 'afternooners' running it all off. But the deep and powerful undercurrent was being confronted by so many ideas, ideologies and belief systems. There was no way one could sit idle and watch from a distant hill; they provoked choice and they demanded questions; one was bundled into the fray.

And the net result? Well lots of hiccups and plenty of mistakes! And now surprise, surprise – I am an ordained priest.

The Rev. William Mather (Forrester '63) is an Anglican priest working with Sharing of Ministries Abroad (SOMA) and is the author of the book, Cry for Sudan.

ART AND THE POTTER'S WHEEL

10

Creative space

Art at Bryanston has a prestigious history despite being run from some unlikely places. Originally located on the first floor of the Main Building in the Portman family's Billiards Room (now the Bursary), it moved in the early 1930s to purpose-built accommodation above and to one side of the Dining Room (later Galley Studies and now mainly offices). In the early 1970s it moved again to the upper half of what used to be the high-ceilinged dining room and then occupied temporary portakabins on the Plateau for a number of years until the new, and current, Art School was ready. Pottery and carving began life in a room below the basement next to the boiler. In the 1930s Walter Jenke built the first kiln, connecting it to one of the large chimneys of the house. The sculptor, Willi Soukop, who taught wood carving and clay modelling, complained that the space was coated in 'black coal dust' and lit unsympathetically by electric light. In 1938 a new sculpture studio in 'Mr Bramall's old garage' transformed his classes. But the Pottery remained in the cellars for many years.

The longest serving and most famous of Bryanston's art teachers was Don Potter, whose expertise lay in carving. He took over in 1940 when Willi Soukop was interned as an alien during the war. Don had worked for several years with Eric Gill before coming to Bryanston and was both an inspiring teacher to many generations of Bryanstonians and a successful sculptor. His nine-foot statue of Baden-Powell still towers over Queen's Gate in south-west London. Don's wife, Mary, also taught weaving after the first girls arrived, and fashion was introduced by Philippa Sayer. Don Potter's long contribution to Bryanston came to an end in 1984 when he retired. No head of art matched Don's length of service,

Right: Lift, by Ian Middleton and pupils, 2003

Howard Hodgkin (Portman '48), Small, Medium and Large 2004 *(oil on wood)*

but talented artists the others were too. They included Elsie Barling and Elizabeth Muntz during the war, Charles Handley-Read who was the first OB (Hardy '34) to join the staff, Eric Rennick, Phil Monk and Mike Suffield.

In 1997 the Art Department moved to a new building appropriately named the Don Potter Art School, and for the first time art, pottery, sculpture, textiles and photography were combined under one roof.

That Bryanston should have so many exceptional artists and designers amongst its alumni is testament to the School's long tradition of encouraging creativity. The art syllabus has evolved over the years, with modern materials and computer imagery opening new doors, but the inspirational qualities of the teachers remain constant. Pupils continue to display outstanding talent and enthusiasm, and we relish the thought of some of them following in the footsteps of Freud, Hodgkin or Conran.

Mike Owens *has been Head of Art since 1998.*

Building the kiln – a risky venture

In 1935 Ronald Muirhead came to the School. The standard of carpentry immediately improved. He had a large, well-equipped workshop in what I think had been garages beyond the Dining Room. Carpentry was on the main timetable for first-year pupils. The workshop was well used and open most evenings for the hobby period. The Art Department at the time consisted only of Reggie Hughes, and quite a bit of time was taken up making lampshades! A book of colour linocuts was professionally printed in Blandford, and posters were made to announce lectures, films, plays, etc. in the Main Hall. There was a small printing room, with a Platen Machine and half a dozen fonts of moveable type. Small jobs were undertaken such as theatrical programmes and poetry. A few of us took the School Certificate art exam.

Walter Jenke, a German refugee, also joined the staff in 1935. His first responsibility was in the German Department but he was a craftsman with many talents and was keen to start a pottery. Those of us who were involved from the start were fortunate to experience not only our own achievements and disasters but Jenke's as well.

There was quite a large area beneath the basement behind the door at the bottom of the stone stairs and opposite the bookshop run by Mr Hare. Local clay from Poole Pottery was bought, and a small kick wheel, cupboards and strong tables were installed. We experimented with slab work and plaster moulds for casting in slip. Jenke was quite undaunted by the building of a kiln. He chose a position in the Pottery immediately below one of the main chimneys. The Clerk of Works, Mr Putman, agreed that the flue from the kiln be connected to the bottom of this chimney. (I wonder if he realised we needed to reach a heat of 1000ºC?) 'Bosun' Acott, who looked after the fires and central heating, supplied us from his stock of steam coal.

When the moment came for the first firing, no one knew which of the vast chimneys on the roof was ours. We soon found out. Black smoke billowed upwards, happily caught and carried away by the wind. The length of the chimney drew the fire powerfully, so much so that Jenke needed to put a damper in to restrict and control the draught. The first muffle cracked and had to be replaced. Controlling the fire meant that someone had to be watching it all the time and occasionally Jenke could not be there himself. This gave some of us an excellent reason for going to bed late, sometimes after midnight. All too soon firing the kiln became routine. Ten years later in 1947 ceramics at Bryanston were taken sufficiently seriously to be included in an exhibition at Heal's on Tottenham Court Road.

***Peter Bradford** (Salisbury '37), after four years running the Photography Department in Naval Intelligence, joined the director, Paul Rotha, and began a career writing, directing and producing documentaries.*

Walter Jenke's kiln as photographed by Peter Bradford, 1937. No-one knew which of the vast chimneys served the kiln until the first firing

An artist looks back

When I came to Bryanston the teacher in charge of art was, quite unfoundedly, called by the boys Pansy Hughes. All the painting in the Art Room was in watercolour and, while technically sound, the subject matter was hardly innovative. Typical would be ploughmen at the bottom of a carefully stretched sheet of paper, coming over the brow of a hill, the rest of the picture being sky made by running thin washes of colour by tipping the board. The other prevalent subject was crinolined ladies, also in watercolour.

Some time later an oil painting club was set up by the boys in opposition to school art. I expect there must have been some benevolence from the staff to bring this about. The studio was a room at the far end of a ground-floor dormitory wing and of fairly light construction.

The only heat came from a Valor Perfection paraffin stove which gave out more smell than heat. I know there were trees close by the windows because I painted them. I am uncertain how many artists used the room, perhaps a dozen. I remember one organised criticism of our pictures given by Miss George, a local artist, and another occasion when Lucian Freud's sophistication was rewarded with the first prize and my picture of *Tugs Beneath a Bridge* seemed very innocent.

There was a trip to see Michael Sadler's collection in Oxford, where I was impressed by Constable's little paintings of sky, and another trip to see Christopher Wood's brilliant flower pieces. These outings, I believe, were arranged by Mr Williams, whose geometrical drawing on the blackboard of perfect circles and straight

Patrick George (Shaftesbury '41), Trees, Sky and Pond, *1994 (oil on canvas)*

Left: Patrick George, Trees at Bryanston, *1939*

lines (the chalk being so ground into the board that it left a plume of chalk dust behind) was such a tour de force that I quite lost the reasoning of the Pythagorean proof that followed.

Encouraged by Willi Soukop, I painted a decoration for St Anthony's Chapel. David Barker, Bill Smith and JC Marris made large reliefs on the entrance walls. Finally I was let loose on the walls of the gallery above the Main Hall.

This, as I try to remember, is how it was. The attitude to art in the School at that time I would describe as liberal and haphazard.

***Professor Patrick George** (Shaftesbury '41) is a figurative painter. He taught at the Slade for many years and still paints landscapes in Suffolk.*

Don Potter

Don Potter was a remarkable man.

Above all he was a great teacher, as many generations of Bryanston students can confirm. His enthusiasm and the twinkle in his eye were quite magnetic and he caused many an uninterested student to become motivated and lit the flame of creativity in many a damp, dull soul.

I was at Bryanston during the war years when life was exceedingly austere. We were all hungry and cold but Don brought a cheerful energy into our lives in the Metalwork, Sculpture and particularly the Pottery Departments. He took our minds off Latin prep and the war by getting us to think and make creatively – you just longed to finish your tedious school work so you could get back to one of Don's departments. They didn't seem like school, they seemed like a hobby and very quickly they became a hobby.

My best memories are of the below-stairs pottery, with its wood-fired kiln, which reached terrific temperatures because of the hugely tall Bryanston chimneys. I remember the all-night firings, keeping the kiln stoked with wood and waiting for the cones to melt to indicate that it had reached the right temperature for our galena or wood ash glazes.

I am sure we shouldn't have been allowed to stay up all night and certainly we shouldn't have been drinking beer or cider, but we would then have missed Don talking about his time with Eric Gill; about wearing kilts whilst carving the outside of BBC in Portland Place; about his enthusiasm for slipware and Thomas Toft;

Lucian Freud (Portman '38)

Don Potter in the Sculptorium

about St Ives and Bernard Leach's pottery; and about his admiration for the work of Michael Cardew.

He talked and inspired us throughout the day and night and showed us how to make things with consummate ease. I certainly would not have been able to achieve the things that I have in my life if he had not taught me the practical skills of welding and forging, potting and casting, sculpting and carving. But most of all, he imbued us all with the pleasure of making things. He showed us the glow you can get from seeing an idea turn into a three dimensional, beautiful object.

He got enormous pleasure from his own work, particularly his sculpture and beautiful carved lettering. I saw him just after his 100th birthday, chipping away at a huge piece of heavy oak, which he proceeded to lift to show how strong he still was. Although I'm thirty years younger, I could only just move it!

He always was a tower of strength in every way. Thank you Don, now carving angels in Heaven I am sure. You were a great inspiration to many generations of Bryanstonians and helped them make their lives much more creative and interesting.

Sir Terence Conran (Connaught '48) is a designer, shopkeeper, restaurateur, furniture designer, writer, property developer and gardener.

Thorold Coade's headboard

Bryanston encouraged us to be self-motivated; in addition to normal classes, we were expected to take up other activities and hobbies. As woodwork was part of the curriculum, it was not long before I found myself in Cecil Colyer's class. At thirteen, I had never done any woodwork before, but I soon found myself getting more and more involved and enjoying making pieces of furniture. During the next few years I made bookcases, coffee tables, a dining table, a dressing table and a special cabinet to take church brass rubbings.

However, the most interesting project was the special headboard I was asked to make for Thorold Coade. During my last year at Bryanston Mr Coade asked me to come to his study and said that he wanted me to make a special headboard for his bed in his retirement cottage. He arranged for his wife, Kathleen, to drive me to Old Bell Cottage in East Knoyle so that I could see where it had to go and take measurements.

The design was quite complicated. It had two large veneered panels and the rest was solid wood. There were shelves for books, a padded section to lean against and a folding table that could swing round over the bed for writing. The bed was positioned next to a window so Mr Coade could look out over the countryside.

Everyone at Bryanston was able to enjoy the work of top national and international artists at first hand when *Sculpture – a Spectator Sport?* was arranged at Bryanston to celebrate the 75th anniversary of the School. The stunning work of Nash, Caro, Woodrow and Ian Middleton could be seen in the wonderful setting of the school grounds.

Ian Middleton, Fools and Footsoldiers *(bronze)*

I had little time to make it during my last term and it all had to be done by hand. On some Sunday mornings I would get up early, against the rules, but I needed the extra hours to complete the work. One Sunday my housemaster, Bill Williams, found me in the woodwork room at 6am and was very annoyed. Little did he know I had been there since 4.30am! I explained about the headboard and that I was running out of time. Nonplussed, he dismissed me with a brief nod and the hope that I would get it finished.

Eventually the headboard was finished and we delivered it on the open school lorry one dry summer day and installed it in the bedroom. Mr Coade thanked me at school assembly and then asked me to come to his study where he gave me a present of a large book on furniture construction. Over the years I have lost the book but the inscription is unforgettable:

'I will remember you every night, Thorold Coade.'

Paul Cornford (Hardy '57) has worked with furniture ever since, designing, importing and exporting. He now runs his own business in Spain.

Teaching art

I began teaching at Bryanston in the autumn of 1986, having previously worked mainly in Higher Education. I didn't know much about the School but I had met Don and Mary Potter a few years earlier. My own feelings about art education were similar to Don's; we both placed emphasis on the development of the individual student and the relationship and dialogue students had with their own work. We also shared a scepticism for the examination system.

Mike Suffield ran the department then. He had a real passion for contemporary art, both as a collector and as a practitioner, and an extensive knowledge of twentieth-century art. Mike helped his wife, Wendy, run the Hambledon Gallery in Blandford where he regularly staged very good exhibitions and each year he hosted a student/staff show from the school. There was a belief in the department at that time that in order to teach art it was necessary to make it yourself and, just as Don had done, I was encouraged to work alongside the students, capturing their imagination with my own commitment and enthusiasm. Teaching by example is still favoured in art schools, where students learn that art is not an easy option but a serious undertaking demanding intellectual, creative and practical disciplines.

The Art Department was a collection of temporary buildings up on the Plateau; there were three, later four painting studios and rooms for weaving and textiles. The sculpture studio was outside the Dining Hall next to the old woodwork and metalwork shops. The room was rather austere, with two wooden walls and a concrete floor. It was always cold. A large sliding door opened on to the courtyard and an opaque glass sunlight window allowed natural light into that end of the room. At the other end a small window made visible a teacher's desk, a collection of battered and well-thumbed books about sculpture on some wall shelves and a very chipped and stained sink with one tap. In the centre of the room, stretching from one end to the other, stood a massive workbench with a thick elm top made from a single plank, its edges and corners worn round and the surface distressed by half a century of fervent creative activity. The room had a compelling atmosphere and although it would get uncomfortably cold (the tap froze regularly in winter), for some students it became a sanctuary and as a teacher I was really happy there.

Drawing was regarded as fundamental in the department, underpinning the painting and sculpture. We encouraged students to look, observe and record,

enabling them to develop the necessary analytical and research skills to explore their ideas and pursue visual investigations in their chosen media. On two evenings a week we ran life-drawing classes and these were so popular that another daytime class was introduced. The standard of drawing has always been very high at Bryanston and each year there were one or two quite exceptional students whose work I will always remember.

In the late eighties Steve Sheridan resurrected the Pottery. He was succeeded by Sue Haslam, who now runs pottery and ceramics, and Jane Hedges arrived to teach painting and drawing. Peter Rush joined the staff a little later. The balance in the department was still in favour of part-time staff and most did their own work. There was a strong belief that art and design should be seen as a core subject, that a sound visual understanding is essential and that all young people could and should be visually literate. The individual student was seen as the focus of the A-level course, which was interpreted to encourage the particular aptitudes and interests of each child, fostering confidence, understanding and a sense of achievement. By identifying and building on their individual strengths, students were able to develop a dialogue with their work, which encouraged an attitude of curiosity and enquiry, self-reliance and independence. The department provided an important pastoral role within the School, offering space for contemplation and reflection and a trusting, supportive environment for students to explore their own perceptions, sensitivities and creativity. Students were challenged to think for themselves and were not heavily directed, the student-centred approach encouraging understanding and confidence without the pressures of continuous assessment.

Ian Middleton taught sculpture from 1986 to 2003.

Ceramics, sewing and monumental sculpture

When friends ask me to describe what Bryanston was like to go to as a school, I normally just reel off a list of every activity I can think of. For sports, tennis, canoeing, squash, cricket, rugby, etc., and for the arts, metalwork, theatre design, sewing, weaving, ceramics, sculpture, painting, photography, life drawing, technical design, stone carving, printing press, etc. The effect this has on the listener is to create an immediate vision of Bryanston as a kind of wondercamp for kids. Which in a way, it was.

Top left: Charlotte Wales (oil paint)

Bottom left: Harry Young-Jamieson (oil bar)

Above: Ellie Kealey (ceramics)

Right: Fiamma Montagu

For myself, my sister and brother and three cousins (Bona Montagu, Olly Montagu, Hetta Hunloke, Ned Hunloke, Tilly Hunloke) who went to school from the late seventies to early nineties this inevitably meant different things at different times. Aged fourteen I sewed myself a pencil skirt so tight I could barely walk; at fifteen my sister handwove two beautiful cushions which she gave to my parents for Christmas. My brother started what was to become a professional interest in photography and animation, and I nearly got suspended (by Mrs Daynes) for staying up until midnight making a birthday card to put on the 24-hour board.

In the mid-eighties the Art Department was still a group of cabins on stilts on the Plateau run by Mike Suffield, the Metalwork Department was a cabin by the old tuck shop, run by the fiery but inspiring Frank Bristow (rigorous about poor soldering techniques and sloppy spoon workmanship), and the Ceramics Department was in a room beneath the basement corridor.

In my memory, they were all separate kingdoms with different philosophies. The Ceramics Department felt rebellious and earthy, with a scruffier vibe from the seventies, whereas the Art Department was slicker and design/advertising-oriented.

Ceramics was what ended up stealing my heart. While my cousin Hetta was happy doing beautiful drawings in the Art Department (she is now an architect), I was at my happiest covered in mud in the small hole that was the Ceramics Department run by Steve Sheridan. The sense of escape and excitement were immediate and wonderful, despite the lack of resources. Fortunately for me, the same mood of relaxed radicalism continued with the arrival of the new CDT centre. This meant a lot more space, a lot of jokes about the screws on the building being left-hand screws (which apparently told you a lot about how much you would really learn about design technology) and also a lot more equipment. This was a very free and happy place to be, with a general view that you should pretty much explore your own path and then take responsibility for the consequences.

For me this meant constructing massive pots and applying copious amounts of glaze. And the glazes were seriously good, not just average dead glazes that would kill anything you made, but (now I know the names) an amazing blue/brown/black Tenmoku and an incredible blue chun. (There was also a rather strange yellow custard glaze.) Whether this was due to the hard work of the Ceramics Department, funding or having had potters of the calibre of Richard Batterham at Bryanston I will never know.

Steve Sheridan was a good pottery teacher mainly because he was relaxed and let you follow your own path. Ian Middleton was a good sculpture teacher because he loved the surreal (I remember his extraordinary sculptures), and neither of them would let you get away with any intellectual laziness. Ceramics was a refuge from the worries of Oxbridge and academic study. Since I was not even doing an art A-level at the time it is amazing they taught me at all, but they did.

Since leaving Bryanston I have realised that Old Bryanstonians are easy to spot in an crowd and are marked out in life as being by far the most likely to say, to the anguish of their loved ones, 'I've just stopped a very successful career as a banker to become a novelist'. Most of the people I am still in touch with do extraordinary things. To name them by their job descriptions: tree surgeon, film script writer, art dealer, animator, architect, dress designer, sex advisor in schools, and my friend Paula, who has been redesigning city centres. Those that have normal jobs do them with a bit of a twist.

In keeping with all of this, I recently stopped quite a healthy career as a documentary maker in television to start from scratch making monumental ceramic sculpture. I'm not sure where I got the confidence to do such a daft thing, and I spent a good two years with my head in my hands in worry about the small practicalities of life like paying a mortgage, but there you go. Ultimately I do think that the best that Bryanston has to offer lies in the extraordinary luxury of being able to try out so many aspects of art. Perhaps this also gives people the ability to relate the various art forms and have a more radical approach to what is possible.

When I was twelve, I remember going to a meeting at Tom Wheare's office to decide whether Bryanston would be a school to go to – this was probably just a pitch, but I remember someone describing it as a school where 'you could build an aeroplane on the games fields if you wanted'. As a child this pretty whimsical idea of what life could be all about delighted me. It still does.

***Fiamma Montagu** (Harthan '89) worked for some years as a documentary producer, making programmes for the BBC, ITV and Channel 4. She is now a sculptor specialising in monumental pieces.*

11

MUSIC SPEAKS

114 Music and maestros

Music departments, like schools, are best defined by the personality of the person in charge. The first director of music was CE Osmond. He had been appointed at the time of the School's foundation by the master, JG Jeffreys, and he immediately started regular concerts in the Centre Room (Cowley). He was encouraged and ably supported by the headmaster's wife, May Jeffreys, who was a competent violinist. There survives a 'third choral concert' programme for 8th June 1929, in which the orchestra has eleven members, the Common Room staff sing male voice items, and Jeffreys and Osmond play the first movement of Grieg's *Piano Concerto* arranged for two pianos. After two years, Osmond's obvious ability took him to the organist's post at St Albans Abbey.

Paul Rogers appeared on the scene after another two years. He was a meticulous organiser. Labels and instructions appeared everywhere. One still surviving on the cover of the Coade Hall grand piano reads 'keyboard at this end'. He was a fluent pianist and excellent organist. He gathered together musical members of staff such as Bill Carpenter-Jacobs (a formidable bassoonist) and Walter Jenke (clarinet) and visiting teachers such as the Allen sisters (violin and cello), Willoughby Smith (horn), Don Potter (cellist as well as sculptor) and Rogers' wife, Pat, a useful viola player. Chamber music and orchestral concerts were frequent.

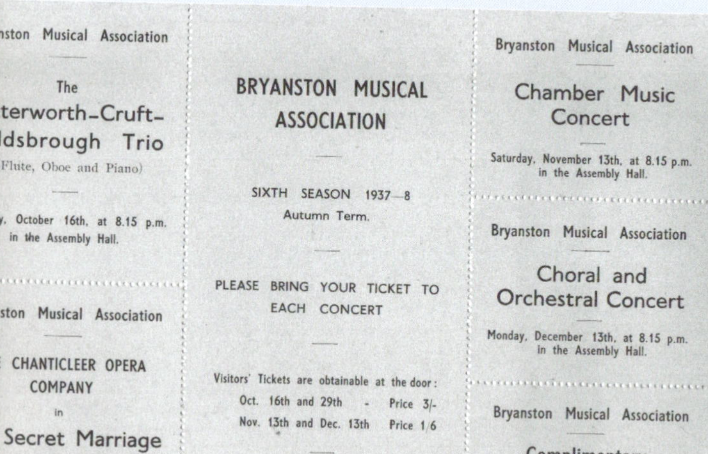
anston Musical Association
The
tterworth-Cruft-
ldsbrough Trio
(Flute, Oboe and Piano)
ay, October 16th, at 8.15 p.m.
in the Assembly Hall.

nston Musical Association
E CHANTICLEER OPERA
COMPANY
in
Secret Marriage
(Cimarosa)
October 29th, at 8.15 p.m.
in the Gymnasium.

BRYANSTON MUSICAL
ASSOCIATION
SIXTH SEASON 1937–8
Autumn Term.
PLEASE BRING YOUR TICKET TO
EACH CONCERT
Visitors' Tickets are obtainable at the door:
Oct. 16th and 29th - Price 3/-
Nov. 13th and Dec. 13th Price 1/6
A Complimentary Visitor's Ticket for Nov. 13th
or Dec. 13th is included.

Bryanston Musical Association
Chamber Music
Concert
Saturday, November 13th, at 8.15 p.m.
in the Assembly Hall.

Bryanston Musical Association
Choral and
Orchestral Concert
Monday, December 13th, at 8.15 p.m.
in the Assembly Hall.

Bryanston Musical Association
Complimentary
Ticket
Available for November 13th, or
December 13th.

Rogers was a competent composer, but his greatest strength was as an actor and producer. Before the war he directed and conducted Purcell's *Dido and Aeneas* and a staged Handel's *Samson*. It is fortunate that we have a complete set of programmes for musical events from 1928 to the present. The master, as Jeffreys insisted on being called, appears as baritone soloist, pianist and cellist. The twelfth Choral and Orchestral Concert of 1933 lists a full orchestra and choir of twenty-four, plus twenty trebles from Charlton Marshall House Prep School, all conducted by Paul Rogers. The long programme included Mozart, Vivaldi, Bach (*The Peasant Cantata*), Dyson (*The Seekers*), Grieg (*Landerkennung*) and the *Pioneers' Song* by Martin Shaw. The evening concluded with the singing of the Bryanston song, set to music by Rogers. The first verse goes:

> The life we live at Bryanston
> Is free and full of fun:
> Not only do we eat and sleep,
> But dig our trenches broad and deep.
> To sow a seed the world will reap
> When Pioneering's done.

A fine pianist named John Sterling arrived to support Rogers before the war and, when Rogers went off to the navy, he became the director. He had the difficult task of steering the department throughout the war years. He coped with fluctuating numbers of pupils, prep schools taking up temporary residence in Bryanston and a teaching staff that appeared and more frequently disappeared. I have always thought that the war limited

HANDEL'S WATER MUSIC

Left: 1964 performance to mark the retirement of Wilfrid Cowley, who dressed for the occasion as George I

Below: The 1971 production formed part of the Bryanston Arts Centre Festival

the scope of the Music Department but the programmes, now headed Bryanston Musical Association, not only maintain a flourishing school repertoire but also feature professional London visitors – Arnold Goldsbrough (organ), Isolde Menges (violin), Sir Thomas Armstrong (organ), York Bowen (piano) and my second-favourite organ composer, Percy Whitlock. There were exchange concerts with Sherborne and Winchester and *The Messiah*, sung by Bryanston, Clayesmore and Croft House in Shillingstone Church.

Paul Rogers took up the reins once more in 1946. John Sterling became responsible for music at Cranborne Chase School for Girls when it was founded in the same year. Despite the distance between the two schools, the musical link was close and the Choral Society, operas and orchestras benefited from the presence of the girls. The boys felt there were other advantages too. The relationship withered when Bryanston started to accept its own girls from 1972.

Bryanston gained a wider reputation for music from the summer school which began in 1948. Five years later it moved to Dartington and still flourishes. The Amadeus Quartet, Janet Baker and other artists were among the students who are now famous. There were also distinguished visitors such as Paul Hindemith in 1948, and Dame Myra Hess and George Enescu in 1949, 1950 and 1952.

In 1970, Rogers retired to Polruan where he was able to indulge his passion for sailing. Prabhu Singh took his place. He was a delightful, charming Indian who was a superb pianist. I remember his stylish performance of Brahm's *Horn Trio* with Bill Norman and Willoughby Smith. He was a sensitive soul who did not like the rough and tumble of boarding school life. One day he named each practice room after a famous composer. He was very shocked when his careful lettering was complemented equally carefully by an imaginative pupil: Brahms and legs, Haydn seek, Liszt and learn, Handel with care, etc. After two years, he moved on to Huddersfield College of Technology.

I had been teaching at Bryanston for a year, when Robson Fisher appointed me director in 1972. By this time the syllabuses of the national examinations were changing for the better and the music syllabus was no exception. The Associated Board instrumental music examinations were integrated with the A- and O-levels and thus were given greater status, and music rightly became a very practical subject. Part of the A-level music exam involved the pupil producing a concert and the examiner appearing for the performance. Out of this beginning, the yearly operatic/musical tradition began. Gilbert and Sullivans moved on to operettas; lighting and effects became more important; and sound amplification is vital for any school performance these days. The Coade Hall is an ideal venue for these occasions and has housed some tremendous performances – *Ruddigore*, *Oklahoma!* (three times), *Kiss Me Kate, Anything Goes*, *Orpheus in the Underworld*, and many more.

St Martin's Church was closed and had become a diocesan storehouse, but in 1976 the headmaster purchased it for the use of the School and began weekly Sunday services. As the dilapidated organ had been removed, brass ensembles provided the music. This sounds like an exciting move but the irritations of brass players playing the wrong hymn, losing their music or dropping their mouthpieces on to the stone floor led to the installation of a new classical French organ in 1980. Regular service singing produced better choirs, and it was slowly realised that the Church was an excellent location for concerts ranging from chamber music, through organ recitals to orchestral or band concerts.

With the encouragement of the headmaster, Tom Wheare, the Music Department became more adventurous. The choir sang evensongs in cathedrals and did tours to Budapest (Mozart's *Coronation Mass* in the cathedral), Paris (a full Madeleine church on a Sunday afternoon), Spain (superb churches with terrible organs) and Venice (unaccompanied singing in those silent but glorious churches). There were many memorable moments on these trips. A grateful Spanish priest presented us with a crate of excellent sherry which we carried around with us for a week, only to have it confiscated by Heathrow customs. The Hungarians were so impressed with our singing that they put on a party for us in which a lady singer elegantly removed her clothes. Such events were character-developing for both pupils and staff.

The abilities of our music scholars were also revealed in orchestral and choral concerts in London, and chamber ensembles were frequently successful in the National Chamber Music Competition.

Electric guitars, drums and saxophones have become more respectable in this last decade. Despite the volume produced (excessive in some opinions), groups, bands and ensembles are fully integrated into the department's activities and even into examination syllabuses, or prospectuses as we have to call them nowadays. Similarly, recording studios and electronic music are now a vital part of twenty-first-century music-making.

Paul Searle-Barnes was appointed director in 2003, having been head of keyboard for twenty-six years. He is probably the most gifted pianist and musician that Bryanston has ever had. Under his leadership the department is once again successful academically and, as a performer himself, he ensures the standard of performances is consistently high and that music has a growing reputation outside Bryanston.

***Peter Lattimer** was Director of Music from 1972 to 2001.*

Discovering the flute

There were certainly musical opportunities at Bryanston in its early days. We had an orchestra and music teachers. Using a battered old school instrument, I used to have flute lessons from a local bandmaster who taught anyone at the School who wanted to learn a wind instrument. On first holding the flute I thought, 'This is my future,' and looked at it with awe, then spent hours by myself working out how the complicated keys worked. But at first I disliked the sound I made, for it was thick, breathy and dull compared with the sweet-sounding bamboo instruments that I used to make for myself; but I saw that the flute was more serious, an advance, and forced myself not to play my bamboo pipes ever again. For a time they were hard to resist and I would sometimes hold them lovingly, but never lift them to my lips.

Each day, after lunch, there was a time when boys could listen to classical records. We took small mattresses to the huge, ornate school hall and lay down, forced to rest and listen to music coming from the speakers on the walls. In contrast to the noisy hassle of school life, I enjoyed quietly lying there with the tranquil sounds washing over me.

One day, expecting just another ordinary, pleasant record, there was one that was quite different; it was of Moyse playing a Mozart flute concerto, and I was at once overwhelmed. The music hit me like a physical assault that seemed to go to the pit of my stomach, not to my ears, and I was no longer aware of where I was but lay, crying without shame, ignoring the other boys.

Afterwards, having packed away my mattress, I walked alone in the sunshine toward the playing fields, with Mozart still singing in my head in vivid bursts of sound that again made me cry. I felt expanded, bigger than my body, and floated along as if not touching the ground. The trees I walked under had head-high upward bends in their boughs, especially shaped for me to pass under them, and the gate into the meadow was open, waiting; the whole world was perfect. Moyse had so shaken me that even my kidneys must have reacted, for I had to stop several times to pee.

That evening, I wrote to my parents, asking them to buy the record and, when at last I got home for the holidays, I greeted no one, found the record, told my family to leave me alone, and played it.

Moyse was again overwhelming – and he'd set the course of my life.

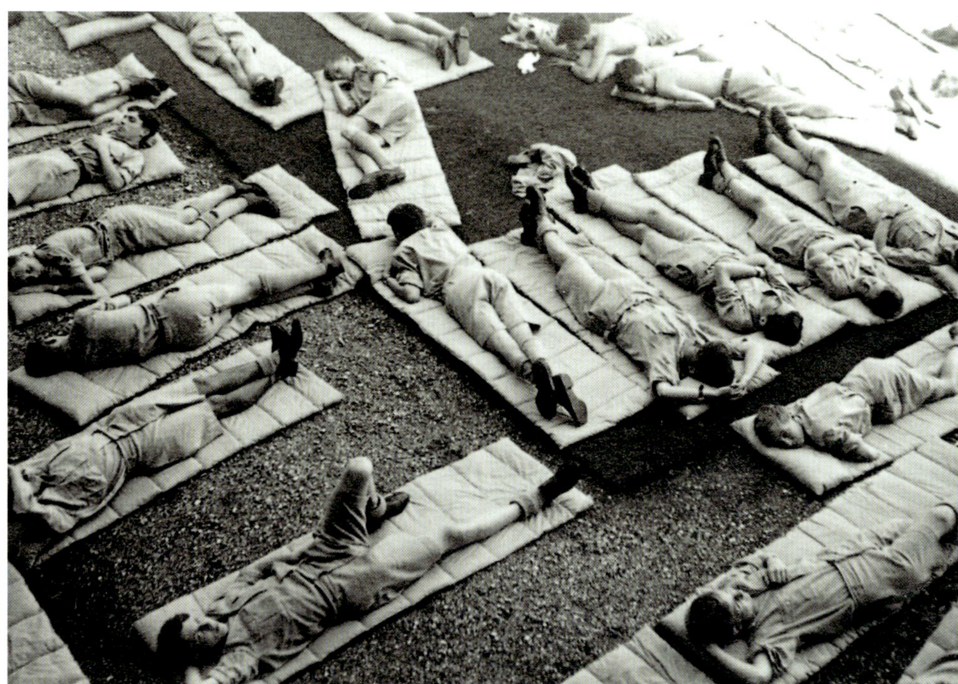

Compulsory afternoon rest, 1935: an opportunity to listen to music

I practised a lot and the day came for my first rehearsal with the school orchestra. We played Schubert's *Unfinished*, which was impossibly difficult, especially the syncopated notes; it seemed that everyone else was playing perfectly and I was the only one struggling. Nevertheless, being in the middle of an orchestra was perfect happiness, something quite unlike everyday life, and I lived through classes, through games, waiting between the weekly rehearsals, longing for the next one.

Already, in 1934, only a year after Hitler became Chancellor, there were Jewish German boys at the School, presumably sons of intelligent parents who had seen what was coming. These boys were different from the others at the School because they accepted the enjoyment of classical music as a normal part of life, and they talked to me about it in a matter-of-fact way that taught me a lot. One of these fourteen-year-olds told me how he prepared himself mentally for a concert, settling himself into a receptive mood. For them, as for me, there was more to life than lessons and games.

The seeds were sown for the rest of my life. I left Bryanston for Dartington and the Royal College of Music and a career as a flautist.

Richard Adeney (Portman '36) played the flute for the London Philharmonic for many years. He has also been a member of the Melos Ensemble, the English Chamber Orchestra and the London Mozart Players, and has played in the first performance of many of Benjamin Britten's works.

Blowing and singing

My first music class, soon after arriving in the autumn of 1941, was taken by Paul Rogers, head of music. We were introduced to a truly rural example of folk song: 'The fly is on the turmut' (and it's all my eye for to try and get the fly off the turmut). Young and inexperienced as I was, this was not really what I was looking for; Rogers soon left to join the navy for the duration.

John Sterling became head of music (unfit for war service due to a decided limp) and I found him really inspirational. He soon had me in the School Chorus and the Chapel Choir (I could already reach low E flat at age fourteen) and everything led from that.

It was still a rule at that time to lie down for half an hour after lunch – but it did not have to be in the dormitories: if you wanted to, you could go up to the Music Room in Portman Roof, roll out a so-called mattress and listen to records. I became totally hooked, soaking up symphonies and concertos – all this long before BBC Radio 3 – choral works and chamber music.

The school orchestra gave a concert in Blandford, with the Grieg *Piano Concerto* in the programme. John Sterling selected three talented players – one for each movement. Being friends with two of them, I heard many of the rehearsals, and decided I must try to get into the orchestra – but I didn't play any orchestral instrument. Taking up a stringed, or upper woodwind, instrument would have been useless as there were others with years' more experience ahead of me. However, the bassoonist left just then, as did the only double-bass player. Taking up either instrument would automatically make me eligible, and the bassoon, being the more portable, was the one I chose. John Sterling let me take the school instrument home for the Christmas holidays, together with a book of fingering and studies, and I spent the vacation working at it, being allowed to join the orchestra the very next term. What a thrill!

Left: A Bryanston quartet, 1943

Below: Roger Stalman

I was also learning the piano with Margaret Morham, and she later married Bill Carpenter-Jacobs, who eventually joined the staff – much to my good fortune as he was an excellent bassoonist himself and helped me greatly.

A very amiable member of the music staff, a pianist called Geoffrey Robbins, was also supportive – though I never liked the song he chose to teach me: *Lullaby,* which hardly suited my rather robust voice! Later on, though, he gave me an introduction to his cousin's husband, the eminent tenor Eric Greene, who thought I showed promise, and who eventually took me on as a pupil some years later, after National Service.

By this time my voice was developing and John Sterling got me to sing a solo verse in Stanford's 'Songs of the Fleet' at a school concert. (Rather too jingoistic for today's tastes, but good experience.) The BBC Bristol Studios became an important centre due to wartime relocation, and Reginald Redman headed the music section. He instituted a series of 'Music from Schools' where schools from throughout the region were invited to submit players and ensembles for short broadcasts. John Sterling got three of us to form a trio of two clarinets and bassoon (Tim Ormerod, who subsequently joined the Scottish National Orchestra, John Clay – I think it was – and myself). I don't recall how we reached Bristol, road or rail, but we did, and of course it was all live broadcasting in those far-off days. A great excitement, playing a Mozart *Divertimento* on air.

There was a very grand lady living in a very grand house some miles away towards Child Okeford. She used to keep 'open house' on a Sunday afternoon, and the chosen few would cycle over and enjoy music, tea and sandwiches in luxurious surroundings. I had long hoped to be asked to join these gatherings, but felt very much a 'country cousin' compared with the sophisticates from Connaught House who were invited regularly. However, the time did eventually come, and I remember singing *Ich grolle nicht* (Schumann's *Dichterliebe*) and accompanying myself on the piano. It seemed to meet with her approval, and I really felt I had ARRIVED!

In my last year, John Sterling undertook a performance of Haydn's *Creation*, engaging the professional soprano Margaret Ritchie (with whom I found myself on platforms in later years) with Angus Thomas and myself as tenor and bass respectively. JS spent hours coaching us through our roles; he was endlessly generous with his time – much to the annoyance of his

Common Room colleagues who expected me on time for whatever it was, only to have me turn up late with an explanatory note! The performance was very well received. Shortly after the interval I had to leave the Gym – much to the concern of Matron, who rushed out thinking I had been taken ill! But no: the soprano's next aria had a passage where two bassoons, in thirds, echo the 'Cooing Dove', and, as the only other bassoonist within miles, I had to dash round to the back of the orchestra to join Bill Carpenter-Jacobs, do the twiddly bits, and get back to the front of the platform in time for my next recitative!

My first oratorio performance, and how thrilled I was to be part of it. It would have been beyond my wildest imagination just then to think that I would eventually be giving more than eighty performances of the *Creation*, one of my favourite works in the repertoire, in a singing career much influenced and inspired by John Sterling and other Bryanston staff. That performance remains unique to this day, being the one and only time I both blew and sang in the same work!

Roger Stalman *(Portman '45) became a professional soloist working with many choral societies. His performances include 275 of the* Messiah*; he continues to play the bassoon for fun and started his own orchestra, the Misbourne.*

Some musical memories

I first experienced Bryanston before I actually arrived. I was up for a music scholarship and spent a couple of days there as a rather nervous twelve-year-old demonstrating what I could do – which wasn't much really. I can still remember the headmaster's study, and being asked by Robson Fisher who my favourite composers were. That was the cue for what little knowledge of music history I had to abandon me. But I recall giving a passable performance of a Handel concertino for trumpet with a brisk finale full of hang-on-to-your-seats-and-pray-to-God triplets. I did enough to get a music exhibition. And without that I doubt I would have seen Bryanston again.

I was one of two trumpet players to arrive at Bryanston in autumn 1969. With my minor scholarship I was seen as the senior but Ben Gaskell, my cohort, was, in truth, almost certainly the better player. The School's lead trumpet at that time was Fabian Bush and I played second trumpet to him. But Fabian was a sixth-former, so after a year or so, Ben and I had the trumpet desk to ourselves. But we made our mark well before that.

Ben had a rather classy new silver Yamaha trumpet and had a good knowledge of popular songs of the thirties and classic jazz. I had *Louis Armstrong Plays WC Handy* and thus knew the classic blues. I cannot now remember how our duo got going. But I do recall our first public performance. There was a sort of school cabaret in the Coade Hall one Saturday afternoon. Now Coade and cabaret seem unlikely bedfellows. But it happened. I recall performing a very silly robot sketch in which we had painted cardboard boxes over our heads and trumpet mouthpieces sticking out with which we held Clangers-type conversations – very silly.

Then towards the end we did our duet – just two trumpets; not exactly promising. Ben had a great ability to harmonise. So I played the lead and he provided the harmony and it fitted sort of hand-in-glove. We did *Daisy*, *Home on the Range, St Louis Blues* and probably one or two others. It brought the house down and a little double act was born that got periodic outings thereafter.

Bryanston's musical life in the late sixties and early seventies was flourishing yet schizophrenic. Official musical life was represented by the School Orchestra, wind ensembles, brass quintets, a military band, a choir and probably other groups I have forgotten. Contrasting with this was a sort of samizdat scene of rock and jazz that bubbled with aspiration and periodically burst into flower.

Once or twice a year Bryanston would have some special assembly or other – it might be an end-of-term do or a Christmas carol concert. Once again the brass section would be wheeled out to add punch and Willoughby Smith would often write a descant. *All Things that on Earth do Dwell* sticks in the memory. Oh, and *Hark! the Herald Angels*. So there we were, a full Coade Hall with 500 boys singing with enthusiasm, the organ with Joyce Wilson at the helm cranked up to full pitch, and over the top of this we trumpets would soar in, playing fit to bust, with a glorious descant that nobody could miss. Wonderful stuff!

Bryanston also introduced us to live rock music, which was for a few years a feature of the annual Summer Festival. In 1970 we had Steamhammer, whose minor hit *Junior's Wailing* is still lodged somewhere in my brain and whose guitarist Martin Quittenton was about to co-write *Maggie May* with Rod Stewart. Gentle Giant, who played the 1971 Summer Festival, were in an altogether different league. Giant were in fact depping for Black Widow (whatever happened to them?). Their music, which we knew well, as someone in my house had their debut album, was sophisticated prog rock with touches of jazz and medieval influences featuring brass, cello and vibraphone, as well the usual rock line-up and strobe-assisted drum solo.

Climax Blues Band, who played in 1972, were chiefly memorable for pupil exuberance which almost broke the Coade Hall's forestage.

The sort of samizdat underbelly of Bryanston's musical life was, I think, second only to the school Motorcycle Club; tolerated so long as we were only tinkering at the edges, but as an officially sanctioned form of cultural transport, no. But from my arrival it was unmissable, if only for the volume at which it was performed. I suspect that the school has been so redeveloped, manicured and sculpted that I would not recognise it today. But in 1969 at the fringe of the area that housed Bryanston's Music School was a smallish wooden hut, which if memory serves me correct was simply called the Wooden Hut. On Saturday afternoons and other leisure periods this nondescript building could be seen physically vibrating from a loud electric blues trio that held court inside. And it weren't arf good. Inside was the the cream of Bryanston music-making. Robin Wood on Clapton-inspired guitar, whose predilection for rock-guitar-in-shorts predated AC/DC's Angus Scott by some years; a bass player called Funky (but musically who wasn't) and whose name is lost in the mists of time; and the assistant art master, Chris Hall, on drums. There was room in the Wooden Hut for a small audience. Impressionable newcomers like me sat at the feet of gods and were suitably impressed.

Bryanston is completely to blame for my becoming a jazz anorak. In fact I really blame Anne Brackenbury who programmed the annual Bryanston Summer Festival at the Coade Hall. That first summer she booked the Mike Westbrook Sextet performing Mike's *Love Song and Variations* suite. It was a wonderful band: Norma Winstone, one of Britain's best ever jazz singers; George Khan on saxes; the rumbustious Malcolm Griffiths on trombone; Gary Boyle on guitar. There was a joyous freshness about the music.

Mike returned with *Solid Gold Cadillac* – a more rockish line-up – a year or two later, but it wasn't quite the same. Graham Collier, the first man to get jazz funding from the Arts Council, performed with his sextet. And for two years running we had the John Dankworth quartet, first with Cleo Laine and then with Marian Montgomery depping for an indisposed Cleo. A few years after this, John and Cleo were to be found playing leading concert halls both in Britain and Australia. Seeing them in the relative intimacy of the Coade Hall was a stroke of huge fortune and of Anne Brackenbury's booking acumen. This early exposure to top-quality jazz held me in good stead and ultimately led to my first job and my career, as I went on to run the jazz club at university and then to work for the national jazz organisation, managing national and regional tours for them.

Left: Fiddler on the Roof, *2003*

Below: Ruddigore, *1976*

Paul Kelly *(Portman '74) has also had his own radio show and has worked in the arts in various parts of the country. He has been Principal Arts Officer for Plymouth for the last twelve years.*

Getting on with it

Write something about my time at Bryanston, you tell me. Well, that should please my contemporaries, some of whom – still my best friends – continually and *cruelly* berate me for never having really left the place. All right, I admit it, I was heartbroken in that summer of 1976 and, let's face it, I am still in regular telephonic contact with my director of music, Peter Lattimer. When he picks up the phone I merely say, 'Ah, well done, Lattimer,' and we're off again, gossiping and giggling, just as it was thirty years ago over coffee and biscuits in his room on the Shaftesbury Floor.

The curious thing is that I do assume subconsciously that I *have* only recently left the School. Mark Perrow (Hardy '76) was explaining to a close friend of mine only the other day that Bryanston instilled in us the understanding that we were God's Gift to the World, and that nothing would stand between us and success. 'I can't imagine anyone not employing you, Tim,' said Joan Potter to me shortly after I left. Consequently, during my third and, to date, most unreliable career (as an actor), I am constantly outraged and hurt when not employed. And when unceremoniously sacked from Foyles Bookshop, my very first menial job, I remember actually weeping with indignation one cold Friday night somewhere in Soho and moaning that I had been head boy and had a bloody degree in French and who *did* they think they were?

But now I come to my real claim to fame. A shrink once said I should be proud of it and so I am. The man's completely screwed up, I hear you cry, but I was the one who insisted on staging *Trial by Jury* as a house play and refused to countenance doing it merely with a piano. Or even two pianos. And here is my point: I stamped my little sixteen-year-old foot and Peter Lattimer said, 'OK, get on with it, then. Here's a list of local orchestral players.' He and Bob Allan essentially enabled me and countless others to 'get on with it', air our egos, and be creatively fulfilled. I conducted *Ruddigore* the following year, with Tim Heath (Connaught '76) producing, and the annual musical became a regular fixture.

Here was a school with a creative environment allowing and encouraging this sort of thing to happen, and I am entirely grateful for those fabulous experiences. For me, there have never been such opportunities since. Where else could I have been first horn in Beethoven's *Eroica* symphony, Dvorak's *Eighth*, or Schubert's *Fourth*? Where could I have rehearsed and conducted an operetta; played a comic role in a Feydeau farce (or worse still, a god in one of Ken Greenwood's countless versions of *The Good Woman of Setzuan*), and all this within a couple of academic years?

Above left: Songs from the Shows, 2004

Above: Kiss Me Kate*, 2004*

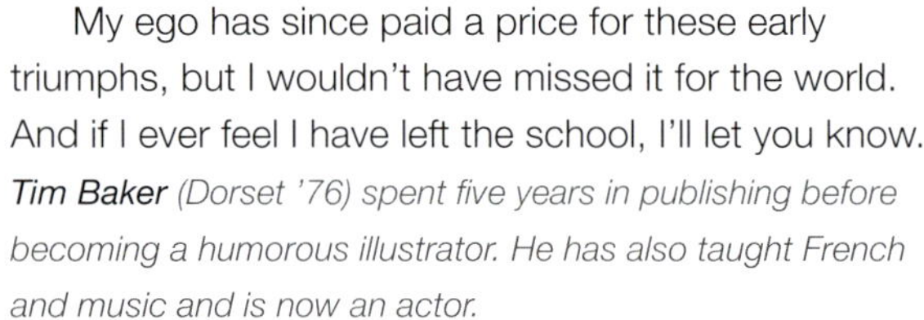

My ego has since paid a price for these early triumphs, but I wouldn't have missed it for the world. And if I ever feel I have left the school, I'll let you know.

***Tim Baker** (Dorset '76) spent five years in publishing before becoming a humorous illustrator. He has also taught French and music and is now an actor.*

Making music

Rugby was the social emollient when I first went to Bryanston, a sport that I rather lamely participated in but had absolutely no interest or enthusiasm for. For the first year at least it was those who could play rugby who got all of the attention, and musicians like myself were considered aloof and perhaps just a little weird. In fact, now I come to think of it, one could have assembled a small orchestra from those in game six rugby, or at the very least, a string quartet.

No, I was more interested and stimulated by what went on in the Music Department which, despite looking like a glorified portakabin, became my refuge where I made some of my closest friends. In my first few weeks of school I soon found that music transcended the otherwise prominent social gap between age groups, and owing to the fact that I played guitar, became friends with people who otherwise I would not have encountered. Maybe everyone thinks this when they are thirteen, but there also seemed to be a lot of great bands around at the time, and many hours were spent working out and jamming the latest tunes with my musical friends when, perhaps, we should have been doing something a little more academically 'constructive'.

For a music scholar there were certain demands to be met and certain little perks too (like not having to do geography GCSE because I was too busy – hoorah!). I was constantly performing for small informal concerts, music exams, assemblies and the occasional last-minute tea party in Sturminster Newton. The latter, at the time, caused much grievance due to the lack of warning and preparation, but in hindsight I can see that this was character-forming stuff and am now rarely fazed when put in a similar situation. In fact one of the unique attributes of Bryanstonian musicians is their confidence to perform, purely because they had the opportunity and encouragement to do it so often. Being now a London-based musician, I fully appreciate the performance opportunities I had at Bryanston. I didn't have to pay to perform, I didn't have to convince some musically illiterate 'manager' that I would fill their dank and smelly venue – I could just play when and where I wanted.

One of my most treasured personal memories is the concert I did as part of the A3 Festival, made up mostly of my own music (by this time music had become a socially respectable pastime!). On hand and at my disposal were a free venue, a large audience, two Steinway grand pianos and enough talented musicians to start a small conservatoire. I also remember fondly the time when my friend Ken Swayne and I did a concert of repertoire for the classical guitar (for which I sported the most hideous haircut). For this we decided to use the beautiful Main Hall of the School which has, as you can imagine, the most fantastic acoustics. I remember in particular Ken saying to the audience, 'Looking around here now, it's rather like playing on the set of *Titanic*, although I didn't think we would go down so well.' Well, I found it funny.

And then there was the Concert Band. The German trip was a particular favourite where every 'activity' organised for us seemed to involve alcohol of some sort. Leading us with skill and panache was the delightful Mr Brown who is to this day one of my closest friends. I remember in particular a concert where Ben Childs, first saxophone to my second, couldn't find a white shirt so he borrowed a female trombonist's blouse. He looked hilarious in this tight white number with boxers hanging out of his grey corduroy trousers. Still, he got a cracking review in the local German newspaper for his solo, *Harlem Nocturne.* Quite right too.

I could go on and on about the musical things I got up to at Bryanston because there were so many (conducting the operetta, playing a guitar concerto, open-air concerts in the Greek Theatre, adapting songs for the Connaught House dinner, blues concerts, etc.). The Paris choir trip, which was so memorably put together by Mr Lattimer, was another highlight. I can't think of many people who have been lucky enough to sing *I was Glad* at the very same church where Poulenc was organist or who have had the opportunity to sing Palestrina in the magnificent Notre Dame.

Despite the occasional unforgivable bouts of Andrew Lloyd Webber I was made to endure, my musical life at Bryanston was an unrivalled pleasure. It was there that I learnt to play and appreciate music for what it really is, and there that I was taught so superbly by so many inspiring individuals. It was there, too, in that rather modest-looking Music Department, that I made easily some of the best music of my life so far.

***Leo Dawkins** (Connaught '00) is currently doing a masters in musical composition at King's College, London.*

12

THE PLAY'S THE THING

Drama with Mr Coade

The teaching of drama when I was at Bryanston? I suppose the first thing to say is that there wasn't any – as such. We just did plays; so whatever we learnt was by doing. I was lucky: Coade was the headmaster during my time and a natural actor and director. He directed at least one play a year, usually by Shakespeare. I was in four of his productions, first as the cream-faced loon in *Macbeth* and finally as King Lear via Ophelia and Cassius en route. I was also in Sheridan's *The Critic* directed by Wilf Cowley, who also wrote and directed end-of-term pantomimes in which staff members needed little encouragement to strut their stuff, and Eric Bramall gave us our earliest glimpses of drag. We were also allowed to stage our own productions at the end of some terms when those of us with at least one eye already on a stage career would angle for the best roles. No girls in those days, so boys played all the female

KING LEAR

By William Shakespeare

anston School Dramatic Soc
June 22nd and 23rd
1944

KING LEAR

By William Shakespeare

CAST

Lear	B. D. Williams
King of France	T. G. Sloane Stanley
Duke of Burgundy	P. W. Nelson
Duke of Cornwall	P. Bramson
Duke of Albany	S. A. Stuart
Earl of Kent	H. R. Macleod
Earl of Gloucester	A. D. Estill
Edgar	I. R. Walker
Edmund	K. W. M. Taylor
Curan	T. G. Marris
Oswald	D. C. Hodgson
Old Man	S. N. Marris
Doctor	T. G. Sloane Stanley
Fool	M. C. L. Black
1st Messenger	H. A. Miskin
2nd. Messenger	H. F. Capener
1st. Officer	A. Wilkinson
2nd. Officer	S. N. Marris
3rd. Officer	M. Walker
Knight	R. A. B. Durant
Herald	H. E. Capener
1st. Gentleman	A. Wilkinson
2nd. Gentleman	P. W. Nelson
1st. Servant to Cornwall	A. Wilkinson
2nd. Servant to Cornwall	R. A. B. Durant
3rd. Servant to Cornwall	T. G. Marris
Goneril	Miss A. E. J. Wilson
Regan	Miss T. Hicks Bolton
Cordelia	Miss C. B. Galton

Knights	Attendants
M. B. Selby Green	R. F. Marshall
C. A. Eagger	G.T. Marshall
P. H. Morris	B. J. Pitt-Pitts
D. M. A. Scott	R. H. ff. Duke
M. Walker	I. Mackenzie Kerr
K. R. Mitchell	G. H. Bush

The action takes place in Britain and will be presented in two parts

Interval of ten minutes after Part One

Incidental music from Sibelius No. 2 and 4 Symphonies

Costumes by Citizen House Bath

Wigs by Bert.

Scenery designed by H. A. Miskin and executed by J. R. M. Tennant under the direction of Miss E. Muntz.

Produced by T. F. Coade.

Assistant producers: Mrs. de Selincourt and Mrs. Caine.

Stage Manager, R. C. J. Hunter. Assisted by J. R. M. Tennant, D. C. Hodgson, S. A. Stuart, A. D. Estill C. E. Townrow

Lighting: A. A. Thomas. assisted by R. N. Barfield, R. E. Hardy

Sound effects under direction of J. Sterling

Trumpet I. R. D. Walker

Incidental music arranged by A. Stobart and G. Trasler

Costumes supervised by Mrs. Coade

Programmes printed by D. C. Robinson and D. R. Hooper at the Bryanston School Press

Right: The Rover, *1998*

roles and I don't remember a single Francis Flute among us when thus cast ('Nay, let me not play a woman, I have a beard coming'). In later life I have noticed that guys enjoy dressing up, whatever their orientation, more than girls do.

Coade was an ideal director for schoolboys: patient, insightful, always encouraging, if a trifle remote in manner. He could coax some sort of truthful expression out of the most recalcitrant material, and, in a few cases, inspire remarkable performances. He never seemed overly interested in decor; none of the productions had a designer and I don't recall anything in the way of scenery beyond a rostrum or two and some steps. Costumes arrived from Bath in big wicker hampers, and wigs from a mysterious chap in London trading as 'Bert' whom we never saw. Coade made us all up himself, occasionally assisted by an acolyte. All the plays were done in the Gym; no Coade Hall or Greek Theatre then.

Not surprisingly *Lear* is what I remember most vividly. Of course the very notion of a seventeen-year-old attempting this Everest of a role is a pretty tall order, but whether it was vanity or innocence (no doubt a lot of both) I jumped at the opportunity. (Miss Givings who was apt to confront one in the course of many subsequent professional situations was nowhere to be seen.) I don't exaggerate when I say it was a time of rapture; nor is this a rose-coloured retrospection for I felt and thought it at the time. Outside circumstances had something to do with that: the Second World War was still in progress and D-Day happened a few days before the first performances; it was a perfect summer – Dorset at its most beautiful – and call-up imminent; *carpe diem*. But I would have felt essentially the same whatever was taking place elsewhere.

Needless to say, even at the time, there wanted not buzzers to the ear that such goings-on were Not A Good Thing. I remember my tutor (a fine scholar and admirable man) writing in an end-of-term report after I had played Ophelia that I must now 'forget all about it' – weirdly impractical advice for a stage-struck fifteen-year-old already secretly set on a stage career. Most of the boys who acted in those plays would become lawyers, doctors, captains of industry, etc.; only a few of us ended up in the arts.

For me the supreme benefit of acting on those early stages, especially in *King Lear*, was immersion in those oceanic texts: to have to learn, for example, rehearse and then act before an audience the speech beginning:

Poor naked wretches, wheresoe'er you are
That bide the pelting of this pitiless night,
How shall your houseless heads and unfed sides,
Your loop'd and window' raggedness, defend you
From seasons such as these? O, I have ta'en
Too little care of this….

To sense this mandate was inescapably to confront Shakespeare's apocalyptic vision. Those were the days when the foundation of my faith in the value and necessity of great art was created, and which has survived the rise and fall of this or that literary theory and the erosions of theatrical productions which, from time to time, mistake distortion for 'relevance'. At this point Miss Givings nudges me and mutters some words of Portia:

This comes too near the praising of myself,
Therefore no more of it: hear other things.

David Williams (Connaught '44) is a director, actor and lecturer, now living in Canada.

Lighting the Greek Theatre

Some time in 1953 my tutor, WE Potter, introduced me to the stage lighting crew at Bryanston, thus starting an interest that has stayed with me for much of my life. There were several highlights and I particularly remember *The Ascent of F6*. But the memories that stay with me most vividly are of Thorold Coade's production of the *Chester Mystery Plays*. The nativity play was mounted in the Church before Christmas, as was the passion play later on. Providing effective lighting with the limitations of the church architecture certainly proved a challenge.

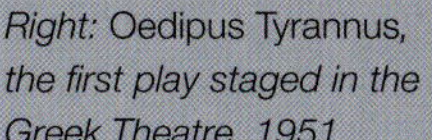

Right: Oedipus Tyrannus, *the first play staged in the Greek Theatre, 1951*

In the summer of 1955 the whole cycle was presented in the Greek Theatre with a dragon stage right representing hell and great arches for heaven erected on scaffolding above the back walls of the stage. But for a lucky escape I wouldn't have made it to the final production. One day I had been up in the scaffolding adjusting spotlights. With the job finished and with the enthusiasm of youth I swung down through the scaffold grabbing a bar with one hand and then a second bar with the other. Suddenly 240 volts were coursing through me. There must have been some faulty wiring. Luckily one of the other lighting guys was standing near the switchboard and when he heard me scream he ripped out the blackout plug.

Once the lights were set we had many rehearsals to get the lighting script just right and I drew the (short) straw to run the main switchboard. I remember my consternation when, a few minutes before the start on opening night, Mr Coade appeared at the door of the lighting box. 'I've decided we need to change the lighting,' he said, and then stood at the door throughout the show as I tried to produce the new effects he was demanding. Seemingly he was satisfied and then it was a matter of documenting the changes for the remaining performances.

A few years later, after National Service, I was involved with a youth group at the City Temple church. I built a small switchboard with six dimmers and the all-important blackout plug for a travelling show which we toured to other churches and to prisons. I can still stop a conversation with a light comment about having been in Wormwood Scrubs and Holloway. Later when my wife, Evelyn, and I had settled in Sydney she happened to mention to a teaching colleague that I had done some stage lighting. That was it. I was shanghaied on to the lighting desk at Pymble Players on Sydney's North Shore. I've been a member now for nearly thirty years and designed the lighting for nearly as many productions.

Clive Harrison *(Shaftesbury '55) worked in the computer industry from its infancy, in London, the USA and Australia, where he now lives.*

Pantomime

Or, more properly, the 'Cowley Pantomime'. By the time I appeared in 1953 they were an established institution and I experienced the tail end of the distinguished run. I think I was in four. What happened was this. About four weeks from the end of term Wilf was to be found in the gazebo tapping away at one of the huge old typewriters. Then every two or three days there'd be a few more duplicated sheets of scripts, and a sort of theme would emerge. We scanned these avidly to see what the

HOSTEL and GROUNDSEL

An original Pantomime by Wilfrid Cowley

preceded by

1.	The Jubberwock	Bill Hoyland
2.	Oriental Juggling	Professor Humperdinck

Overture	"Correlation Blues"	*Paul Rogers*

Characters in order of appearance :

Hostel	Geoffrey Morris
Groundsell	Timothy Cobb
High Tea, the Fairy Pig	Ronald King
Anti-Social	Eric Bramall
Uncle Crisis	Wilfrid Cowley
Clancy	Bill Hoyland
Father Christmas	Dickin Moore

Porter	Bill Hoyland
Sewer	John Henderson
Lady Macbeth	Eric Bramall
Macbeth	Wilfrid Cowley
Duncan, King of Scotland	Dickin Moore
Malcolm, his son	John Upward
Chief Inspector Banquo	Leif Maine
Ross	Anthony Pratt
Lennox	Charles Read
Angus	Henry Pope

Spirit of Rowing	Dudley Coventry
Spirit of Rugger	Michael Tyssen
Spirit of Eating	John Upward
Spirit of Training	S-Major Howard
The Tutor	Harold Greenleaves
Spirit of Salem	Bernhard Buhl

At the piano : Paul Rogers.

Lighting by Guy Worsley.

Sound by the Leyton-Tanner System.

Left: Wilfrid Cowley and Eric Bramall in Aladdin

maestro had in store for us, and soon rehearsals would begin in the Old Gym, often starting after 9pm. The great thing was that these scripts were only the starting-point, as it were. We were not simply allowed, we were positively encouraged to develop, elaborate, ad lib. Thus the relaxed atmosphere of uncertainty was projected into the performance itself (last night of term). On one famous occasion Ronnie King and Bill Williams wandered far away from the script and when there was a sudden hiatus, Bill led Ronnie (gently) by the ear to where the bemused prompter was desperately trying to find a place, and said, 'Come on, dear boy, it's time we had a prompt.' It must be admitted that Wilf was pretty unscrupulous in plundering Common Room and school gossip, and his scripts sometimes went (for those days) close to the knuckle. The show ended with a verse review of events during the term, each verse adorned with the chorus referred to above:

> Give him alpha, give him beta, give him red or give him
> blue, You may not care for him and he won't care
> for you,
> So produce a nice lead pencil, give him gamma to
> annoy,
> And then go and tutor a far nicer boy.

(NB: marks entered on boys' charts were colour-coded: red for satisfactory effort, blue for poor, pencil for bad.)

And then the finale, to a catchy tune allegedly written by Wilf himself in the thirties:

> So that's the end of the pantomime,
> We wish you all a good Christmastime,
> Happy ever after as the story-books say,
> On your hol-i -- day.

Incidentally, that tune was played solemnly, slowly and in the minor, as Wilf's coffin was brought into the little church at Worth Matravers. Not many people noticed.

Rodney Dingle *was a member of staff from 1953 until 1970. He was later Head of Modern Languages at Exmouth Comprehensive and is author of the biography of Roger Altounyan.*

Much Ado about Nothing, 1964

Thirty years of drama

At the time of my arrival to teach at Bryanston in 1956, my expectations of school drama were based on the programme at my own excellent grammar school comprising a single Gilbert and Sullivan operetta every year. My dramatic contribution to these had been to be in charge of the front of house. Gratitude is due nevertheless for a sound knowledge of Gilbert's words, especially for their illumination of life in 2004, as for instance in the surge in top grades at A-level ('When everyone is somebodee, then no one's anybody'); and in our national distaste for Continental Europe, epitomised in *Ruddigore* by the 'hardy British tars, who had pity on the poor Parlez-voo. D'you see?'. But I was stunned to be confronted with Wilf Cowley's *Henry IV* and Thor Coade's *King Lear* in the old theatre and a pupil's production of *Othello* if you please. In the Greek Theatre I saw Thor's *The Lark* of Jean Anouilh and Peter Brewin's *Romeo and Juliet*. Certainly some ancient classics too – Euripides' *Alcestis* and the first production anywhere of Seneca's *The Troades* for the last seven hundred years! Who remembers the traditional producers' appeals to the audience as the light evening drizzle began to drain the dye from the togas and drapes: 'Shall we go on?' 'YES,' we would all shout, wriggling surreptitiously closer to the shelter of the trees on either side of us. More usually as the hour of performance approached, the gusting summer breezes would die away. The rustling of the leaves would cease, leaving nothing to mar the acoustic. The sun setting behind the audience would warmly illuminate the stage, and at some later magical moment the spectator would realise that the artificial lights had taken over from the sunlight.

Change was afoot, we thought, with new HM Robson Fisher's arrival, so we sang 'Let's hot up Alcestis; You must admit that's best as – Fings ain't what they used to be', but in truth it was *plus ça change*

on the drama front as Robson was very quick to present a fine *Hamlet* in the Greek Theatre. And Wilf Cowley's pantomime tradition – continued by Brewin, Baker and Greenwood in the sixties, Sayer in the seventies and eighties and Elliot in the nineties – continued to supply Xmas doggerel and bathos of unfathomable depth.

In the early sixties the theatre in the old wooden gym was abandoned. Boys perched in precarious boxes to work spotlights were being repeatedly stung by electric shocks. The stage was collapsing by degrees, itself shocked perhaps by the oh-so-innocent amorous adventures underneath its boards involving actors and the actresses from Cranborne Chase School who came to perform in all the senior productions. Consequently I managed to have a temporary stage erected in the Main Hall for my *One Way Pendulum* which obliged everyone traversing the Main Corridor to clamber across it, thus symbolising the central place of drama in Bryanston!

Speaking of our gifted actresses from Cranborne Chase in the pre co-ed era, with girls being such a rare commodity I had to get used to penetrating the third bush on the right behind the Greek Theatre to extract an actress from her tryst whenever her last call on stage became imminent. And in *The Birthday Party* our two actresses performed heroically despite one having broken her leg and the other having been expelled for overindulgence in illicit sojourns in London.

Enterprising pupils Marc Karlin and Nick Hutchinson developed an acting area for presentations of contemporary plays under the rafters of the 'servants' wing' in the interim between the Music School vacating this space in favour of the Plateau and the later building of study bedrooms. The bare boards and cobwebs were just the ticket for *The Caretaker* and Beckett's *Krapp's Last Tape.*

1966 saw Robson Fisher achieve the completion of the Coade Hall. The Duke of Edinburgh opened it and looked in on our last-minute rehearsal of *The Alchemist.* Bunty Hunter, such a tower of strength overseeing the work of the stage crews, insisted that the marvellous facility of the Coade Hall must be shared with the public and so he led the formation of Bryanston Arts Centre, which was to bring professional theatre and music here for the next thirty-eight years. For instance, the RSC came and loved playing in the Hall, filling the house for four performances by their first team, which included Ian McKellen and Bob Peck, in *Twelfth Night* and *Three Sisters.*

Bunty also set the House Drama Festival under way in 1961, since when six or seven plays have been

Left: Galileo, *1965*

Below: The Alchemist, *1966*

mounted over a single weekend every autumn. It was never competitive. No prizes. Lots of plays by Brecht, Ionesco, Stoppard, James Saunders, Chekhov, Arden, Ayckbourn and not a few original efforts. Audiences of 300 packed into the Edwin Evans Music Room, spilling everywhere onto the acting area and generating exciting intimacy. Inevitably we later moved to the luxurious spaces of the Coade Hall, finding less intimacy and greater technical challenges for players and directors. At the close a distinguished commentator would show us what had been achieved and what more could have been achieved and how. The style was set in 1961 by the utterly inspirational John Blatchley whose successors have included Michael Blakemore, Bill Alexander, Adrian Noble in his shiny white shoes, Robert Bolt, Joanna David and Edward Fox.

Anne Brackenbury (daughter of Aubrey de Selincourt and sister-in-law of Christopher Robin) was the temptress who persuaded many of the commentators to come here. She trained a line of very professional pupil stage managers; she also ran the Arts Centre and devised 'Forum Theatre', in which we staff, with neighbours and OBs, exposed our powers and our shortcomings in her presentations of *Three Sisters*, *The Cherry Orchard*, *Twelfth Night*, *Midsummer Night's Dream* and *The Magistrate*.

Alan Shrimpton in Staff Review, *1972*

With more and more pupils wanting to experience the buzz of dramatic performance there were in the eighties probably fifteen to twenty plays put on every year – senior, junior, house plays, plays by Garry Sayer's Dramatic Society, plays in the A3 Festival launched by David Jones, with a couple more squeezed into the gaps. Lest any soul couldn't get into some of these I launched LAMDA acting exams; these were open to any pupil of any age and any or no experience, with free coaching from a team of staff volunteers. More exams? Surely not! Ooooh, yes please! Scores of folk every year jumped at the chance of polishing two or three pieces to audition standard and gaining medals up to Gold and Diploma.

An annual pupil-run operetta or musical has become a favourite fixture, from *La Belle Hélène* to *The Merry Widow,* from *Oklahoma* to *Grease*. Students often gained the know-how to undertake such ambitious projects by learning from Garry Sayer's model direction of some high-powered Forum Opera presentations and his characteristically confident choreography, inventive staging and lightning scene changes in *Journey's End, Equus*, *Wild Oats* and Feydeau, and in Shakespeare's *Loves Labour's*, *Much Ado*, *Comedy of Errors*, *Hamlet* and *The Merchant*.

Tom Wheare's arrival extended the line of dramatic HMs. I've a lasting image of his first sight of the Coade Hall which triggered Tigger-like *joie de vivre* as he bounced elatedly down the gangway towards the stage, and his productions have exuded exactly this vigour and sense of fun in Feydeau, Wilde and Coward.

In the gales and power failures of 1987 the School spent long hours in the Coade Hall thanks to its having its own electrical generator, but meanwhile the Greek Theatre was suffering grievously. The trees providing a beautiful backing and surround to the stage collapsed and the arena has not yet regained its former atmosphere. Not that it is completely out of favour. Duncan Fowler-Watt notably has been able to use it to generate work of great power. Equally at home indoors, in his series of writings designed to suit specific groups of pupils, he invariably secures fluent performances in a novel genre, and he has inspired to a level of excellence a host of candidates for LAMDA awards.

My most admired performers down the years? Invidious to say, but they themselves must surely know. The productions in which I've taken most pride? Probably *Galileo*, *The Alchemist*, *Much Ado* and *All's Well*, *A Slight Ache*, *Look Back in Anger*, *The Rose*

Tattoo, three versions of *The Good Person of Setzuan* and two versions of *Three Sisters*.

When I retired after 120 terms in 1996 it seemed to this Grumpy Old Man that Bryanstonians' appetite for engagement in drama was as all-pervasive as ever, but that the challenge of seducing an audience away from the delectable pleasures of evening socialising elsewhere on the campus was increasingly testing. Now eight years on, my tenuous connection demands that I adhere to the dictum 'That of which we cannot speak we must consign to silence' and instead I contentedly immerse myself in the sounds of Rossini.

***Kenneth Greenwood** was Director of Studies, Senior Master and a member of staff from 1956 to 1996.*

'Resident Alien'

Bryanston! *Et nova et vetera*. Grey shorts and grey open-necked shirts. Runs in the early morning, runs in the afternoon as punishment, no caning, no fears, all sweetly reasonable, first names from the masters, artistic natures encouraged. The perfect stage for my melodramas: hysterics in the tuck shop – pork pies thrown and dip pens too (the nib quivering from my best friend's brow); revolution in the Art Room, centre of my world, with 'Action Painting' currently the rage and me pinning up my latest poster statement, still wet and dripping, in the Main Hall, then the Beak (*sic*) coming up against my art and getting paint all over his jacket and telling me it's neither art nor funny, and me telling him he's a phillistine and marching off in a huff, running when he tells me to stop, and when I'm cornered he says, 'You'll be expelled for such outrageous behaviour!' Expelled! By a headmaster famous for his progressive ideas, his spirituality, his burning bow!

I faked a mental breakdown and they sent me to the Sanatorium and summoned the school psychiatrist. Outside the window they were off on a cross-country run; by my bedside was a common-sense man in a cardigan and tie. He said, 'Think of the Cyprus situation and Sir Hugh Foot, our governor. Think of his terrible predicament – Greeks and Turks and us, as usual, stuck in middle. I'm sure that your problems with, arguably, this century's greatest headmaster will shrink to their proper size.' After supper I said I was feeling better and could I see the headmaster.

He sat me down in his comfortable study. On the shelf behind him I saw a copy of his book, *Manhood in the Making.* Then he said, 'If the volcano has cooled and we can expect you to behave like a young man and not a spoiled child … by all means stay on here. And try to be creative.' For several minutes we talked of acting. 'I'm told your impression of King Lear – not to mention a scoutmaster – is quite funny. I shall be there at the school revue tonight … and I wish you every success!'

I was a success, a real howling one. It was the high point of my life. Everybody was transformed and they loved me. Never a prefect, never in any eight, eleven or fifteen, never even a Junior Colt; taking lonely walks through the woods to find a spot where I could read a comic as I ate from a tin of pork and beans …. Now in the dark and fusty gym – a place transformed into a theatre of magic – I was getting their attention, there was laughter and cheering and clapping. 'Good old fatty!' yelled somebody. 'You're an ass, but you're a funny one!'

***Ian Whitcomb** (Salisbury '59) extracts from* Resident Alien *(Century, 1990). Ian, the original host of* The Old Grey Whistle Test, *is an author, performer and songwriter, living in California.*

Ian Whitcomb in 1956, and some years after his first stage success

Plays and films

Personal history and world events do not always quite run in synch. It is generally agreed that the 1960s peaked in summer 1967 with the 'Summer of Love' only to slide thereafter into increasingly acrimonious disorder that hit its nadir in the 1970s.

But, as one might expect, the sixties took a little longer to reach Dorset than elsewhere, and at Bryanston in the autumn of 1969 they seemed still to be in full bloom.

The House Drama Festival yielded extraordinary work. In my first year I saw a hysterical version of Orton's *Erpingham Camp*; Georg Buchner's *Woyzeck* with Robert Saxton as the aggrieved and cuckolded doctor; Brecht's *The Irresistible Rise of Arturo Ui* starring the Boulting brothers and Charlie Hanson; a malevolent piece of Restoration comedy titled *Anything You Say May Be Written Down, Twisted and Used Against You*; and a home-penned drama by Mansil Miller somewhere between *King Lear* and Samuel Beckett, with a largely silent fool on the top of a high tower responding wearily to a series of soliloquies from the stage. Later Greg Herzov staged the most imaginative production of Max Frisch's *The Fire Eaters*.

The school cinema programme, which I was briefly involved in, was just as imaginative and we were graced with classics from Fellini (*8½* and *Juliet of the Spirits*), Satyajit Ray (*Panther Panchali*), François Truffaut (*Quatre Cent Coups*), Kurosawa (*Seven Samurai*) Lindsay Anderson (*If* – very popular! And *O Lucky Man*) and Kevin Brownlow's *It Happened Here*. We would have enjoyed Menzel's *Closely Observed Trains* if the Coade Hall cinema projector hadn't blown up half way through, leading the projectionists (I was one) to make a swift exit from xenon gas fumes.

The Coade Hall Festival programme was also stimulating. We had several visits from 'The Barrow Poets' featuring Jim Parker, whose music has been heard on countless TV programmes since. I recall the Ken Campbell Roadshow causing something of a stir: a series of brief sketches, and Ken's madcap humour culminated in a piece involving live ferrets being put down one of the performers' trousers – a sort of forerunner of Japanese TV game-show endurance tests – which prompted a number of the Dorset squirearchy present to get up and leave.

The past, as LP Hartley once wrote, is a foreign country. But periodically, I am reminded how it has shaped the whole course of my life. A few years ago a planned trip to Bilbao turned into an unplanned week in New York. I was there when the Charles Saatchi/ Norman Rosenthal 'Sensation' show was at Brooklyn Museum of Art. This was the show that Rudolph Giuliani tried to close down on the grounds of profanity because of a Chris Offili picture that featured both elephant dung and a picture of the Virgin Mary – ridiculous as there were far more offensive items on show if Giuliani had bothered to visit and look. That I was visiting the show, that I could both enjoy and critique its content and laugh at its periodic self-referential jokes, was largely a result of the liberal arts education I had received at Bryanston.

Paul Kelly *(Portman '74) had his own radio show and has worked in the arts in various parts of the country. He has been Principal Arts Officer for Plymouth for the last twelve years.*

Dramatic moments

Shakespeare and I went to the same school in Stratford-upon-Avon, though not at the same time, as some pupils thought in my latter years. I was even in Shakespeare House, and Chipper Woods, our admirable English master, staged a play by the eminent Old Boy nearly every year. I once played a – er – wooden Prince Hal on the rickety platform stage wedged into one end of the sixteenth-century Big School. This cost £49 to build way back then. Bryanston, therefore, came as a shock when I arrived in 1966 shortly after the opening of the splendid £100,000 Coade Hall. My first year passed in a blur: there were seven house plays directed by pupils, a Junior Dramatic Society production directed by Peter Brewin, and the major summer play staged by the imperturbable Kenneth Greenwood. In addition, there were other occasional productions and the amazing staff Christmas entertainment. In my first term, this last was loosely modelled on a Salisbury House version of *Everyman*: the hero was Eric Rennick as Everybod and I was cast as a manic, athletic Batbod (Batman was all the rage on TV at the time). In rehearsal I made a highly athletic, flying entrance and on landing went through the newly constructed forestage much to everyone's delight.

Pupils had more time on their hands then because Bryanston was much further away from the delights of London since the M3 was still at a planning stage; the age of the video was yet to dawn; and Tower Park was still a piece of scrubland outside Poole and Bournemouth. Even so, what struck me in my first year was the pupils' genuine passion for putting on plays and their apparently inexhaustible energy when it came to working late into the night. The pupil stage crews under the relaxed management of the devoted Anne Brackenbury and the genial Bunty Hunter worked hours that would have had a trade union shop steward frothing at the mouth. I remember Ben Lefevre, Chris Ford, Andrew Bridge, Adam Daum, Jonty Arendt, Nick and Matthew Burge, Boogie Corke, Bo Steer, Tim Faulkner and Jo Daynes and many more, all of whom took on responsibilities of an extraordinary order and carried out their work with exemplary commitment. This may not always have been good for their A-levels and as tutor to many of them I often had to wear two hats: wearing one hat I urged them to cut prep and work into the night, wearing the other I ticked them off for late or non-existent assignment work.

No one was more committed to making the Coade Hall a centre of excellence than Anne Brackenbury. She was the absolute factotum: theatre manager, wardrobe mistress, set designer, production manager of Forum Theatre and Forum Opera and latterly director of some truly memorable productions: *Cider With Rosie*, *Amadeus* and *Bedroom Farce* spring immediately to mind. I spent some of the happiest hours of my life with Anne – working late into the night on productions. And so did generations of stage crews who found in her a witty, sometimes wicked, caring, indefatigable and occasionally subversive fellow spirit.

In my early years at Bryanston I was a little deranged and tried, I think, to turn the School into a repertory company with productions from D to A1. I did *Journey's End* with my A-level English set because it was on the syllabus – only it wasn't, it was the previous year. There was *Tiger in the Bath* (a Polish political satire) by Mrozek, *Eunuchs* and *Ballcocks* (*Little Malcolm's Struggle Aginst the Eunuchs* by David Halliwell and Charles Wood's *Tie Up The Ballcock)*, the inevitable Brecht, the *Wild Westminster Show* and *TitUS VietnamicUS* and *Bomb*, keen and biting satires all.

One enduring problem at this time was girls or, if you like, actresses. The School had none. Boys could be quite stunning as women: in Joe Orton's *Erpingham Camp* a beautiful slim blonde in an elegant blue skirt and jacket drifted on stage to guffaws of astonished laughter – for it was none other than Edmund Boulting. And once, on stage, a quattrocento Virgin gave birth to the infant Jesus during a blackout; the lights went up again and the male Virgin and Child were greeted with loud cheers. So, if we really wanted actresses, we had to borrow them. On one production of *The Tempest* I spent more time ferrying girls to and from Cranborne Chase School in Tisbury than I did actually rehearsing the play, and it showed. For the Thomas Hardy Festival Play – *The God Cursed Sun* – in 1968 we co-opted girls from Blandford School. This epic was scripted by two young lions who had recently worked with Peter Brook at the Royal Shakespeare Company. The script offered a theatrical compilation from *Tess*, *Jude the Obscure* and *The Mayor of Casterbridge*. As a publicity stunt we rehearsed the arrest of Tess in front of TV cameras at Stonehenge itself and this appeared on Southern TV. Hoorah! In the interval of the play we performed 'The Death of Nelson' from Hardy's *The Dynasts* below the steps outside the Coade Hall. Hardy and the compère of the whole play was played by Richard Quarshie, the most dynamic actor I have ever seen at Bryanston. Nelson was played by Nick Kavanagh who also directed Richard in a house play production of *The Emperor Jones* by O'Neill. Nobody who saw this production will ever forget Richard's power and artistry. 'Girls' continued to be a problem, which is how my wife (Titania) came to be suspended in a bed twenty feet above the stage sharing a bed with William Quarshie (Bottom). When the wires holding the bed began to slip … well, we are still married.

Then girls came to Bryanston and all was sweetness and light, particularly when it came to the annual Gilbert and Sullivan operetta or full-blooded musical in which there ain't nothing like a dame. The musical rose to ever more giddy heights thanks to a nucleus of astonishingly talented performers: Hal Cazalet, Simon Chesterfield, Mary Childs, Rupert Felsing, Matthew Hargreaves, Jo Hensel, Lucy Tregear, Mark Wigglesworth, Zoe Willis and many others, the majority of whom are now performing professionally. These stellar pupils lit the Coade Hall stage in remarkable productions of

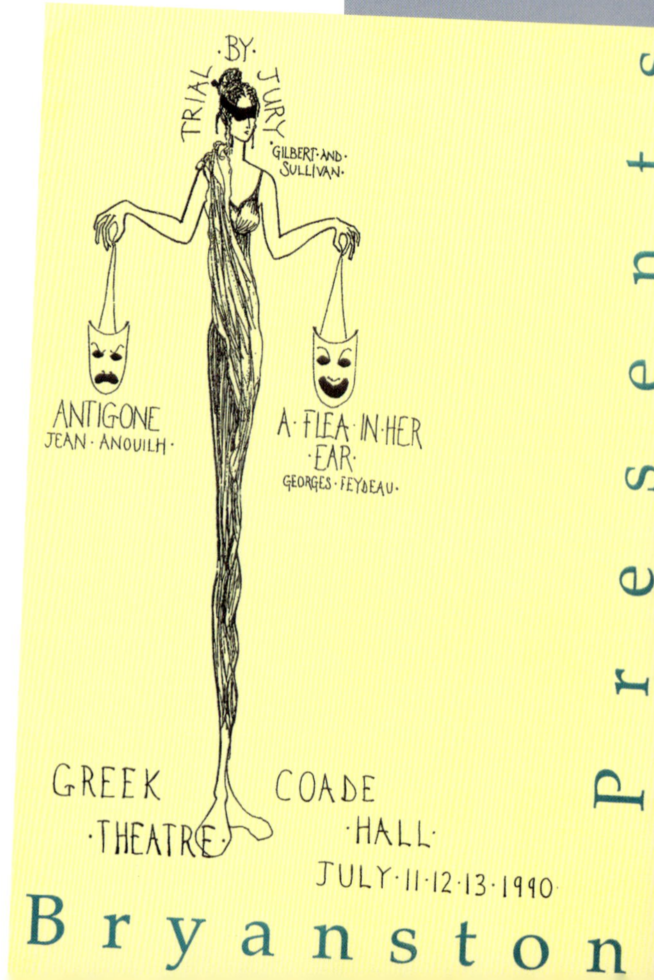

Die Fledermaus, *The Pirates of Penzance*, *Kiss Me Kate* and above all *West Side Story*. Mark Wigglesworth abridged and directed a hugely powerful version of Pirandello's *Six Characters in Search of an Author* as a House Play: it was far better than the National Theatre production of this play some years later.

In the eighties discontent among the newly arrived A3 pupils who tended to miss out on the House Drama Festival gave rise to the A3 Festival. Performances took place all over the school – in fact, everywhere except on the main stage of the Coade Hall itself. There was a *Bedroom Farce* in the Cowley Room, *La Cigolli* (like Dylan Thomas' *Llareggub* it makes sense if read backwards), dance in the Main Hall and a very rude piece by Sue Townsend in the upstairs foyer of the Coade Hall. All very jolly and so it continued each year.

As we moved into the late nineties the shape of the dramatic year was gradually altered. The House Drama Festival and the musical were squeezed into the Autumn Term to the potential detriment of both. The altered demands of GCSE and A-level exams placed increasing pressure on staff and pupils alike, and only the most devoted senior pupils would commit themselves to the end-of-year play after A-levels. A pity.

Yet despite these obstacles some astonishing productions still emerge, most notably Duncan Fowler-Watt's production of his own play *The End,* which brilliantly married video and live on-stage action as it followed the end-of-school adventures of eight A2 pupils. The Greek Theatre was still used to good effect: again Duncan Fowler-Watt directed a stunning flame-lit production of *Antigone* and there was a wild play entitled *Bryocles* which is not to be found in the classical canon. It was scripted by those staff *enfants terribles* Graham Elliot and David Jackson.

Looking back, I think I remember most happily the end-of-term Staff Play. I took over from that redoubtable pair Kenneth Greenwood and John Baker and for many years wrote and produced an hour-long farrago loosely linking the plots of the house plays and exploiting the remarkable histrionic skills of the staff cast. Kenneth Greenwood and Peter Brewin were the two stalwart stars around whom the action developed. Kenneth played magisterial, headmasterly figures and Peter Brewin played dastardly villains or guileless innocents, Tony Taylor and Alan Shrimpton turned themselves into a Morecambe and Wise double act and a good time was had by all. In one of the earliest plays Peter Brewin was a villainous ex-pupil leaving Bryanston which he cursed for ruining his educational virginity and vowing revenge. He and his gang linked up with a motorbike gang consisting of Bob Allan, Michael Scoular and Dick Poulton who arrived on stage on their 50cc scooters. They proudly announced that they had taken twenty-three O-levels between them and failed them all. Later, all these and their motorbikes and two molls and two members of Peter's own gang emerged one after the other from a single yellow bivouac tent while The Magnolia Temperance Ensemble played 'That's why the lady is a tramp'. This ensemble was faultlessly and unflappably led by Douglas Heffer. One of Peter's gang was Brack the Brick ('cos he's as thick as') who emerged with his teddy bear:

A Midsummer Night's Dream, *1997*

> I have a little Teddy/I keep him in my bed/And whenever he is naughty/I bite his bleeding head.

These fine lines were impeccably delivered by Ian Brackley, who is now Bishop of Dorking. This play ended with a huge punch-up between the forces of good (Bryanston, naturally) and evil (Peter and company). Evil triumphed and twenty trusty teachers and true were laid low on the stage until the Six Million Dollar Man (Eric Rennick in heavily padded Bryanston rugby gear) came to the rescue with 'Fear not, dear boys, I will save you all!' And so he did. In another staff play, following a house play *Dr Faustus*, Peter Brewstus summoned up the spirit of Helen of Troy and onto the stage marched the redoubtable Miss Harrison, feared chief caterer for many a year: Peter seized her work-reddened hands and reverentially intoned, 'Are these the hands that fried a thousand chips?' And not only can the staff act and sing, they can do ballet. We rehearsed an elaborate sequence of mimed rugby: line-out, maul, ruck and pass down the line with an invisible ball, all in slow motion, and when at the dress rehearsal the Magnolia Temperance Ensemble accompanied this with a full-blast rendering from Tchaikovsky's *Swan Lake*, why, it was magic!

Magic is the word. That rare and wonderful transformation from rehearsal to performance when the audience is transported and forgets to breathe. Crispin Redman's dying Hamlet, Alex McBride's agonies in *Equus*, Simon Lys capering naked in *Having a Ball*, four excellent and different productions of *The Browning Version* over the years, Janan Kubba and Simon Day in *The Rose Tattoo*, Zoe Willis and Ed Carver in *Antigone*, Simon Wheeler's *Another Country*, Tom Wheare's double bill of *A Woman of No Importance* and *Hay Fever* all come to mind. In our Forum Opera productions of *The Magic Flute*, *The Marriage of Figaro*, *Acis and Galatea* and *Fidelio* there was something very special and we climbed some way up the Everest each presented. My favourite play remains *A Midsummer Night's Dream* and I have made four attempts of one kind or another at it.

But the most memorable production of all for me was of *Peter Pan* performed before an audience who themselves were about to say or had just said goodbye to that world Peter refused to leave. I have left the world of Bryanston; whether I have grown up is not for me to say. But much, so much of it, was magic.

Garry Sayer *was a member of staff teaching English and producing plays and operas from 1966 to 1998.*

Oklahoma, *1981*

Fashion and wardrobe

It cannot be often that a product of one of my or anyone's classes receives a standing ovation in the school Dining Hall. But Jerry had finally completed the pair of trousers he had made in my needlecraft lessons and no sooner made than worn. Jerry joined the lunch queue glowing with pride and oblivious to the mounting whispering and stifled giggles. He had lots of friends and word had got around, and as he stepped away from the counter with loaded tray he was greeted with loud cheers and clapping.

Jerry was exceptional. Usually boys contented or discontented themselves with making a pair of boxer shorts and just occasionally a shirt. Boys were more impatient to achieve results and generally were quicker than girls in picking up the practical side of sewing. This was fine by me as I believed in teaching the easiest way to make a garment with no tailor's tacking and what-have-you. Two boys even won the OB Leisure Activities Prize for making a garment: one of them was my youngest son who is now a surgeon and whose skill with the needle is much appreciated. Girls tended to be more ambitious and sometimes ambition outstretched ability when it came to making that dress for the Leavers' Ball. I then became very popular and it was, tearfully, 'Mrs Sayer, I think I've done something wrong, do you think, dear Mrs Sayer, that you could …?' And I usually could and did.

My classes as a humanities option for the senior girls on Tuesday and Thursday afternoons became something of a hilarious social club, highly therapeutic, constructive and gossipy. I enjoyed these sessions very much, and found my earlier career when learning my trade in a West End couturier's, the constructive wardrobe of the Royal Shakespeare Company and later the Old Vic Theatre Wardrobe, stood me in good stead.

When Anne Brackenbury retired I took over the school theatre wardrobe and found myself dressing upwards of a dozen productions a year. The School had

The Rover, *1998*

acquired a considerable wardrobe of its own and many productions were dressed from stock, but large-scale musicals and the summer play were another matter and frequently entailed visits to the National Theatre, the Royal Shakespeare Theatre and the Bristol Old Vic for raids on their wardrobe departments. I think my proudest achievement was to track down not only the costumes, but also the gauzes and pirate ship from the wonderful post D'Oyly-Carte production of *The Pirates of Penzance*. The first entrance of Matthew Hargreaves and his motley crew in the mobile ship brought the house to its feet and made the hours on the telephone and chewing the ears of middle persons all worthwhile. For other productions I found myself making several pairs of satin corsets to be worn by the chorus and (male) compère of *Cabaret* and washing and ironing each night sweaty shirts and other garments to be donned fresh and clean by the cast at the next performance. Sometimes, backstage could resemble a striptease joint as two girls helped another to make a lightning change in the wings as they was no time to go into the dressing room.

There was often one dress or particular garment that I could not find anywhere even after rummaging through umpteen Oxfam shops. This meant I had to create something at the last minute, which put extra pressure on everyone during the last week before performance.

My toughest time was the year Tom Wheare produced an excellent double-bill of Wilde and Coward at the same time as a tyro English teacher decided to make an adaptation of most of Jane Austen's novels to be performed on the school terrace. The cast was immense and nearly a hundred costumes were required. In the event rain drove the production into the Cowley Room and it was a great success.

It is a thankless task being a wardrobe mistress who is always taken for granted, but whose unglamorous attention to detail is essential: she must ensure that hair is neat and orderly rather than Bryanston wild, that jewellery and shoes are all correct, that petticoats do not show and that garments fit properly, even if this entails altering the costume without damaging it. Even then, there was always someone who looked more like a scarecrow than a king and required my services as a dresser. At the end of the production every wardrobe item has to be checked and repacked for return to the hirer, and missing garments which have been 'borrowed' have to be tracked down and repossessed from the reluctant 'owner'. The wardrobe mistress's reward? That everything looks right and the satisfying feeling that her duty has been done and – usually – an appreciative note from the director and a bunch of flowers.

Philippa Sayer *was teacher of needlework, Wardrobe Mistress and member of staff from 1976 to 1997.*

part three : the great outdoors

13

THE GROUNDS

From Portman parkland to school grounds

The first detailed written description of the grounds comes from the *Journal of Horticulture and Cottage Gardener,* 1st August 1867, following a visit to them by the author of the article, Mr D Deal. Here we find descriptions of the park, house, gardens and the ornamental pleasure ground. The park, about three miles long, is described as being 'fine and well-timbered' and 'of a much diversified character', with some 'very fine specimens of trees'. In front of the house, there is a 'very pretty sweep of river, and just opposite the house this is considerably widened, and a pretty fall of water is well arranged'. Behind the house, 'The Cliff, as the eminence running at the back is called, contained some very fine specimens of Cedar'; and a 'perfect forest' of evergreens, principally box and yew, intermixed with some fine deciduous trees, including plane trees, a tulip tree and a maidenhair tree.

The garden and ornamental pleasure ground were located in the 'somewhat deep valley', at '...some little distance from the house...' and were a '...happy combination of the stiff and natural styles of gardening', comprising terraced walks on one side of the valley with '... various beds planted in different styles, and giving some pleasing combinations of colour...'. The main features of the garden owe more to the picturesque and landscape styles than to reliance on a 'blaze of colour for a few months'.

At the time of Mr Deal's visit, Bryanston was already noted for its kitchen gardens. A wide range of fruit was grown including apples, cherries, pears, gages and, under the protection of glass, peaches and a variety of vines, the prominent grape being Black Hamburghs. The Bryanston Gage originated here, a cross between the greengage and Coe's Golden Drop, and 'said to be a fruit of very great merit'.

Clearly the woodland, many specimen trees, both walled gardens and the pleasure garden were well established many years before Bryanston House was

Constructing the terraces in the 1890s – a 'monumental undertaking'

built on its present site by Norman Shaw, the famous architect commissioned by Lord Portman. Construction of the mansion in the early 1890s was a monumental undertaking, as was the construction of the terraces and the magnificent flight of steps leading from the 'Saloon' down to the pond and main lawn – some sixty-nine steps in all.

Historical documents reveal the huge ambition of the landscape proposals. If the building was to be grand and impressive, then so too was the surrounding landscape. Consequently it needed to be altered and shaped on a massive scale, and so it was. A contemporary photograph conveys the scope of the project with the huge amount of earth-moving required to form the desired levels for the generous terraces, steps and main lawn.

The *Gardener's Chronicle*, 17th December 1898, reinforces our understanding of the scale of the earthworks and the skill with which the work was executed: 'The mansion was completed about five years ago, after several years had been spent in its erection. It stands on high ground, involving an immense expenditure in the alteration of the old, and formation of new pleasure-grounds and shrubberies. The groundwork at this part of the place must have been very heavy, some parts having been raised four, six, and even ten feet above the old levels. So skilfully, however, has this part of the work been carried out by Mr Allsop, and the planting performed with such judgement that only a very critical observer could tell the new work from that previously existing.'

The main terrace, 'a 125 yards long and a 100 feet in width', boasted flower gardens immediately in front of the two wings of the mansion. Visual harmony prevailed despite the different design of each garden. The borders were filled with the 'best kinds of bedding-plants'. Finally the gardens are praised as being 'managed by a skilful gardener, who not only cultivates plants under glass and out-of-doors in a very creditable manner, but who has an artist's feeling in all matters pertaining to landscape gardening'. A tribute indeed.

The purchase in 1927 of the mansion and 450 acres of the estate from the Portman family by JG Jeffreys, founder of the school, marked a major change of direction in the management of the gardens and grounds. Gone was the need for extensive orchards,

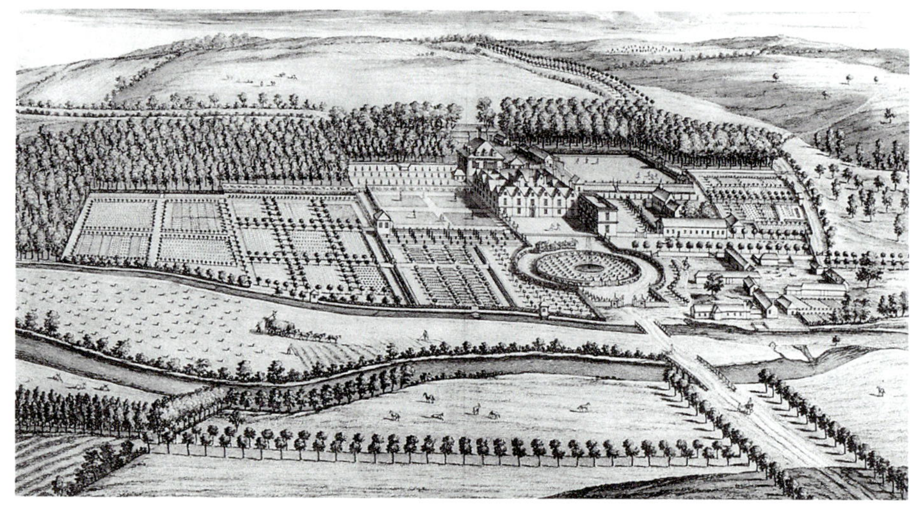

The earliest depiction of the gardens, by Knyff-Kip (1708), above, is thought to be somewhat idealised. Only the woods remain. The 1780 house lay roughly on the site of the present church

abundant grapes, thousands of carnations, intricate bedding displays and the intensive labour all this entailed. Instead the requirement was for teaching and dormitory space, sports pitches and, as the School grew, sites for new building development. With such a change in use it was inevitable that fewer resources were available for the gardens and that a low-maintenance policy would be adopted.

Major changes or improvements to the landscape would now be driven by either a special event or a new development. Of these there is space to comment on just a few. The construction of the Greek Theatre between 1949 to 1951, one of the first major projects undertaken by the School, involved sensitive site planning, carving into the hillside and skilful 'cut and fill' to blend the theatre into the landscape.

The development of the Music Department and later the former Art Department on the Plateau fundamentally changed the character of this area and encouraged a new landscape initiative, adorned with planting and a collection of interesting sculptures to soften the buildings.

Shortly after the Science Labs opened in 1958, the science garden was created by the biology teacher, Dick Harthan, with an interesting array of plants, dominated, in the early 1960s at least, by the genus *Euphorbia*. Pupils were asked to study the unusual flower structure and to beware of the white sap – a poison that could cause allergy on the skin and severe stomach pains or worse if ingested.

The landscape adjacent to the Bramall classroom block (named by some pupils as the 'Bridge over Tarmac') was better in concept than in execution. It was a bold and imaginative idea to allow the space to flow under the building and to terminate in generously wide steps that front on to the parkland, with the magnificent view of the lime trees and beyond. What a pity such an important pedestrian space should be let down by the use of poor-quality materials: concrete flags and a sea of tarmac. Thankfully, Don Potter's *The Tree of Life* sculpture, the juxtaposition of the Coade Hall and some recent planting enliven the area.

The Hunter House landscape is of a different order in terms of materials and visual effect. In spite of the tricky levels, the attractive paving and thoughtful planting, combined with the strong open courtyard form of the building, make this an attractive garden space.

The walled garden has taken on a new lease of life with the conversion of part of the space to manège, and it is now much used by a growing number of pupils to exercise horses.

Today, after seventy-five years of changes and school developments, including numerous new buildings and sports facilities, the gardens and grounds still retain their overall structure and essential landscape character. And they are, in a word, impressive.

The magnificent terraces and steps are perfectly wedded to the mansion in arrangement, materials and scale; and they tie the building, despite its palatial size and elevated position, comfortably into the landscape. The main terrace with its long gravel walk, flanked by lawns and bordered by balustrades, commands wonderful views over the gardens, the parkland and the surrounding countryside. Descending the flight of steps to the middle terrace, the near view is enriched by the main border, skilfully replanted by Richard Joyce in

A food chain on the terrace

2002. The middle terrace is laid to grass with grass embankments above and below. A further double flight of steps curves down to the main lawn, leading to the circular pond with fountain and gravel surround. A strong axial line informs the design with hard and soft elements disposed more or less symmetrically on either side. A large but discreet sculpture, a rhino, sited at the rear of the lawn and to one side, adds incident and a hint of humour without disturbing the formal symmetry of the layout. The immaculately tended grass tennis courts fit well with the grandeur and magnificence of the design and in the Summer Term tennis enlivens the landscape. Views from the main lawn up towards the mansion are equally impressive, with the sheer mass of the building projecting a sense of power and drama.

The parkland landscape continues to evolve with sensitive new planting replacing trees lost to gales or old age. The attractive qualities mentioned more than a hundred and fifty years ago still hold true today. The 'Cliff' retains its mix of evergreens and deciduous trees and still boasts some fine specimens. One of the veteran London plane trees has graduated to national fame and is listed in the publication *Champion Trees of Britain and Ireland*. The Hangings are still dominated by beech and carpeted with a diverse range of ground flora. The meadows, backed by the river, continue to make a major contribution to the beauty of the landscape, despite the intensive use of the area for sport.

No doubt every Bryanstonian has a favourite memory of the grounds: a special moment and place. The pride and privilege of playing tennis on the grass courts, a sense of freedom at 'End of the World', walking the 'Secret Path' with a friend, wonder at the play of dappled light in Beechwood after leaving the Art Department, the currents and eddies in the river, bluebells enjoyed along Middle Cut, playing at the ruins and on the river swing.

And, finally, as a spur to those involved with the future planning of the Bryanston landscape, inspiring words from Frank Fraser Darling:

> The near landscape is valuable and lovable because of its nearness, not something to be disregarded and shrugged off; it is where our children are reared and what they take away in their minds to their long future. What ground could be more hallowed?

Rik Sturdy *(Dorset '64) is a landscape architect specialising in school landscapes and the design of large gardens.*

Red squirrels, roe deer and the river

In the 1940s red squirrels still existed in the school grounds, and there were otters in the river. I saw one while fishing by the sluice that led water off to the Pump House. This carrier was full of crayfish (the native white-clawed sort). We caught some with the aid of one of the school woven-wire wastepaper baskets baited with a dead fish. Edible Roman snails occasionally appeared on the bank going up to what was then the Science Block. I wonder if they still do. Even in our wartime state of perpetual hunger, I never heard of anyone eating them. I did find a grey partridge caught by the leg in a rat trap under a corn stack when out on a natural history expedition with Willie MacNae, the biology master. He was a bit horrified when I killed it, took it back and subsequently roasted it in front of the Common Room fire. Frogs for biology were collected from an abandoned water cistern near Bloody Shard Gate in Cranborne Chase.

There were roe deer in the Hangings – the beginning for me of a lifetime spent studying them. All the woods within bicycle range were regularly scoured for butterflies and moths, and there were a great many more of them, in number and variety. The woods, too, were larger. Houghton Wood, now reduced by bulldozing to a couple of small coverts, was over 1,000 acres. The woods between Ashmore and Gunville, too, were enormously reduced in the post-war era in the name of rabbit clearance by two war-surplus Sherman tanks.

The vast majority of the woodland was species-rich hazel coppice with standards, a relic of the enormous hurdle-making industry originally serving local sheep farms. Much of what survived the bulldozer was felled in the post-war years and replanted with beech or conifer. When I returned to Dorset it was difficult to realise how much the landscape had changed.

Hurdle-making is a lonely job. The hurdle-makers were often glad to talk, even to a schoolboy. They bought the right to cut half an acre or so of coppice in one of the annual 'Sales of Underwood' and established a rough camp on the spot to make them – a skill that is

'The scent of philadelphus still brings back rides down the Blandford Drive on June evenings'

still fascinating to watch. One old chap working in Broadley Wood told me he could remember the arrival of the very first reaper-and-binder. 'Mr Browning, he had seventeen of them – and three horses for each: two harnessed and one resting. He could put twenty-two teams out ploughing in the autumn – t'were like a battle! – like a battle!'

The Round Pond was used for practice by non-swimmers. For the rest there was a bathing place at the river with a rickety diving board and somewhere to hang clothes. This was before the School was built opposite, so everyone swam naked. The river was cold and muddy but nobody came to harm. Bill Williams was in charge and put a notice up showing the temperature. Hard to believe, but I think we started when this reached 64° (18°C). Early-morning swims were a delight – a charge down the fields in minimum wear, to be flung off in flight as the bathing place was reached.

On my last night at Bryanston we had a midnight (or thereabouts) swim at which Eric Bramall, Wilfrid Cowley and one of the school governors were present. The first two submitted with good grace to being thrown in, but there was a noticeable hesitation among us about the governor suffering as well. Wilfrid, dripping but true to his vocation, quoted 'There's such divinity doth hedge a king…' He was right.

Bicycles were our magic carpets, and of course apart from army traffic the roads were empty. The scent of philadelphus still brings back rides down the Blandford Drive on June evenings. All the surrounding countryside was open to exploration, and in spite of wartime rationing, one could still get tea and buns or even a Welsh rarebit at various teashops from Gunville to Wareham.

Latterly my home was in Devon. At the end of term a trunk could be piled with all the rest to go off by rail as 'Passenger's Luggage in Advance' and one could slip off on the bike around midnight to make home by breakfast, making a whole extra day on the holidays. The railway never twigged that all the trunks were not legitimate passenger's luggage, so it turned up in due course full of dirty clothes. I was never caught taking French leave, and on a fine night the ride in a sleeping countryside through Sherborne, Yeovil, Crewkerne and Chard, watching the flags of dawn appear on the hills behind was an experience I shall never forget.

Richard Prior *(Dorset '47) began work with the Forestry Commission as a trapper and finished as a conservancy wildlife advisor. He then became a freelance advisor on deer management and has written many books on the subject.*

This river runs through me

By the time I left Bryanston early one summer morning in 1966 – after a friendly goodbye from a dressing-gowned Mark Elder in the courtyard of the old Forrester House which he then headed – the sixties were getting into their stride. Me too. After a year's freewheeling, I would spend five years at two very different universities, increasingly immersed in the emerging counter-culture. Yet, in retrospect, if any one institution was my alma mater it was Bryanston. Not so much for what it did to me as what it allowed me to be and do for myself.

So what do I remember most, apart from the shorts – and the shirts whose shoulders we would surreptitiously rip so that the poor matrons would gradually build up impressive chevrons of stitching? Top of my laundry list would be two things: the freedom of choice and the River Stour. In terms of freedom of choice, after a prep school where the cane-fetishist headmaster eventually ended up being committed to an asylum, and a childhood spent in hotbeds of religious and inter-communal intolerance like Northern Ireland and Cyprus, perhaps anything would have felt like progress. But Bryanston allowed me to test out values I was still struggling to understand and express. Oddly, whilst the uneasy dynamics of several years as a notional Protestant in a Catholic convent school embedded in a Protestant community in Northern Ireland had put me off religion and rosaries for life, the lessons learned at Bryanston somehow ended up linked in my memory by the Stour's winding course, beaded along that sinuous thread.

In a school committed to the Church of England, no-one protested when I said no to Confirmation. Next, with a father who had been a Battle of Britain pilot, I was amazed to be allowed to be a conscientious objector when it came to the Sea Cadets. Later still, when (greatly to my surprise and his) I had a stand-up disagreement with my tutor in a hushed library, I was allowed to change to another tutor who – by accident or design – kept me on a much looser lead.

Much of my personal study time I spent delving into the history of religious and civil wars, whether on the curriculum or not. And in the end that around-the-margins study in Bryanston's libraries was what propelled me, pretty much despite myself, into university. Like many people, I had discovered that I learn best when allowed to follow my own lines of inquiry.

Of course, the freedom to choose is also the freedom to make your own mistakes. I had no thought of going to university, for example, which meant that I was allowed

TREES

My happiness at Bryanston was interwoven with love for the school grounds, especially the woods. I started painting trees at Bryanston, and have continued ever since – in oils, drawings and watercolours. I used to spend hours on my own painting in the Beechwood below the eastern corner of the school, and then in 'Desolation Valley' beyond it. I enjoyed the solitude. I did my only oil painting completely with a palette knife in Desolation Valley. There was a beautiful chestnut tree near the Science Labs that I particularly enjoyed drawing.

There was tragedy, too, amongst the trees. I remember a stretch of woodland by the River Stour called the Hangings where a boy had committed suicide. I remember this because my brother (who was very happy at Bryanston) took his life not long after leaving school.

I think the plays in the Greek Theatre amongst the trees contributed to the bonds so many of us felt towards the beautiful school grounds. Trees have always cast their mystery and joy, and nowhere more so than at Bryanston.

David Hay-Edie (Shaftesbury '61) is a diplomat and artist.

to drop subjects like Latin early on, ruling out Oxbridge. I also skittered away from most of the sciences, even though years later I would do a good deal of science writing for the likes of *New Scientist* and *The Guardian*.

The upshot: I ended up (language deliberate) at Essex University. Thank God. When it erupted in student protests in 1968, *annus mirabilis*, I learned more about social and political dynamics than at any other time in my life. Indeed, when I later spent two years doing a postgraduate degree at UCL, I woke up to just how lucky I had been to have found myself, time and again, on the edge: growing up in the unravelling fringes of Empire, then at Bryanston (outside the traditional academic mainstream), moving from Dorchester House to Forrester (which, as part of a large batch of new inmates, I remember being told we were meant to help civilise), then Essex and my immersion in the gathering tides of environmentalism. New things emerge – and best evolve – on a system's fringes.

But if any one thing unites my memories of the Bryanston years, it is the slow-moving, valley-hugging River Stour. These were days when so-called 'detergent swans' would still foam below the weir, forming great masses of bubbles. But I remember watching barbel, chub, dace, perch, pike and roach in clear eddies and rills under shaded banks. By moonlight I watched a graceful silver fish arc up over the weir. I don't know whether it was a salmon or sea trout, but its flanks flash far brighter in memory than anything experienced in biology lessons.

Meanwhile, the real pleasures – and the source of my most intense memories – lay several miles upstream. One more thing we were allowed to do was to cycle off into the landscape. Though I still loathe most sports, cycling (alongside skateboarding around the Science Labs) was soon an addiction. Despite my having to be carried back to the School unconscious after one cycling mishap on Durweston Bridge, this became a lifelong (and on occasion almost life-ending) passion. I have now cycled in London for over thirty years. Things may be better now, but for years this was my war. I was twice left unconscious, once – on a day when I flew to Egypt to work on the Nile ecosystem – with three broken ribs.

Anyway, cycling down through Durweston, we would cross the bridge, heading for the confluence of the Stour and Iwerne. From there, we would strike out either to Hod Hill or Hambledon Hill, haunt of glow-worms, from whose magisterial summit and ramparts we would look down on the backs of circling hawks, quaffing from a half-gallon flagon of illicit cider.

I recall one sun-hazed afternoon when we unexpectedly met up with a pair of Bryanston sculls on the river winding around Hod Hill – and the glorious, slow-rending crack when a tree-vine on which one of us was swinging out over the river broke and the would-be Tarzan described an astonished arc into the current. That, looking back, was what leaving Bryanston was like for me, mainly because I had little idea what course I really wanted my life to take.

All of this came back to me recently, courtesy of a psychotic peacock that had taken to attacking its own reflection in parked cars and shrieking through the night from the roof of the Spread Eagle Inn, hard by the Stourhead estate. Sleepless in a room directly below the squawking, my mind reflected on those halcyon days along the Stour. Whose main source turns out to be the Stourhead springs. And that fact I learned in 1998 when one of my favourite conservation groups, Common Ground, launched its 'Confluence' project. Over three years, Common Ground organised music workshops, courses and concerts for people living in the Stour catchment, from Somerset and Wiltshire where the river rises, through Dorset, alongside Bryanston, and thence to the sea at Christchurch, where schools of bass and grey mullet glide.

Today, only one river rivals the Stour in my affections: the Thames, particularly its London reaches. We have lived alongside it for thirty years, raising our daughters Gaia and Hania in Barnes. And I am often struck by the way our lives make more sense when viewed from a considerable distance, just as rivers do when you can look down on their entire catchments.

It's now nearly four decades since our old Land Rover growled through Forrester's gates for the last time. What I value most about the Bryanston experience is that it made it much harder for me to go with the flow. Instead, like the Stour or Thames in turbulent weather, I have felt a growing urge to break through banks and explore new tributaries, new eddies, new courses. And in today's free form, do-it-yourself economy, that drive has proved more valuable than anything we ever sat an exam on.

***John Elkington** (Forrester '66) is co-founder and Chairman of SustainAbility and the author of sixteen books, including the* Green Consumer Guide.

Fishing

Within days of arriving in the spring of 1965, I was out fishing the river, unsuccessfully at first, but with improving results as time progressed – particularly after reading *Fishing the Dorset Stour* by Owen Wentworth several times in prep (well it was natural history!). The first catch was a chub, just after the 1st VIII had passed by on the S-bend, about a pound in weight on a Blae & Black. Having been brought up on fly fishing I found it quite natural and continued to use flies, though after a while I progressed to live mayflies, of which there was an abundance in the Summer Term. Spinning for pike also became a favourite pastime, and I recall being absent from the weekly house meeting on account of finding the pike in a feeding frenzy above the weir one evening. The excitement was worth every minute of the extra work my housemaster, Mr Chirgwin, handed out!

The Dorset Stour at Bryanston was basically a coarse fishing river abundant with roach, pike, perch, dace and chub which could be readily caught on spinner, live bait or worms from the sewage works. There were several of us who spent considerable time on the river bank, and I probably spent more time there than I should have. However, the resultant knowledge gained was extremely useful when, as a cox, I had to turn the eights up underneath the rubbish dump avoiding the sunken cars.

Wentworth's booklet stated that trout could be found, and I spent many hours scouring the river in search of this elusive game fish and finally caught up with one underneath the arches of Spetisbury Bridge; unfortunately it got off before I could land it. Eventually I did manage to catch a lot of trout in the River Tarrant, a tributary of the Stour, which I then sold in the local villages to buy cider at the Langton Arms! I have made a career out of this and now have my own trout farm on the upper reaches of the Stour (Mere Fish Farm). We still sell trout to the Langton Arms thirty-five years on!

I think it was the Spring Term of 1967, it had been raining hard for a few days and the Stour was high and swollen with fast-flowing brown water, not a very good prospect for fishing. Undeterred I gathered my fishing tackle together, hopped on my bike and headed down to the Church. On arrival I found the farm fields partially flooded but I reckoned with a bit of luck I could work my way across. Abandoning the bike I carefully skirted the pools of water and eventually got across to the now thundering weir, feet soaked and the distinct possibility of being cut off by the rising water. But who cares, a few hours fishing was at stake. I settled myself on the stones beside the weir and tackled up: an 'Ardsley bomb' and a bunch of brambling worms from the sewage works.

Then it happened. A large fish swam straight out of the pool and catching the curve of the waterfall made it over the weir. It was so close that if I'd stretched out my hand I could have touched it. There was no doubt in my mind that was the king of fish, the salmon, making its way to the spawning grounds. This happened several times over the next hour or so by which time I had abandoned my fishing rod and resorted to lying on the iron platform, landing net in hand, hoping a salmon would jump into it! No such luck, but I got close.

I don't believe salmon run up there any more but on the trout farm we have upstream in Mere, we hope one day to rear salmon parr for release into the Stour. So who knows, if the Environment Agency cleans up our rivers, perhaps salmon will once more be seen jumping the weir at Bryanston.

Chris Wood (Forrester '69) studied marine biology at university and has been running the Mere Fish Farm since 1982.

Natural history at Bryanston

The estate was and remains one of the glories of Bryanston. For me it was not just a place to visit at weekends but an essential escape, a release from the charged atmosphere in the School itself and, with the surrounding countryside of Dorset generally, what made Bryanston possible for me.

First, the Bryanston estate meant the river and the woods immediately beside it. The path from Middle Lodge to the boathouse was my regular walk and became a familiar friend. The steep wooded banks, a few open spots and the beauty of the river itself surely nourished many a boy's, and subsequently girl's, adolescent need for a connection with a natural environment away from the School itself. It became particularly precious, when I was there, on some early mornings in May as a place to keep up a Common Bird Census for the British Trust for Ornithology, run by Margaret Harthan. There was, as always in the early morning, an atmosphere of frenetic singing and activity

BATS

Bats have been observed in the Old Kitchens since the 1930s. In the 1970s Ben Gaskell (Shaftesbury '74) and Andy McLeish (Shaftesbury '77) made a study of the colony and found an adult population of 120 geater horseshoe bats (*Rhinolophus ferrumequinum*). Since then the roof has been restored and a bat cave has been created in the chalk

base behind the Kitchens. Now over ten of the sixteen British bat species use it, including the rare barbastelle (*Barbastella barastellus*) and even rarer grey long-eared bat (*Pelecotus-austriacus*). The Kitchens and the surrounding woodlands have been designated a Special Area of Conservation and the site is managed by the Vincent Wildlife Trust.

among the birds and absolute calm among the watchers, treading delicately in familiar territory that seemed so unfamiliar when we were the only people about and the non-human world was so busy. A wide range of birds was there including summer visitors like blackcaps, willow warblers and spotted flycatchers mixed with the numerous residents, and I shall never forget the thrushes; the song of song thrushes varies a lot, and Dorset thrushes sing better than anywhere else in Britain. It was along this path and in the woods around in October that we followed the occasional fungus foray. The range we found was impressive with the great dinner plates of *Ganoderma* threatening the beech trees, mounds of sulphur-tufts, parasols and numerous others and a particular treasure, the *Geastrum* earth stars.

The river itself frequently gave good views of kingfishers rushing up and down and I saw mink on two occasions that I remember; sadly no otters, although they were said to be there. *(After their recent decline there are certain signs otters are returning. The School plans to build an otter shelter near Middle Lodge. – Ed.)* Often the only people I would meet would be the fishermen on the other side, sometimes with a friendly greeting, quietly waiting, as only fishermen know how, for a catch. The numerous plants, such as the bulrushes and yellow water lilies, showed how healthy the river was.

There were some good badger setts; a few evenings in my A-level term were spent waiting and watching, and trying not to disturb any badgers by swotting too many of the midges. The 'River Path' to Blandford along the edge of these woods could produce kingfishers, and large clumps of river dropwort grew mid-stream, but the river never seemed as rich as further up.

Another early morning haunt in the Summer Term was the Hangings, at that time mainly young beech plantations near the School and mature coppice-with-standards further away. This was the haunt of numerous garden warblers, and a few nightingales in the coppice. How I hope the nightingales are still there, although they are declining nationally. We would usually scare a roe deer, or often several, up there. Early spring days with sunshine would produce a brimstone, once in early February, and there were a fair number of early purple, spotted and greater butterfly orchids in places along the rides.

The progress of spring could always be followed for

me in the beech wood right beside the School. The naturalised winter aconites and snowdrops were the obvious early spring flowers, but the one that always pleased me most was the spurge-laurel with its deliciously scented but inconspicuous greenish flowers in January. Several bushes grew there. It was in the beech wood too that I tried moth trapping with beer and sugar kindly supplied by Alan Shrimpton one summer evening. I caught two moths on one tree, nothing on about six others and an entire colony (or so it seemed) of by then totally inebriated ants on another. I never tried it again. But I did go down to the terraces on summer evenings to find my first glow worms.

In the immediate surrounds of the School the grey wagtails that regularly appeared on the Science Labs pond, especially in autumn, were always a lovely sight, and once a hawfinch came down to drink in the Music School pond just before my lesson. The only real bird rarity at the School itself during my time was a fabled snowy owl. I caught a tantalisingly brief sight of an extraordinary large whitish bird from the main stairs of the school one morning during the time it was meant to be about. I rushed up past the San but never saw it again. It could have been one, though.

I did not shine academically at Bryanston and, on recollecting a few aspects of the natural history for this account, I realise that there were numerous temptations not to work. But the legacy of the estate and the Dorset countryside and the experiences I have described here last; they made Bryanston for me and, along with a few staff, they are what I remember with greatest affection.

***Andrew Lack** (Salisbury '71) is a writer and lecturer at Oxford Brookes. His area of expertise is pollination and plant population genetics.*

Toads, birds and Lady Portman's Pleasure Garden

In 1985, when I was sixteen, I teamed up with Len Taylor of the grounds maintenance staff to restore Lady Portman's Pleasure Garden from its derelict state. I spent each games period doing this for the next two years. Fortunately these were the days before stifling Health and Safety Regulations, so we were equipped with chainsaws and got on with the job of hacking through almost impenetrable undergrowth and scrub woodland. The safety equipment was too hot to wear so we didn't bother. Len Taylor taught us how to use a chainsaw safely, so I left school with the same number of body parts I had arrived with.

As we progressed, we uncovered the remains of two ornate fountains and a few of the ornamental plants that had survived nearly a century of neglect. It's the nearest I've got to hacking through the Central American jungle and encountering a lost Maya civilisation. We restored the landscape to an open woodland setting. During the summer we spent hours cutting back nettles and scrub with strimmers. Of course, discreet lobbying from smokers meant that we left a few favoured corners untouched, strictly for 'conservation' reasons.

Nearly twenty years later I still recall Len's kindness, and the pleasure of spending afternoons in the world of woodland management before returning to school smelling of wood smoke.

Keen ornithologist Tony Taylor of the biology staff ran a wonderful Bird Club for enthusiastic pupils. His main focus was an area of reed bed on the far bank of the Stour downstream from the boathouse. On winter weekend afternoons we would take a boat downriver armed with bow-saws in order to cut back the ever-encroaching scrub. We also created four lanes within the reed bed for mist nets to catch birds for study as they came in to roost.

My overwhelming memories of this are the stinking mud of the Stour, the dodgy duck boards that we needed to walk on in order not to sink into the slime, and the freezing dank conditions of misty November evenings as the sun set and birds came in to roost. After dark, we would delicately unravel the reed buntings and other birds that had been harmlessly caught in the nets before taking them back to the Biology Labs for measurement and ringing. Once fitted with a unique identification ring the birds would be released back into the reeds where their movements could be tracked. I remember that one of 'our' birds was subsequently re-caught in central France.

During summer, the Bird Club's focus was on ringing chicks of birds that had used the many nest-boxes that had been put up in the woods. Tony was in particular looking for marsh tits. I remember one day we opened a nest box and found a rare dormouse curled up inside.

As soon as the pond in the centre of the Science Labs was built, it was colonized by toads. On wet March nights these toads would emerge from hibernation in the woods and make their way back to the pond to breed. How they made their way up a flight of steps and into the pond via the one small gate, heaven knows. Many of the migrating toads would be squashed by cars as they crossed the drive. I took it

Beekeeping, 1950s and 2002

upon myself to rescue these toads before they were squashed and even bought some Toads Crossing Road signs (yes – such things do exist) to alert drivers. Eccentric yes, but it did succeed in dramatically reducing the number of squashed toads.

***Desmond Hobson** (Dorset '87) has worked as an ecologist throughout Britain. He was Director of Conservation at the Countryside Alliance and is now an environmental policy consultant.*

Swiss bees

When I left my home town, Basle, in Switzerland in 2000 at the age of seventeen, I left behind about 200,000 bees and five queens. From the age of thirteen I had learnt not only how to keep bees and encourage them to store as much honey as possible, but also how to breed queens.

During earlier holidays at the Park Farm in Milton Abbas Mr Burch, a veterinarian, introduced me to a passionate beekeeper in Sturminster Newton, Bill Summers. Bill promised to help me instal beehives near the School and to look after them when I was either too busy or back in Switzerland. When I came to Bryanston there was only one bee colony in the grounds. Bill Summers provided beehives and soon we had ten colonies near the School (we had to relocate later on). My teacher in queen rearing in Basle had supplied me with highly bred Swiss queens, mated high up in the mountains of the Engadin, which I brought to England in my jacket.

Swiss bees are very good workers and it was interesting to observe how they used their abilities in Dorset. I taught Bill how to rear queens and we were pretty successful. We managed not only to collect a lot of bright yellow honey, but also to produce new bee colonies ruled by real Swiss queens and their daughters. We sold quite a lot of queens to interested beekeepers. For the honey jars my father designed a special label 'Bryanston School Honey' and my tutor Gordon Leadbetter helped to sell the honey jars quite *seduliter*. After I had finished my A-levels, I had once again to leave a lot of bees behind. But I am very glad to hear that with the help of my friend Bill Summers, Bryanston has become a great place for busy bees and sweet honey. At the moment I am in my third year of veterinary medicine at the University of Zurich, which unfortunately keeps me from looking after bees … for the time being.

Dorian Bindler *(Salisbury '02)*

14

SPORTING COLOURS

Passionate delight: the rise of Bryanston rugby

> Every September the whole of Bryanston's Rugby Club returns to school having forgotten the game completely. All teams have to be trained from scratch, and talent or brilliance recovered from a welter of far-off, forgotten things. The cure?… To be haunted by a passionate delight in rugby and to concede to the game the intelligence, imagination and practice you would give to painting, acting or playing the flute. Too keen altogether? Then you must be content that Bryanston should be, in respect of Rugby Football, second-class. (Andrew Wordsworth, *Saga*, 1955)

Like so many teenage boys I virtually lived for sport. However much I enjoyed my music, drama, prefecting, socialising and, at certain times, my academic work, it was sport that defined my schooldays – and I was by no means alone.

After all, I was a part of the meteoric rise of athletics under the young Harold Tarraway, who stole a march on other public schools, stuck in traditional ruts of 'major and minor' sports. I enjoyed good hockey on the velvety Hearne pitches and accomplished gymnastics in that Old Gym whose walls breathed in and out with the wind. But, above all, there was 'Rugger' and membership of the most successful 1st XV yet produced, frolicking on the wide acres of a brand new James Ground. Although in the fifties rowing was Bryanston's most prestigious sport, the School's philosophy of choice encouraged all options to hold their own, with tennis, squash and cross country flourishing equally with the more prestigious games. Conscientious objectors could even opt out of sport altogether and choose Pioneering, demonstrating their building prowess on Greek theatres and music schools.

But Andrew Wordsworth was right: Bryanston competed successfully in the two most popular sports of cricket and rugby, but at a level below that of 'top' schools like Sherborne, Marlborough and Blundell's. Those schools achieved their dominance by dedicating resources to these two 'major' sports and placing those heroes who succeeded in them on a pedestal. However, at most schools it was rugby that stirred the blood, stimulated youthful adulation and brought prestige to the establishments. At Bryanston most of us were bitten by the same bug, and we would have given our right feet to be able to defeat the likes of Sherborne and Marlborough. But in those days it was not to be – not even in sevens.

Sixteen years later, after coaching in the fevered intensity of South Africa and the stirring expanses of Scotland, I was appointed to the Bryanston staff by Robson Fisher the week after my Canford Junior Colts had defeated their Bryanston opposition by over fifty points. Bryanston, in gentle Dorset, had considerable leeway to make up. I am sure that fundamentally it was a matter of attitude, of the will to approach sport with an ambition and a dedication that drove you forward to achieve your potential, both as an individual and as a team.

When, in 1975, David Jones asked me to take over the 1st XV he gave me a remit to put Bryanston rugby on the map. I readily found a group of talented players at the top of the School who were longing to be whipped into shape: Gregg, Tedford, Tozer – and others. There was also a young new boy in B, somewhat overweight and untutored, but with a rich vein of genius in his running: David Trick. He, of course, went on to win England caps and thrill the crowds.

The summer of 1976 was incredibly dry; when we returned to school in September the fields looked like the African veld. We could not possibly play rugby on those rock-hard grounds, so there was only one alternative: to train frantically hard for fitness and for skills. By the time the drought broke two days before the first match, the boys were superbly prepared and

thirsting for a game. They swept all before them, including that Canford side that had taken fifty points off their Bryanston opposition three years earlier. By mid-November, however, they were becoming anxious about remaining unbeaten. A narrow loss to King's Taunton taught us an important lesson: better to lose an unbeaten season than to lose the enjoyment of playing. From that match on the boys relaxed, and the season ended in a creative manifestation of the team's capabilities: they were a joy to watch.

Some players found the tough training regime difficult to adapt to in those early days, before the traditions had been laid. Along with the humour, wit and camaraderie, I always believed in old-fashioned discipline to gel a side and drive it onward. A big lock forward once admitted how much he hated me during those arduous training sessions. I told him I was happy about that, provided it helped him train harder and play better! A group of individuals needs this structure of discipline if it is to achieve proper unity of purpose. The evidence is there in all team games – and in the best music and drama and mountaineering. Such focus has not always been known as a prime Bryanston attribute, but a team, a crew, an orchestra or a cast will not fully succeed without it.

During those three years, 1977 to 1979, Bryanston's 1st XVs were indisputably amongst the best in the country, with fast, skilful backs playing off dominant packs. Marlborough, Abingdon, Taunton, Blundell's were walloped. Names like Cox, Sayer, Rochmankowski swirl with many others in the mists of memory. A third unbeaten season was celebrated in 1982, thanks to another team studded with gifted players. The performance of those backs, Phillips and Gale to the fore, when King's Taunton were cut to shreds on their ground, was as accomplished as any schoolboy three-quarter play you are likely to see. And then there was our first defeat of Sherborne by Lovell-Smith's team. Sherborne had declined to play us until Trick and Cox had left. We travelled there for the first time in 1981 with motivation high and won with a superbly controlled performance. Before the match a Sherborne parent was overheard to say, 'Well, if we can't beat a side from a girls' school….'

The impact of an outstanding side in a high-profile sport is immense. It raises the whole school's morale. A community 'feel good' factor feeds off it. The most unexpected people support and identify with it. It raises the national profile of the School. It attracts the prep schools and their good pupils. There is also another, more altruistic benefit: prestigious teams frequently draw the best from their opposition. Kingswood and St Paul's defeated us against the odds in 1978, and they won widespread respect for it. It is hugely creative to lose from time to time: one learns so much more in defeat, and arrogance contaminates even the best.

In rugby one is aiming for victory, yes, but more than that: a kind of aesthetic purity of teamwork. The hours of training for fitness and skill, the repetitive practice of team and unit play, the marriage of individual flair to the team's purpose, the balance of rigorous control with expansive creativity: these and so much more contribute to all team games. The moments of truth, of perfection, though achieved only rarely, are unmistakably fulfilling to both players and spectators. They are akin to the perfection of harmony that can be achieved in music, on the stage and in the studio. In competitive sport, however, there is an opposition bent on breaking you down, spoiling your designs, subjugating your efforts. So there is a continual need to regroup and support, a need for spontaneity, for instinctive creativity. One move can never be the same as the next, so the mind as well as the body is always at work. It can indeed be poetry in action.

The seven-a-side version of the game places abilities, fitness, resilience and teamwork under the microscope. To achieve victory a team has to pace itself over a tournament, with a confidence and calmness to ride the crises and take opportunities. It is for this reason that I draw particular satisfaction from Bryanston's sevens

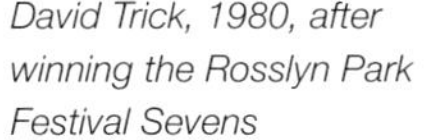

David Trick, 1980, after winning the Rosslyn Park Festival Sevens

triumphs. In 1979 Bryanston reached the national final at Rosslyn Park for the first time. We played consistently throughout but made rather heavy weather of beating a strong Monmouth seven in the semi-final. A few uncharacteristic errors meant that our trump card, Trick, had to extend himself rather than being protected for the final. The impact of this on our performance in the showdown against Rossall was probably decisive. But it was a marvellously competitive final, with the advantage seesawing with each score to the last gasp.

The following year our expectations were even higher; we had suffered injuries and were somewhat disjointed in the early rounds, but we had something in hand. On the second day, once Shoebridge had arrived in the nick of time from a traffic jam, and a faith-healer had unexpectedly offered his services, we carried all before us. Frankly, we were never truly tested. We had, however, been tested in a previous tournament at Taunton – by Millfield, who were determined to dent our reputation. That was a bone-crunching final between two top-class sides, which we won in the end with a little to spare. At Roehampton that year Millfield won the Open tournament, while we were victors in the Festival (for one-term rugby schools), so we could justifiably claim to be the best side in the country.

As I left Bryanston for pastures new, Philip de Glanville, England's future rugby captain, was emerging as a very good, but not exceptional, Colts scrum-half, skilful but light in build. Over his playing career he transformed his prospects – by dint of great motivation, by dedicated work on his skills and physique, and by maintaining an admirable mental balance. Phil remained true to himself and his priorities. I can think of no better sporting ambassador for Bryanston. For nearly thirty years I have rejoiced at the School's continued rugby success. And to the young Bryanstonians, and those yet to be born, I will quote the great Mike Gibson: 'If your mind is fresh, your conscience clear and your body fit, just go out there and give expression to your talents.'

(Dedicated to HGT, QC, GR (Colonel Pressups) and AJM – and John Griffin, our most loyal supporter, who would doubtless have put me right on a number of details!)

Malcolm Green *(Salisbury '58) was a Housemaster, 1st XV rugby coach and member of staff from 1974 to 1984. He became Headmaster of Warminster School and then Eltham College, retiring in 2000. He was a President of the Old Bryanstonian Association.*

Rowing – a personal story

Looking back(wards), as rowing folk do, I am amazed at the huge part that BSBC has played in my life. I have often referred to rowing as an octopus; once it has you in its grasp, it doesn't let go. My first rowing memory is of listening to the wireless commentary on the Boat Race in the late 1940s. A small prep school boy, I stood in the Staff Room with my fists clenched, desperately willing Cambridge to win – which they did, of course. I had never seen rowing, but somehow it had glamour for me and I was immediately a fanatical Cambridge supporter. How fortunate I was that my parents chose Bryanston. I had been useless at all the other sports – football, hockey, cricket and rugby – and was not likely to make the grade in athletics. Rowing saved me from being a total wimp and has given me a huge store of wonderful memories.

When I arrived at Bryanston in 1950, it was, as a non-Bryanstonian once wrote to me, '*The* school for rowing'. Jeffreys had been determined that his new school would be a rowing school and, to that end, he appointed Ronnie King, whom he had met at Westminster, to take charge of the Boat Club. Rowing took place initially from under the trees at the 'Old Rope Place', but in 1930 an ex-army hut was purchased (for £15) and served as the boathouse for over thirty years. Bill Phelps arrived as boatman in or about the same year, a member of the famous family of London watermen. A 1st VIII was formed in 1931, the first entry to Henley came in 1937. Ronnie was away on service during the war, but the club was kept afloat by Arthur Bull and, once the war was over, things soon blossomed. The *annus mirabilis* was 1948 – at Henley we contested the final of the Ladies Plate with Eton (the only time since 1893 that two schools fought that final, and it has never happened again), Charles Swithinbank rowed for Isis (coxed by Douglas Cox, future member of staff) and Mark Bodley Scott rowed in the Olympic Games at Henley. Our first Cambridge Blue followed in 1952 (George Marshall), the year in which we won the Schools' Head of the River Race (coach Douglas Cox). In the next four years we had six more seats in Cambridge boats; no fewer than three in the 1954 boat. For Oxford Blues we had to wait till the 1960s. At the

Eton beating Bryanston by two-thirds of a length in the final of the Ladies Plate at Henley Royal Regatta, 1948

Many years after leaving Bryanston, living in the top floor of a house, staring out at some huge branches of a tree looming up from below, I began a large watercolour. After a while, the branches became oars and a large limb turned into a boat; soon, the whole thing had become a rowing eight, a memory of times upon the river with Ronnie as cox – probably the most exhilarating of experiences at that time.
Stephen Spicer (Dorset '61)

1948 Henley, Bryanston had entered for both the Ladies Plate and the Princess Elizabeth Cup. After winning a race in the PE, Bryanston reckoned their chances brighter in the Ladies and scratched from the PE, leaving Radley to 'row over' in their next race. The next meeting of the Regatta's committee of management put a stop to such skullduggery.

As a new boy, I signed up for rowing and plodded along until the Autumn Term of 1953. Rodney Dingle had just arrived from Cambridge (winner of the Grand at Henley, Gold Medallist in eights at the European Championships, and a Cambridge Blue) and put me in his Winter Term eight. The following term I was in the 1st VIII, displacing Dick Batterham from seven to bow (the bow man has to be the best oarsman in the boat). My father met one of my prep school masters in London who, asking after me, was amazed to learn I was in the 1st VIII – 'What! That little squit!' Possessed of no great physique and not being physically competitive, nevertheless I loved the action and feel of rowing, the 'deities of wood and water'. Henley 1954 and 1955 introduced me to a world of excellence I had hardly dreamt of. All this took me to St John's College, Cambridge, and Lady Margaret Boat Club, where I found a new fulfilment in coaching – 'The great thing about you, Alan, is that we can always hear you.' However, my first job was in a non-rowing school and I was soon absorbed in other pleasures. Had the octopus loosed its grip?

Appointed to the Bryanston staff in 1964, I was expected to take charge of Pioneering. The octopus had other ideas. A colleague wanted out of rowing. Would I swap? A new member of staff always obliges. I began coaching in a club that was riding the crest of the wave generated by the great Ronnie King. Ronnie was still coaching, but the lead was taken by Bob Allan in charge of the club (an Oxford Trial Cap) and Rodney Dingle coaching the 1st VIII, soon to hand over to John Sutherland-Smith (Cambridge Trial Cap and excellent sculler). I was allocated to the Colts (under-16s) and, after a hesitant beginning, my enthusiasm knew few boundaries. Each year we did a little more, developing our own training without realising that we had re-invented various wheels, e.g. interval running. Bob had invited down the ARA's first national coach, who showed us how to do weight-training, and we instituted a full training scheme. This soon paid dividends; for example, in 1968 we had three eights in the top twenty at the Schools' Head of the River Race.

Bill Phelps had left to become boatman to the University of London in 1952. His replacement was 'Mac', a fine craftsman who hailed from Oxford and commonly spoke in monosyllables. The crews he coached needed to fathom his characteristic instruction, 'No! Not like that. Like tha-a-a-a-t!' When my Colts VIII was due to have a new boat in 1967, Bob Allan asked me how we should name it. 'Let's name it after Mac', I said. Bob and I approached Mac while he was sweeping one of the boathouses. After talking of this and that, Bob said, 'Mac, you know this boat that Alan's Colts are getting? We were wondering if you'd mind if we called it after you?' Mac was leaning against the wall, massive forearms folded over the handle of his broom. 'No-a-o-a-o,' he said, and walked out. We knew he was deeply moved. The smile on his face when he broached the champagne said it all. Later that summer, we won the Colts event at the National Schools' Regatta, Bryanston's first national schools' champions. The only let-down was that the previous year's winners had neglected to return the cup, so we were presented with a small cardboard cup, decorated in pink gingham. I treasured it for many years.

In 1970, Rodney Dingle's Junior Colts (under-15s) followed suit, more or less the same crew as my 1971 Colts who won their division at the Schools' Head and, in 1972, as John Sutherland-Smith's 1st VIII, they won the Child Beale Cup at the National Schools' Regatta. Weight training certainly built that crew. In 1971, all of them were doing sets of power cleans with more than their own body weight. However, we didn't follow our

Schools' Head win with another at the National Schools' Regatta. Maybe we wouldn't have done so anyway, but there was a rare summer flood, and we were racing *up*stream; Eton drew the faster lane, we drew one of the slower ones. Poetic justice; Eton had lost an oar in the Schools' Head – but we had beaten them in a fair race at Gloucester!

Promoted to 1st VIII coach in 1974–75, I was again lucky to have a remarkable bunch of boys – strong, talented, competitive, great friends, and beneficiaries of John Sutherland-Smith's emphasis on sculling at all levels of the club. That year, we won most of the events we entered, and reached the final of the Special Race for Schools at Henley. Despite losing, we were invited to represent England in the Home Countries International. Sadly, the boys all had their holidays fixed and we had to turn down the invitation. Most of this crew were with us in 1976. Through that season we won less, but Henley '76 left another happy memory. Meeting Radley in the semi-final, I saw they were six seconds faster than us in each of their previous races, so our target was to 'tweak the lion's tail'. This we did to good effect, leading Radley to Fawley (where we still hold the record, for a course that is no longer used) and pushing them to equal the record to the finish. We lost by just two seconds, and it felt almost as good as winning. I learned then that what matters is not beating the other guys, but excelling yourself. That is what the other guys are there for, to bring that excellence out of you, and vice versa. The best races are win-win events.

Come 1977, Rodney Dingle had gone, John Sutherland-Smith left, and Bob Allan was destined for higher things. It was my turn to run the Boat Club. My great boon was the arrival of Michael Ricketts as Mac's replacement. Michael, a cabinet maker and son of Harry Ricketts, the School's original painter and handyman, was a complete newcomer to rowing. I soon discovered we had won a diamond. He kept us going until we could afford new boats and oars, and he took an immense pride in the condition of the whole boathouse area. A shrewd judge of men and boys, he was the ideal right hand man. David Jackson's speech on his retirement was a delightful reworking of Wordsworth's poem, *Michael*!

If to the Stour's side you turn your steps, you will,
On dewy mornings and sun-soaked ends of days,
Encounter Michael, strolling down the river's length,
Seeing things only knowing eyes can see.
He and the river hold the knowledge of time,

Left: The 1st VIII celebrates its success, 1972

OPENING THE JAMES MEMORIAL GROUND

On 9th June 1956 the new James Memorial Ground was opened, at Harold Tarraway's invitation, by the legendary Olympic gold medallist Harold Abrahams. He brought an Achilles Club team of Oxbridge blues (including four internationals) to compete against the school team in a handicap match. The highlight of the afternoon was the 880 yards run by one of the greatest British middle distance runners, Derek Johnson. He was the British record holder at the time, and he ran against our sprint relay squad, recording 1 min 51.6 secs, the fastest 880 yards on grass that year. All who witnessed it marvelled at Johnson's combination of effortless grace and power, beautifully captured in this photograph taken by a pupil as Johnson was being paced round the first lap. Regrettably, as one of the relay squad, I saw very little of this exhibition until Johnson flew past me on the final bend. Sadly Derek Johnson died of leukaemia on 30th August this year.

Malcolm Green (Salisbury '58)

The wisdom of nine thousand days,
Constant both and equally true.

We have been lucky with all our boatmen. Not only men of stamina, staying twenty-two, twenty-five, and twenty-four years, they have been exceptional craftsmen. Michael's replacement, Mark Lilley, is another gift from the gods. With his experience of modern sailing craft, he can recondition all our modern plastic boats, saving us thousands of pounds in repair fees.

In the later 1970s, it was apparent that the sort of success we had regarded as natural was no longer going to come so easily. To help maintain standards, I founded the Buffaloes in 1979. Originally intended to provide expertise and coaching assistance from successful rowing OBs, this developed into more of a general support club. Our income has enabled us to provide BSBC with items the School might have regarded as luxurious, though actually vital. Our social events, combining coaches and pupils, parents and OBs, have all grown over the years, providing a leavening of the spirits to crews and coaches, as well as heart-warming reunions for past crews. Perhaps the biggest change to 'hit' us was the arrival of girls, but their story and that of recent years is for others to tell.

Alan Shrimpton (Hardy '55) formerly Head of Biology, master in charge of rowing and member of staff since 1964. He edited the OB Yearbook and is School Archivist.

Harold Tarraway

Harold was one of the star athletes of his generation. He was the gold medal winner for the 800 metres in the 1947 World Student Games in a time of 1 min 54.4s. The silver medallist's time was 1 min 54.6s, and the bronze medallist's time 1 min 54.7s. A pretty close race, but Harold WON, and as he often said, 'winning is sublime'. In 1948 he was selected to represent England in the Olympic Games. He won through to the semi-final, but disaster struck when the favourite, running just in front of Harold, suffered a ruptured Achilles tendon and fell, taking Harold with him.

Having qualified as a teacher he was recommended by someone to Thorold Coade of Bryanston for the new post of director of physical education. Harold's wife Mary insisted that Harold went for the interview, and Harold met a kindred spirit in Thorold Coade (a man he admired immensely). He was appointed director of physical education – an innovative step in the public schools of that era.

Harold was a round peg in a round hole. He loved Bryanston, and was immensely proud of the achievements of its pupils. He was a brilliant athletics coach, with endless champions to his name in many different disciplines. He cajoled, persuaded and charmed youngsters into getting the most out of themselves. He inspired people and built Bryanston athletics up so that

the School was one of the top, if not the top, athletics schools in the country. Anyone watching him coach could see that he was amazingly tactile. He would push and pull boys' bodies into the correct position, and sort of wrap himself round them to get them into the right stance. He gave them a kinaesthetic sense of what they should be doing; it was a sort of 'laying on of hands'. He gathered individuals and groups around him and his stock phrase, 'Well blokes', used to ring out as he persuaded them to do as he wanted. He hated losing.

He brought the same qualities to rugby coaching, and his time in charge of the Rugby Club was one of the most successful in the School's history. During his time in charge he persuaded the headmaster David Jones to give a young lad from Tiverton by name of David Trick the first full sports scholarship to the School. Harold could spot prodigious talent and David went on to play for Bath and England.

Harold's stage did not just consist of Bryanston. He was the chairman of Dorset Schools Athletics, and Dorset Schools Rugby. He was team manager to British athletics teams, travelling mostly to Eastern Europe. He had the distinction of playing basketball with Fidel Castro and his cabinet, and who do you think won? And of course there was Parkstone Sailing Club. He loved and excelled at ballroom dancing. He was also a founder member of the Public Schools Physical Education Conference, and in 1979 he was awarded the Physical Education of Great Britain Gerald Murray Award for outstanding services.

However, Bryanston was where Harold's heart really lay. He was so proud of Bryanston and the children he taught. He was a friend to them all and they were part of his extended family. Of course he could be exasperating and too single-minded, but people respected and admired him, and recognised a rare talent. Harold was a schoolmaster par excellence, with a warmth and compassion that made him a friend to all. Bryanston was fortunate to have him, and he was fortunate to have Bryanston.

David Crawford *taught at Bryanston from 1966 to 1973 and was later Headmaster of Cokethorpe School. He is currently Headmaster of Colston's School, Bristol.*

The Bryanston Butterflies

The early fifties were halcyon years. They were also pioneer years. There was not much to luxuriate in during that post-war decade, but there was delight in what there was. I never enter a marquee on a sunny day but that my thoughts enter another one; I never catch the tang of linseed oil and coconut matting but that I am called back to a simple wooden pavilion deep in rural England. 'All life is an echo of first sensations.' David Hearne and Bill Andrews were groundsmen worthy of their work, and Dorset in manner and speech. Their pronunciation of 'badgers' had just the slightest hint of an 'h' after the 'b', and their conversational syntax has been forever preserved by Thomas Hardy. There was cricket against Bryanston and Durweston, always in the

sunshine of the Butterflies memories, on that superb ground created by Tom Hearne, David's father. The village side was full of worthy characters like Jack Adlem who manned the Porter's Office. The cricketing details of those years were chronicled by my brother, David, and reside in the school archive. It was a suggestion from David that led to Tom's ground being officially known as Hearne's Ground.

John Harrison (Hardy '51)

Tennis in the 1950s

To the left and right of the ornamental pond the five grass courts were blocked off most Saturday afternoons. The 1st VI were playing a match. The sun shone, the smell of freshly mown grass pervaded and the white marking lines were pristine. Visiting teams arrived from Canford, Sherborne, Downside, Clifton, Marlborough, Dauntsey's or Millfield.

Watched over by a bronzed and relaxed Wilf Cowley (probably with his shirt off) or a more serious but intensely interested Bill Carpenter-Jacobs (certainly not with his shirt off) the doubles battles commenced. Best of three sets. During the course of the afternoon the shadows lengthened as a full test ensued with each pair playing each of the visiting teams' three pairs. No tie-breaks in those days. Each set went the distance – I recall one at 14–12.

After it was all done around six or seven in the evening, the best drink in the world was a pint of cold milk! We all slept well that night.

My partners included Quentin Guirdham, Kevin Crossley-Holland, James Wright, Robin Blandford, Peter Loebinger (now Duckworth) and many others.

Charles Maynard (Portman '59)

The swath-cutter

As I drive along the banks of the River Charles in Boston, Massachusetts, where I live, I often see the elegant sight of sleek eights masterfully slicing their way with the precision and seamlessness of a well-oiled machine. As often as not, these boats (and the motor launch running alongside) are composed entirely of strong young Amazonian women, and in these days there is nothing exceptional about that.

This was not at all the way it was when I was at Bryanston. When John Sutherland-Smith decided to start a girls' eight in 1975 he had a veritable motley crew of takers: we were the tallest, smallest, heaviest and lightest. As memory serves some of us weren't even that gainly in the slender rig! There were no requirements for uniformity or rigorous standards here – sufficient interest was the price of admission. The fact that we were the third year of intake of girls with only thirty-eight girls in the school at the time helps explain the height/weight differential, and why as the lightest girl in the crew, rather than being given the role of cox I was in fact placed in bow.

Races? There weren't many. We entered all the races we could that year, making a total of three or at most four. There simply weren't many girls' races in existence in those days. Despite crossing the country we ended up rowing more often in single or double sculls with some fours, because given that this was a fledgling enterprise, smaller numbers afforded greater opportunity.

We didn't come to Bryanston specifically to start girls' eights or soccer teams, act in plays or musical performances with a co-ed cast, although each of these activities illustrate why we were there. We came for something more abstruse; we came for the opportunity

Bryanston offered us, opportunities we could not have found elsewhere. There were no eights for girls in Britain then, and this was one of three schools in the country that offered those kinds of opportunities – one that was pioneering the vanguard as England began to open up to change.

I think there was a sense, speaking personally, that we were searching for more than was currently available, and we went to Bryanston because we were champing for more – more/better teachers, facilities and so on. We wanted to make the best of ourselves and there was no opportunity in our world. Or rather, at Bryanston there were the beginnings of opportunity, but no established path. This provided the freedom of a blank slate, making it a highly creative time for us individually and I believe for the School as a whole.

Recent visits to the School give the impression that thirty years on things are run so smoothly between the sexes that, as Tom Wheare put it to me, one is 'gender-blind'. This is a tribute to how well the institution has integrated girls into the fabric of school life. In a way that's how it was in those early days before the unique needs of girls were established. We played in a boys' school in a boys' way because that was the only way available to us, just as many women slightly in advance of us did in the early years of the feminist movement in law, politics or academia. Undoubtedly the boys didn't see us, or our intrusion into their world, in this way, but for us it was rather a gender-free experience.

When I went to Bryanston and saw myself in conjunction with my peers and within the setting of the School's ethos, I realised I was a pioneer. That sense informed me of one of the deepest tenets of my being which has never left me, and guides my actions to this day. 'Bryanston is a hard place to leave,' we say when we meet up with old friends: it may be truer to say that one does not leave Bryanston. It is certainly hard to replace. Like the water ploughed by the oar, it ripples up from my unconscious each day offering new gems to fathom.

As I watch the parades of boats from major academic institutions across the US at the annual Head of the Charles regatta, I recall some advantages of being one of the first, the swath-cutter.

Harriet Bridges *(Greenleaves '76) has worked as a music teacher and in business development, and she performs in professional ensembles in Boston, Massachusetts.*

MATCH(ES) OF THE DAY

National Schools Netball Championships 1995

As sporting teams go at Bryanston, the 1st VII Netball Squad of 1995 was arguably the most dedicated, hard-working and charismatic bunch of girls ever to grace the Carpenter-Jacobs courts. Years of hard work by Alison Leigh building up girls' sports were achieving results. The National Championships that year was remarkable. Emerging as County Champions, unbeaten for a place at the West of England Championships, they continued their unbeaten run and succeeded in qualifying first and earning their place at the National Championships in Middlesbrough in March.

Arriving at the Nationals after a night on the town with a diet of water and spaghetti, the team were faced with torrential rain and an opposition built like the 1st XV. However they had a secret weapon; Bryanston packed lunches including forty packets of pickled onion-flavoured Space Invaders between nine girls. As Julie Saunders, their coach, remembers, 'We proceeded to blast our opponents off the court, in more ways than one! The semi-final was a close call as we went into the last seconds of the game all square, when a long throw from the centre reached our shooter who dunked the ball into the net to clinch victory as the whistle blew for full time. The final was a different story as our patched-up, tired team faced a sea of pink in the name of "Our Lady Chetwyn" and their abundance of England players. To their credit our girls gave it their all and fought to the end. A bedraggled, battered and exhausted team received their runners-up medals with honour and pride and with the realisation that out of the hundreds of schools entering the initial stages of the competition they had gained the title of England Reserve Champions.'

National Squash Championships 1974

As with many school sports, the National Schools Squash Championships begin regionally. Bryanston is unlucky to be in the same section as the formidable Millfield. However, in the 1973–74 season a determined five roamed southern England in pursuit of the National Championships. They played twenty-three matches, winning them all – usually 5–0. The final, played in north London against Huddersfield New College, was extremely close. We just lost 3–2 in the fifth game of the fifth match.

The Youll Cup 1966

Success in tennis came in the mid-sixties when Bryanston was on a winning roll in the Public Schools tournament (the Youll Cup). The team reached the semi-final ('64), quarter finals ('65) and finals ('66). The 1966 tournament was plagued by relentless rain. The team battled for hours against Westminster in the semi-finals and came within two points of defeat. The final followed immediately, courtesy of Wimbledon Champion, Margaret Court, and Bob Howe giving up their indoor court practice time to allow the final to be played. With a thunderstorm echoing around the courts a rather exhausted Bryanston lost to Emanuel. The following day – despite a rather more prestigious football match played in north London (the World Cup for those too young to remember) – a Public Schools team, captained by Bryanston's Jonathan Potter, had the excitement of playing the All England Club.

National Schools Festival Rugby Sevens at Rosslyn Park 1996

The VII, under Ben Leigh, won the Rosslyn Park Festival Tournament. They were an outstandingly talented and skilful all-round side, comparable with the brilliant team captained by David Trick, winners in 1980. The 1996 VII won all their games at Rosslyn Park by convincing margins, apart from the semi-final against the holders, Wellington College – the most remarkable match of the whole tournament. Losing 5–19 at half-time and 10–26 down with four minutes to go, Bryanston then scored a goal and two tries, the last one in the final seconds, to win 27–26. After this, a comfortable win (26–14) over a strong Cheltenham side in the final seemed almost an anticlimax.

The Devizes to Westminster Canoe Race

Bryanston has an outstanding record in canoeing, so much so that the Devizes to Westminster Canoe Race has been dominated by the School over the last twenty years. It is a gruelling 125-mile race, with three overnight camping stops, which takes place over Easter weekend. The race rules are strict: canoeists must carry essential survival gear in their canoes. Meals are pre-packed in sealed containers and cooked by the competitors themselves. Racers first follow the Kennet and Avon Canal, fifty-four miles of flat water and fifty 'portages' where canoes have to be lifted out of the canal and carried, running, round the locks. At Reading, they join the Thames where progress is speeded by the flow of the river, but there is risk of capsize from the washes of pleasure boats or the roughness of the water. The race finishes by Westminster Bridge, after some eighteen to twenty hours of paddling. The event is always enthusiastically supported by parents and friends on the river bank. To their delight our canoeists have won the Schools' Prize an outstanding sixteen times and the Junior Team Prize thirteen times.

15

BROADENING HORIZONS

A full circle

On the first Tuesday of every academic year, I tell the whole of the D year that the real value of education is what they're left with after they've forgotten almost everything they learned in the classroom. Just as Tom Wheare tells parents that Bryanston education trains children for their retirement, I point out to these thirteen-year-olds that for many people it's the things they were encouraged to do in their spare time, working on their own initiative – the Extra-Curricular Activities – that stay with them and give them much of their satisfaction and enjoyment for the rest of their lives.

I own up that I was myself a pupil at Bryanston; in fact I was an academic scholar; but what I really got out of the School was not academic learning (at least not what the syllabuses required) but the opportunities to develop and indulge in my hobbies. I already loved natural history and accompanied my parents on Far Eastern and alpine holidays with binoculars and plant guides; but butterflies had become my overriding passion, ever since my architect father was sent on a secret mission to Borneo and my mother made him a butterfly net as part of his disguise. Butterflies were *my* speciality, not foisted on me by teachers or parents, and the Dorset countryside – especially in those days when the Summer Term went on until the end of July – provided an ideal hunting ground. I'll never forget finding form *valesina* of the Silver-Washed Fritillary at Stubhampton Bottom nor the emergence of Marsh Fritillaries in my Music Roof study. In the winter months at school, I went birdwatching: my memory of seeing a nightjar on a December day is more vivid than any of the chemistry I learned! It was the birds and butterflies that made me determined to be a biologist, even though my very worst O-level grade was in biology – and now I'm a biology teacher whose doctorate was on the effects of noxious butterflies on bird discrimination and who still takes pupils on field trips to Fontmell Down.

My photography – I tell them – started at Bryanston, and the dark room in which I processed and printed my early pictures is still there in the basement, now an unused (but perfectly usable) cubby-hole. My camera and lenses became as much part of me as my butterfly net on my eight butterflying expeditions to the Andes, and my pictures graced articles in geographical, exploration and even airline magazines; I still receive the odd royalty payment for my photographs at a slide library. And I went on to run Bryanston's Photographic Club for years and to take scores of pupils through the magic of watching images appearing on rectangles of

JVC
Vinten
Vision
3
Vinten
Vinten

paper under the orange darkroom light; and I had hours of happy creativity watching countless dress rehearsals of plays in the Coade Hall through the lens, printing into the early hours and then taking orders for hundreds of copies. Many of these pictures from the eighties, taken without flash on push-processed fast film, hang in the Main Hall as mementoes of past School Plays. It's all digital and colour these days, but my recent use of publishing software to get my photos into a new Bryanston Extra-Curricular Activities booklet has a comparable mystique of its own.

The birth of our son (now in A2 at Bryanston!) put an end to the South American trips, and I transferred my energies into creating a plant-packed garden at our Shillingstone home, including things grown from seeds collected on our continuing travels abroad, from the Alps to Malaysian mountains. During my twelve years as Hardy housemaster, it was time spent in this garden – propagating, weeding, pruning, mowing, edging – that helped maintain my emotional equilibrium, and Jennie and I now open it three times a year under the National Gardens Scheme charity.

My violin playing also began at Bryanston, after my piano teacher (Doris Hooker) had given me up as 'the most frustrating pupil' she had to contend with and my parents came up with the news that both my grandfathers' violins were in the attic at home! Peter Chamberlain, my assistant housemaster in Forrester, became my teacher immediately after I'd watched him perform in Mozart's *Sinfonia Concertante*, and after eighteen very enthusiastic months I was sitting next to him in the first desk in the School Orchestra, playing in *Princess Ida* in the Coade Hall pit, and performing in a Boccherini quintet on the stage.

When Dick Harthan invited me to apply for a biology post at Bryanston – to replace, it turned out, my ex-tutor and biology teacher John Sutherland-Smith who was moving to Sherborne Boys – he said that David Jones wanted a resident biologist who could run the Natural History Society and coach rowing. Even though I'd never even dreamed of becoming a teacher, this was clearly my niche. Needless to say, my love of rowing had begun at Bryanston too: I was a spindly lightweight who only started in the B year, but all the academic work for my degree at Cambridge was emotionally overshadowed by my time on the water (and, as Captain of Boats at Caius College, on the towpath coaching other crews).

That's how I came to run the Extra-Curricular Activities programme. Somewhere among the eighty or so different activities on offer, I hope there will be at least one for everyone which will give lifelong pleasure and, who knows, maybe even guide a future career!

Mike Adams *(Forrester '67) joined the staff in 1977, was Hardy Housemaster from 1988 to 1999, and has run Extra-Curricular Activities since 1994.*

Below: building a hovercraft

Peter Bradford's hut. By 1937 huts like this were no longer secret but listed and inspected

A very special hut

From the first moment that I saw the School, at thirteen, coming up the main drive and round the corner, I had the theatrical buzz of excitement that Norman Shaw must have planned. The better I knew the building, the more I appreciated the dramatic views inside and out, together with the formal areas joining with the Dorset countryside. The smell of philadelphus still reminds me of the walks to Blandford, passing a bush that might have escaped from a shrubbery near where the gardens of the original old house ran down to the river.

It was in these grounds that I learned some of the most valuable skills I took away with me at the end of my schooldays. Thorold Coade told us that we were getting an education that prepared us for life, so that each one of us could make use of and enjoy the various abilities we had. I was never any good at exams and the modified Dalton system was hopeless for me, a slow reader. What might have seemed, at the time, an escape from academic life, later proved to be fundamental to my education.

One day John Mandy and I were asked to help remove a partially collapsed shed at the end of a member of staff's garden abutting the large area of woodland that lies between the drive and the village. As we began the job I sensed there could be a future for the shed if it was repaired. We asked if we could move it into the wood and see what we could make of it. We took it some fifty yards into a hidden part of the woods where the land was dry and there was a good outlook.

Inside we found old tools, a saw, brackets for shelves, rusty nails and screws, much of what we needed to give a new life to the old shed.

Bryanston village still had a working saw mill where we bought imperfect planks for a few pence, which we used to repair and enlarge the shed. We found various piles of builders' remains left from extending the village when the new mansion was built forty or so years earlier. We salvaged a metal fireplace, bricks and the hinged side of a lorry which we fixed instead of a long window – like an eyebrow, it kept both the rain out when open, and when closed prevented anyone seeing what was inside. We each bought a small primus oil stove and later fitted one with a double walled tin oven. We evolved a pattern for most weekends which lasted for two or three years until we both left at the end of 1937.

As soon as Saturday lunch was over, our weekend began by walking to Blandford to buy food, usually herrings to fry or, as we became more skilled, meat for Sunday lunch. Bryanston village home farm sold eggs at a penny each, and milk at a penny a pint, but this went up to three ha'pence if you did not return the bottle. As we were not having Sunday lunch at school, it was possible to order from Mr Chevis, in charge of school catering, either sandwiches or half a large loaf and a generous pat of butter. Sometimes we invited a visitor for a meal. During these weekends at the hut, I developed a self-sufficiency and love of cooking that has stayed with me ever since.

During our last year huts, some even built up in the trees, became so popular, it was felt their proliferation should be controlled! They were to be listed and inspected. This did not worry us as our energies had been spent in improving our innocent and quiet life (no alcohol, sex or drugs). We were lucky to be on Alfred Woodley's list. He was a new and an imaginative member of staff. We fixed for his visit to be at tea-time. At first he seemed to be a bit surprised by our sophisticated service, but left having quite enjoyed himself in spite of the earth floor. (Sadly, he was to be killed towards the end of the war in 1943.)

Ten years after I left, and had joined the film industry, I was doing some research and came across the 1708 engraving by Knyff-Kip of Bryanston. I doubted the magnificence and extent of the formal orchards, parterre, woods and avenues displayed. But when I was next in Blandford, I went into the field east of the river and opposite to where the engraving showed the former mansion had been. Amazingly, there were still three or four very old trees and as many tree stumps marking out where the main entrance avenue had been. Sadly, when I searched the wood near Bryanston village no trace remained of our hut, not even a path to it, just impenetrable scrub.

Peter Bradford *(Salisbury '37) after four years running the Photography Department in Naval Intelligence, joined the director, Paul Rotha, and began a career writing, directing and producing documentaries.*

Expedition Days

I believe that Expedition Days were a feature of pre-war Bryanston. They were suspended during the war because of lack of petrol for transport, but reinstituted about 1946. They happened either once a term or once a year. The idea was to give boys a glimpse of the great outside world and how it functioned. You could choose your expedition, which might be to a factory of some kind, a brewery, a railway depot such as Swindon, or docks like Southampton, or any other enterprise which the schoolmasters might think up. There was also a country house expedition taken by Michael Morgan or Ronald King. I remember Ronald King taking us to a delightful small manor house called Binghams Melcombe. It was mostly Tudor and had preserved much of its original form, with a dovecote for supplying meat in winter, and a yew hedge dating from the reign of Henry VIII. Lady Grogan, who lived there, gave us a tour of the house and showed us a wonderful collection of souvenirs acquired when she had been nursing in the Balkans during the First Balkan War against the Turks.

Other destinations were found by a younger boy than me, Tom Ponsonby (*later Labour Chief Whip in the House of Lords. – Ed.*), who always came up with a relative willing to show us round a stately home. The lifestyles still stick in my mind. We went to Bowood in Wiltshire where we were fortunate enough to see the great Adam house before it was demolished because the family could not afford to keep it up. But they still kept up a recognisably aristocratic way of life. We boys were given most generous helpings of sandwiches and cakes while the butler conducted Michael Morgan and Tom Ponsonby to have luncheon with the family.

A later expedition spelled out some of the contrasts in life in post-war Socialist Britain. We went to Brympton d'Evercy, a house with a garden front reputedly by Inigo Jones. We were greeted and shown around the house by a delightfully informal but dignified old aunt of Tom

The Motorbike Club, mid-1970s

Ponsonby. We duly admired the state rooms which were dusty, and the kitchens were full of dust, rat and mouse droppings and cobwebs. Eventually we came to a bedroom with a great four-poster bed. This was where Tom's aunt slept and lived. She had a primus stove for cooking, and several candle holders for illumination, and a torch. There was no electricity in the house since the National Grid had not yet reached Brympton d'Evercy.

Our choice of country house expeditions may have sounded effete and esoteric compared with visiting factories, docks, or railway yards, but it taught us another side of English social history.

David Winfield *(Portman '48) divided his time between Byzantine studies and conservation and has published extensively in both areas.*

The Gramophone Club

A Bryanston master once called me the most prosaic boy in the school. That slur hurt at the time but maybe it was a reflection of how very creative and arty other boys were. The School encouraged creativity in a tolerant but strict environment compared with today. One of Bryanston's strengths was the choice of extra-curricular activities. There were sixty clubs ranging from beekeeping to wireless, from motor cars to gastronomy, and catering for more intellectual pursuits too. Although never arty (maybe the master was right) at least I had the chance to try my hand at pottery and painting. My strength, though, was in languages and in these I was encouraged by my various tutors. I ran the 'Cercle Français' and the Modern Language Library.

My other great interest lay in classical music and I joined the Gramophone Club at a cost of 3/6d a term (17.5p) which, from memory, had around fifty dedicated members. Through the club I was able to discover classical music in a relaxed and exclusive way. The range of music varied from Palestrina and Byrd to twentieth-century composers such as Stravinsky and Kurt Weil. This, coupled with an amazing programme of concerts held in the Edwin Evans Room and the newly opened Coade Hall, gave me a real sense of privilege.

A room in the Music School was kept for the club. We could drop in whenever we wanted during our free time; the first to get there chose the records. Thoughts about the music were shared and debated. I was possibly more gullible than some. Comments like 'Haydn doesn't have much depth', 'There's not much to Beethoven', 'Tchaikovsky isn't very original' and 'Rachmaninov's music's not very good' flew around. For many years, until my tastes really developed, I took these views seriously and didn't choose to listen much to some composers (especially Tchaikovsky and Rachmaninov), instead of standing up for the music that I genuinely enjoyed.

I still cannot get enough of classical music. My listening repertoire is wide-ranging and for a while I broadcast classical music in South Africa. Languages have helped me in an international career and given me an insight into other European cultures. This was largely thanks to inspirational teachers such as Michael Scoular, Rodney Dingle and Ken Gillett.

As a rather shy pupil I disliked certain aspects of the school but the Gramophone and Language Clubs gave me much enjoyment and I gained knowledge in a rewarding environment. For this I am grateful to Bryanston.

Ashley de Safrin *(Connaught '68) has worked in tourism and broadcasting and is now a business advisor to small and medium-sized companies.*

The Car Club, 1950s and 1970s

Bryanston Car Club

The 'Car Club' as we knew it started in about 1975. Brian Stebbings was trying to rekindle the club after it had been out of operation for a while. He needed to recruit members and show there was an interest in the club before the building was commandeered for another activity. (I think, looking back, he needed a workshop with a pit and some naïve apprentices to help keep his Morris Traveller on the road!)

The club building was a three-bay wooden hut on the right-hand side of the track up to Forrester, the Gym and fives courts from the main drive just behind the small-bore rifle range. So with a need for speed, I decided to become a founder member of the 'New Car Club'. The other members were Nick Lowein and Andrew 'Perv' Hawes (the name being given to him after the monthly subscription to *Penthouse* magazine was found out).

Included in the building were many tools, and a Ford Popular E93A, which had been converted into a kit car known as a Ford Siva. Siva was the company that made the original yellow Dr Who car used by Jon Pertwee. Our car looked just like it except it was blue. Previous members, alas anonymous to me, had done much of the work on the car. However, when we got hold of it there was still plenty to do.

We set to finishing the vehicle and every spare minute was spent in the club – grinding valves, changing piston rings and the clutch, etc. Eventually, we got the thing running. I remember Brian Stebbings turning up on the first day the vehicle was operational and appointing himself official test driver. He was so hard on it that he broke a half shaft in the back axle. However, he made amends by taking me round the scrap yards of Dorset one Saturday morning instead of double PE and geography. We eventually found another Popular to remove the bits from; Brian even paid for the new back axle.

When the car was as reliable as it could be, we drove up and down the track doing timed runs and having more fun than should have been allowed. We then ventured on to the Drive. No one seemed to mind. Life was good; we could drive our car whenever we had free time and petrol. However, things were about to change.

Trouble started when we did 'hot laps' up and down the track, turning round a large pile of manure near the fives courts. We found that by just hitting the pile with the back wheels, it made for a quicker and more sideways turn. Soon the pile had all but become at one with the ground. No more was thought about it until the next day when Brian summoned me to the Gym where he told me that Mr Scoones was none too pleased about his pile of dung being destroyed. Nick and I ended up in Mr Griffin's office (our housemaster at the time). He couldn't believe we were driving this car around the grounds. The reason we had got away with it was that there was no rule saying that we could not. The powers-that-be quickly made one: we were not allowed to drive the car on our own without adult supervision.

We then came up with a wheeze that we needed it for Pioneering, especially forestry. We were told we were allowed to use it for Pioneering and school business but only when we'd passed our driving tests and had some kind of insurance. Quickly driving lessons were ordered (thanks Dad) and I got my licence in record time. The others also got theirs and a magician in the Bursary arranged some insurance. We were back on the road. The car was converted into a pick-up. I think we even collected and delivered some logs in it once – school business of course. On one occasion, Perv Hawes, driving back from the main gates at speed, having picked up a 'log' the size of a shoe box, was going for an all-out speed record on the downhill section before the old stables when the bonnet flew off up into the trees. Terminal velocity guessed at about 98mph; however some debate over speedo calibration (it only went up to 70). It certainly felt quick....

In the last week of school, our exams all over, we used the car to transport food and drinks to the boathouse for the Salisbury House binge. Later we were left to clear up. When finished in the early hours, we decided to have one last blast around the grounds. I don't know how it happened but the grass was very dewy and at very high speed the car spun; it rotated several times as it continued on its journey. Unfortunately we were in the middle of the athletics field. The grass was torn up in neat figure-of-eight patterns across the field.

The last words Brian Stebbings ever said to me were at the leaver's church service. 'You weren't out in the car last night were you?' He raised his eyebrows and winked.

My enduring memory of Bryanston was the freedom allowed to students (this was the school that allowed a sixteen-year-old to keep several shotguns in his study for use at the Clay Pigeon Club!). I hope some freedom still exists. We also had the two best teachers money can buy: Brian Stebbings and Frank Bristow. I hope that they are still flourishing.

***Brenton West** (Salisbury '77) has had a joinery business, done some property development, organised racing and restoration of Historic Formula 1 cars, and is now training to be a sailing instructor.*

Pioneering

Pioneering began in the Summer Term 1933, with Harold Greenleaves in charge and motivated by contacts with Schule Schloss Salem in Southern Germany. To begin with it was voluntary, though most of the School joined. It had much in common with today's Duke of Edinburgh Award Scheme, with an emphasis on useful skills (first aid, camping, life saving – for which certificates were awarded). There were holiday work camps, for instance, in South Wales with out-of-work miners, and useful projects organised around the School. What was possibly the very first Pioneering achievement, a ditch dug to drain the playing fields, still exists today, seventy years on.

Pioneers wore a uniform of grey shorts and open-necked shirt (which later became the school uniform). Pioneer Parades were held to foster unity and teach self-control. These involved marching in front of the School and were supposed to be non-military. By the

Pioneering, 1950s

Building the Greek Theatre, 1950. Below: David Briggs is in the background

early 1950s they had become occasional break-time meetings at which boys who had undertaken enterprising 'pioneer holidays' told their story. The original holiday work camps were a thing of the past and even these 'parades' had, I think, petered out by 1955.

Tim Cobb, who took over Pioneering from Bill Hoyland, said that it was very difficult to find genuine jobs for everyone even in those idealistic days. By the 1980s, when I sat with two other senior members of staff on the 'Afternoon Activities Commission' and examined Pioneering amongst other things, it was clearly unrealistic to employ every member of the School on Pioneering. The D year took 'Sport on Trial', getting a 'sniff' of each of the following term's sports, so that they could base their choices on experience. A2, the final year group, were excused altogether; hardly any of them had been doing any Pioneering and most had a good deal of pressure. More recently, D have been taken for 'Study Skills', C with Adventure Training, and the Duke of Edinburgh's Awards occupy an increasing proportion of the B year.

The great constructional period of Pioneering came under David Briggs. He saw to the construction of the Boathouse (1949), the Greek Theatre (1949–51), the Observatory and the Music School (1955–59), not to mention starting with his own house. The Music School was a far more sophisticated task than the concrete block constructions that preceded it. It was architect-designed, many of the parts were pre-fabricated, and the School employed a skilled builder to prepare the work for the boys, supervise them, and put it right after they had gone. What proportion of the work was genuinely done by boys is hard to guess, but we were involved and we got a music school that is still functioning half a century later.

My own memories of Pioneering were various: early on, probably in the Spring Term of 1951, hauling heavy wheelbarrows full of wet concrete up planks to tip over old iron bedsteads in the growing auditorium of the Greek Theatre. Gratifying work in hindsight, but very heavy for a scrawny thirteen-year-old! Some horticultural tasks had their own reward, such as picking huge, pink gooseberries in the Walled Garden. Pulling up old cabbages and chucking them into a trailer was less agreeable on frosty days, when fingers could pierce the frozen crust of the cabbage into the yellow and foul-smelling liquid inside. Forestry was a favourite for many of us. Not only useful, it also brought us under the care of the forester, Len Taylor, a wiry man, immensely skilful with axe and saw, and who generated a deep natural respect from all. There are OBs who still keep up with him fifty years later. One of the best features of Pioneering was that you could invent your own job.

Tim Sheldon and I were interested in trees and, seeing around us a beautiful but neglected estate, got approval for 'Tree Maintenance' and set about pruning dead branches, transplanting saplings into clear areas, etc. The effect was probably very small but for both of us it cultivated the seeds of lifelong interests. Tim became a chartered surveyor and I maintain a role in the enhancement of the estate through the Gardens Committee.

Alan Shrimpton (Hardy '55) formerly Head of Biology, master in charge of rowing and member of staff since 1964. He edited the OB Yearbook and is now School Archivist.

Running the Pioneers

To this day I have really no idea how it came about that I was put in charge of Pioneering for the ten years 1947–57; but in retrospect it seems to have been quite a neat arrangement. Timothy Cobb, who had been master in charge of classics, left in 1947; and he had run Pioneering for the previous ten years. I succeeded him in both jobs, and thereupon ran the activity for a further decade. I did not leave until 1959, but the records seem to show that Michael Bagenal took over Pioneering in 1957, though I continued to help out.

However, to get the full picture I must go back to 1946. In that spring I returned to the UK after a year in India, and completed a Certificate in Education course begun in 1939 but interrupted by six years of war. In the summer I applied for a post at Bryanston which I had seen advertised. I was duly interviewed at the School by the headmaster Thorold Coade, who told me that he would shortly send a telegram to my home in Bushey (Herts), advising me of his decision. The telegram, alas, was eaten on the doormat by our puppy; but the Post Office obligingly supplied a duplicate, informing me that I had been appointed, to start in September.

The immediate problem for my wife, Mary, and myself was to find somewhere to live near Bryanston, because accommodation in the post-war era was exceedingly difficult. We initially found rooms in the top floor of Stourpaine Vicarage; and one day a telephone message came from Chrystabel Procter, the then Estate Steward, who became a dear friend and colleague. 'There is a Scandinavian pigsty in the school grounds which is empty. The pigs all died of swine fever in the 1930s. Why not live there?' This is where the Pioneers came in; helped by gangs of energetic young boys,

Below: Pioneers Parade, 1938

I was able to clear the massive undergrowth that had accumulated during the war years, and prepare the site for a local builder to instal partition walls and convert the main sty into an attractive bungalow, with the outbuildings available for coal, bicycles and garage. It was there that our four children happily spent their early years; our neighbours, in the Old Stables on the other side of the Drive, were Don Potter and his family.

I explain all this because it provides a typical example of what I found Pioneering to be all about. Timothy had built up an elaborate structure of multifarious activities designed to give up to 300 boys, mostly on one afternoon a week, the opportunity of being practically useful. Forestry, bookbinding, gardening, the building of an observatory and a causeway come to mind. Being thrown in at the deep end as his successor, I did indeed benefit personally by acquiring a home!

The next thing that I remember clearly is the building of the Greek Theatre by Pioneers. One of my classics teachers in the 1930s at King's College, Cambridge, was the Provost, Sir John Sheppard. He was an inspiring teacher, and producer, of Greek drama, and I recall as an undergraduate appearing as a frog in Aristophanes' play at the Arts Theatre there. When I arrived at Bryanston years later, I was keen to have a go at producing Greek plays myself, and I put on a performance of Euripides' *Bacchae* in Greek in the School Gym in 1949. After the performance Thorold said to me, 'I have an idea that we might have an open-air theatre here, and I have my eye on a suitable site. What do you think?' Thus: Greek Play plus Headmaster plus Bursar plus Pioneers plus site equals Greek Theatre. QED.

The Theatre (originally called the Festival Theatre, as it was finished in 1951, the Festival of Britain year) took two years to build, and the whole enterprise was huge fun. With the exception of the wings (added at a late stage by professionals to meet a deadline) the whole stage structure plus orchestra area plus auditorium were built entirely by Pioneer labour, helped by members of staff. Thorold marked the Theatre's opening by putting on Sophocles' *Oedipus Tyrannus* in English. In due course, I was privileged to use it for putting on, mostly in their original Greek and Latin languages, Euripides' *Iphigenia in Tauris* (1952), *Medea* (1954, with Nicholas Phillips in the name-part) and Seneca's *Troades* (1957). Girls from Cranborne Chase School admirably provided the chorus for these plays.

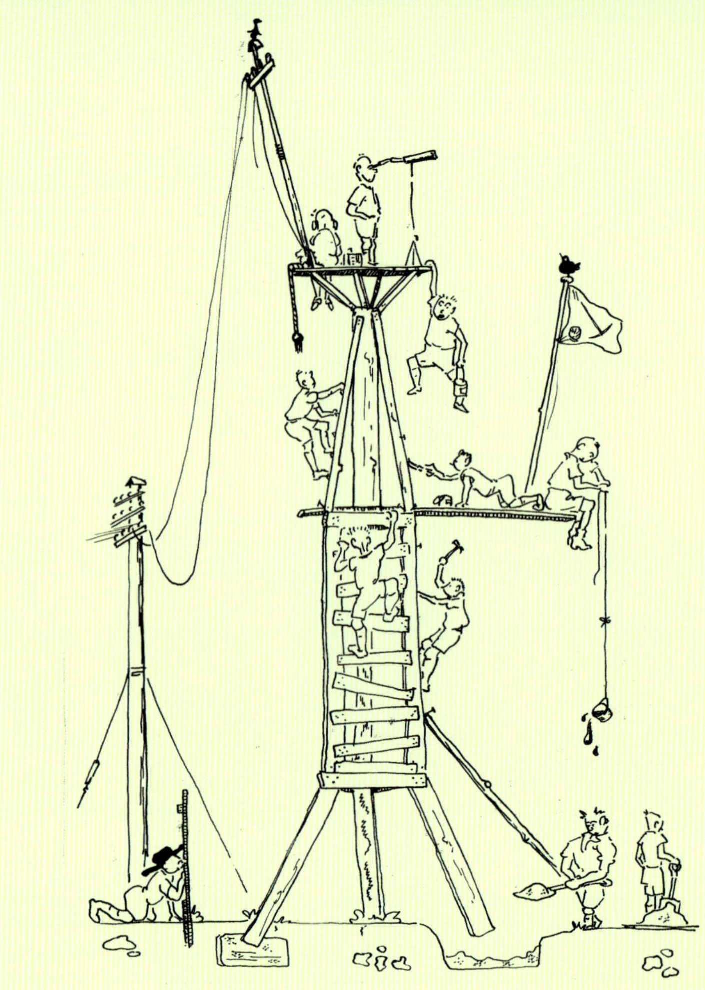

Finishing touches to the Theatre went on for another year or so; and the Pioneers were then ready to embark on another major building project. The idea this time came from the director of music Paul Rogers, who suggested that we build a music school, on the Plateau facing the front of the School. Pioneers started work on this in the autumn of 1952, by building a concrete ramp to enable lorries to reach the site. This time, we had professional architects to design the building, and a highly skilled handyman, Bill Dyer, who tactfully put us right when we made significant errors. (On one occasion, we built the walls of an entire room in the wrong place, and had to knock them down the next day). The first two sides were completed by Speech Day 1955, when it was opened with due ceremony by the Earl of Verulam with music specially written for the occasion by parent and composer, Julius Harrison.

These were the highlights of my own experience of Pioneering, half a century ago. I am conscious that, in this brief article, I have not done justice to the countless less spectacular but nonetheless valuable jobs that were conscientiously carried out by boys and staff.

The term Pioneering can of course be ridiculed as pretentious: but every school has its own jargon, and rightly so. To my mind, it simply means community service, and that is, arguably, an even more pompous description!

David Briggs was a member of staff from 1947 to 1959. He then became Headmaster of King's College Choir School, Cambridge, and is now retired.

Building blocks

I was interviewed for the post of biology master in 1960. Robson Fisher asked me the usual questions about academic matters and previous teaching, but eventually focused on the ways I might involve boys in my research (on minuscule fungi contributing to the decay of beech cupules) and on my skills in building. My father had been a first-class stonemason and builder, and from an early age I had been taught the skills to fit the Pioneering role into which Robson saw I might fit. I remember when he asked, 'Can you build a straight wall?' I could truthfully answer, 'Well, yes, I can'.

Pioneering at that time involved a number of different activities, planting trees, cutting down overgrown vegetation, maintaining paths, etc. My contribution to building 'straight walls' was confined to the completion of the dressing rooms at the back of the Greek Theatre and the main walls of the Edwin Evans Music Room.

Bill Dyer was the Pioneering foreman, a memorable character, invariably cheerful, thoroughly reliable, competent and patient. In building the Music Room, Bill always had the necessary tools ready for when the boys arrived. They used small pointing trowels, not the large brick trowels. My task was to supervise the boys mixing mortar (generally by hand, but the cement mixer was used for big jobs) and laying the breeze blocks; I placed the line pins and line, and showed the boys how to use the spirit level. Bill devised a wooden gadget that helped the boys to fill the gaps between the blocks correctly. It saved us time and mortar!

Inevitably the taut line was snagged, or the amount of mortar beneath the breeze block was too little or too much, resulting in the block having to be removed and replaced. Consequently a boy might only lay one block in an afternoon! At the end of the session I might set the corner blocks for the next day's work, and 'eye' the row of blocks for level and plumb; and then a judicious tap here and there with a lump hammer was sufficient to settle the row into acceptable straightness. The boys left the scaffold quicker than when they climbed up, and made some effort to clean their tools, before racing off to change.

In general the boys worked hard and achieved a very reasonable standard. I checked the main wall recently and was satisfied that it was as plumb (upright) as it should be. The Pioneers' efforts were facilitated by the architect's design, which was effectively simple.

For many there was an understandable reluctance to build, especially in the damp and cold of the winter months. To their inevitable question, 'Why do we have to do this?' I had two stock answers. The first was that the skills might be useful in later life. The second was about the need to change their focus – they were not placing blocks on a wall, they were building a wonderful music room. I suspect that my lines of thought about DIY (for many that was not something they would ever have to consider), and the 'greater picture', were far removed from their feelings of being 'slave labour'!

Clive Carré was a member of staff from 1960 to 1964. He then taught biology at the University of Sydney before returning to become Senior Lecturer in Education at the University of Exeter until his retirement.

Pioneer observation tower, and Pioneering of the future: bridging the river. From Saga, *1939*

16

BENDING THE RULES

Clandestine activities

Three of us founded a Roof Climbing Club. We kept a commonplace book with minutes of our activities and the routes we took, which included the internal spaces of the buildings that were not public. Norman Shaw must have been amongst the most profligate of architects in his use of building space. If he wanted a particular proportion to his reception rooms and that meant walling off quite large building spaces, he did so. As a result Bryanston had quite a lot of hidden spaces to which you could find access by trapdoors. We found one such trapdoor in the basement in the Chapel. A single metal rung was fixed to the wall below it but above the trapdoor was an iron ladder. When we first decided to try it, the three of us were more than a little frightened. We went up the rungs in pitch darkness without knowing where we were going, up and up, higher and higher, with dust and cobwebs adding to the drama. Eventually we emerged in the central attic of the Main Building with direct access from there to the roofs.

It became a favourite climb but one evening nearly culminated in our downfall. The three of us had quietly entered the Chapel and were about to ascend through our trapdoor when 'Whisky Jack' Winslow, the chaplain, entered. 'Ah!' he said, 'You were going to say some prayers. Come, we will kneel and make our supplications together.' We did so, and lingered until 'Whisky Jack' left for other duties. We quickly made our exit up through the trapdoor.

I still ponder over the original purpose of this vertical Jacob's ladder. My best guess is that it was left from construction. The Roof Climbing Club's closest escape came when we climbed up one evening into the rafters of the Music Wing above the Portman dormitories. We intended to go up through a trapdoor on to the Music Roof, when one of us slipped and made a noise. Mr Sterling, the music master, happened to pass by at the same moment. He shouted up into the darkness: 'I heard you, come down from there at once!' We froze. After several repetitions of 'Come down!' he said, 'Right, I'm leaving someone here to catch you if you come down, and I shall fetch the Duty Prefect.' We were trapped. After some whispered confabulation we decided to go on up through the trapdoor on to the roof. Not having any

NORTH POLE 2270
5990
ONG 6080
NEW YORK 3390
10660
DUBLIN 240
OSLO 850

further plan of action we sat on it. It was a very heavy trapdoor and when the prefect and helpers eventually responded to Mr Sterling and got up into the attic spaces below us, they could not shift it since the three of us were sitting on it. Eventually they gave up. We expected them to climb out onto the roof through one of the dormer windows and catch us that way, so we decided on a speedy flight up across to the main roof and over to the roof of the Hardy wing. We got in quietly through one of the dormer windows and walked back to our basement changing room to get rid of our plimsolls. Even the walk back over the parquet flooring was risky. Plimsolls were forbidden as they marked the polished surface. We were lucky … that time.

These escapades served me in good stead forty years later when I became the first Surveyor of Conservation to the National Trust. One of my duties was writing reports on the state of conservation of NT houses and their contents, and my early explorations of Bryanston's structural make-up proved useful.

David Winfield *(Portman '48) divided his time between Byzantine studies and conservation and has published extensively in both these areas.*

The Great Arms Scandal and other tales

Biologists, teachers and parents know that the adolescent male spends much time challenging authority throughout these tricky years. Bryanston was no different from any other school in this respect – the battle was on from the start!

Each boy knew the rules. The challenge was not to get caught for breaking them. But humiliation was around for miscreants – wearing a white shirt for an allotted time. That could make one either a villain or a hero amongst one's peer group. For simple 'mistakes' it was so many runs down to the gate and back. Needless to say, there were methods of mitigating the pain and one rich person was said to have got a taxi in to help him out!

In all schoolboy stories, smoking and drinking are the two great sins – how many youngsters have had that first 'drag' behind the bicycle sheds? There were fewer cigarettes around in the war years and smoking was not much of a problem as I remember it. But drinking – quite another matter!

One day I was persuaded into joining a friend – Duggie Hogg – on a sortie to have lunch at the King's Arms in Wimborne and we set off on this very hot

extract from …

TO ALL WRONGDOERS

With these two small graphs I want to prove that all the ingenuity fertiile brains have spent on devising good punishments has been in vain. That Keate, the terror of Eton boys, wore his arm out in vain when he flogged the whole school for rebelling against him. I want to prove that these poor, maligned defaulters, and YOU were probably one at some time in your life, just couldn't help breakig the rules. The graphs I mention speak for themselves. On the larger one runs given each week of the term are charted. The lower curve gives the termly rainfall. Anyone can clearly see that these curves are almost exactly synonymous. If much rain falls one week then more offences are committed and the run curve rises with the rainfall. The smaller graph representing latenesses since half term (records have been lost for the first half) is better still. It is almost exactly similar to the rainfall regime.

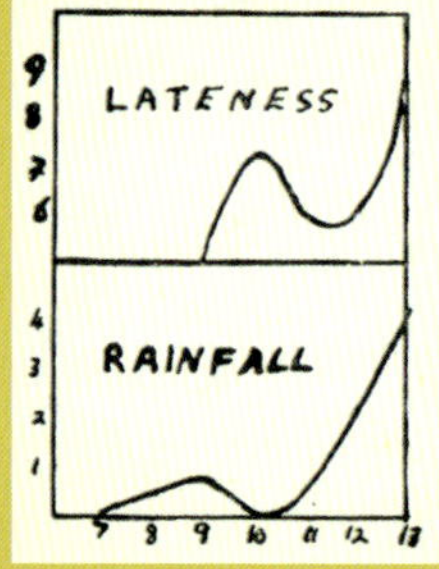

This similarity is very striking. Whatever may be the cause, the fact that it exists throws some doubt on the usefulness of giving punishments for offences.
DGL

Sunday after church. It was thirsty work and as we approached half way, desperate for a drink, the Anchor Inn at Shapwick hoved into view. A half pint of cider helped us on our way, a good lunch for a few shillings and back to school later. The end of the matter? Not so. A few weeks later I was summoned to the headmaster's study. Baffled, I duly reported and was ushered into the sanctum, never seen before.

That great man – Thor Coade – held all the cards. In his usual, dreamy way he drifted round the room, calmly saying, 'I think you have been breaking a school rule…' I answered, perhaps not very convincingly: 'Not me, Sir, must be a mistake.' He soon trumped this: 'Oh? … I think you should tell me about the visit to the Anchor ….' Game, set and match. So it was a white shirt till the end of term. I later discovered that friend Duggie had been all over the place drinking with friends. One of them had got caught and all the names came out a la domino!

Throughout my time at the School – 1941–45 – the country was at war. It was a primary rule that we were not allowed 'out of bounds' but there was a pull that far exceeded this: the lure of getting hold of all sorts of war souvenirs, from crashed aircraft in particular. A visit to a site miles away was best, returning with booty to be flaunted and swapped.

But for some there were more ambitious trophies; arms and ammunition. The chief of this ring was one Kuniczak. Once when I was stroke of the eight and we were just at the upstream turning point with Ronnie King as coach and cox, there was a loud explosion out of sight further up the river. Ronnie K just said: 'Ah, Kuniczak fishing…' Truthful, too, as he used real hand grenades.*

Great excitement when the police arrived to search the school woods and a cache of ammunition, including a Sten gun, was found. All of this led to a prominent paragraph in *The Times*: 'The Headmaster of Canford School wishes it to be known that it was not boys from the school who were involved in the recent find of arms and ammunition at another school.'

The aircraft bombing range near Sixpenny Handley was another magnet: a short bike ride, nip round the back of the range, sidle under the wire and there was a treasure trove of cannon shells fired into the butts, parachute flares and other items to be collected. One Sunday, I convinced Desmond McDougall that he should see this wonderful place. All went well. We thought we hadn't been seen from the watchtower but a loud shout and airmen running towards us soon proved we were wrong. After a wait in the guardroom we were taken back to school in a truck with our bikes. The outcome of this saga was that Desmond – who was older than the rest of us – got the blame as he was told that it was highly irresponsible of him to lead younger members of the School astray! Some sixty years later, we still laugh about this, but I don't think he has really forgiven me yet!

Leonard Dickson *(Dorset '45) spent twenty-four years in the RAF before taking on executive roles in various charities.*

** In 1976 a pupil, Tom Kealy, found something he thought might be a bomb in weeds in the river. Under the supervision of a sceptical Alan Shrimpton the 'bomb' was isolated, the police were called, notices warning people to keep away were erected. When the Bomb Squad arrived, the bomb had disappeared. Bryanstonians' fascination with arms, it seems, was not confined to the 1940s! – Ed.*

The Midnight Race

During my time (1948–52) it was forbidden to cycle round the Plateau for fear of colliding with a car. In about 1950 someone in Hardy House who was also a member of the stage staff decided there should be a race round the Plateau at midnight. The race would be ridden naked and the winner presented with the Scrot Trophy, a very old, battered-looking silver vase. The utmost secrecy had to be maintained before the race for fear of its being reported.

The first race took place and the Scrot trophy was duly presented to the winner. However, the next race met with disaster. The leader came round the final blind corner within sight of the School and collided head on with a car. He flew off his bicycle, landing on the bonnet of the car, fortunately without serious injury. The car owner got out to examine the damage to his car, the bicycle and the very embarrassed naked boy lying on the bonnet.

At this point the Scrot race leader realised he had collided with the headmaster. Coade was really more amused than cross which is one reason why he was such a great headmaster.

But that was the end of the Scrot trophy.

Michael Kingerlee *(Dorset '52) is enjoying an active and productive retirement after a career in manufacturing and shipping.*

Trying not to be seen

My first Spring Term at Bryanston started out rather miserably: I hated team sports and you weren't allowed to opt for something enjoyable (such as cross-country running) in your first year. I was also fairly shy, and somehow failed entirely – probably owing to fear – to show up for my introduction to what we here in Canada call 'field hockey' (to distinguish it from the real thing).

Then I made a remarkable discovery: I hadn't been missed. No one came after me, no one demanded I account for my absence, or even showed a sign of meting out punishment.

Breathing slightly more easily, I did the same thing again. Once again I wasn't missed, and it dawned on me that among the many bountiful blessings of a Bryanston education was a less-than-perfect organisation of the game of hockey.

I can't say that this experience was in any way relaxing; quite the contrary, for I reasoned that the longer I failed to show up and do my duty, the worse my punishment would be when finally I was discovered. And of course it was necessary for me to maintain an extraordinarily low profile every afternoon that I spent without a hockey stick, lest my presence somewhere I oughtn't to be alert someone to my absence from where I should be.

As the term progressed, therefore, I believe I developed a necessary – and increasingly refined – skill: that of *not being seen*. Sometimes I *was* seen, and further refinement was subconsciously perfected to ensure that, seen or not, *I was not noticed*.

This went on, surprisingly, for the entire term. I never was discovered, and the ability I thereby acquired (entirely under my own instruction) – of quietly going about one activity while everyone supposed me to be involved in quite another – has been invaluable to me ever since.

Oh … and I received a first-rate hockey report, though to give credit where it is due, I think the report was intended for my cousin Anthony, whose surname I shared. To this day I have no idea what *his* report was like.

Peter Greenhill *(Shaftesbury '60) studied printing management and technology, worked in the US in computer applications research and now runs his own business in Toronto.*

Smoking was always banned, but some managed to evade the smoking patrols

A moment of foolishness

One moment stands out. It was April Fool's Day in about 1962. At the time it had seemed a funny idea to put a dustbin over one of the chimneys of Forrester House. My friend Jackson made a grappling hook in metalwork and with the help of a long rope this was hooked over the roof ridge at the back of the house over the back dormitories.

Wearing Forrester's dark green rugby shirt as camouflage but otherwise in shorts and gym shoes I clambered up with the bin over my shoulder. For some reason none of my accomplices turned up.

A dustbin is much heavier and colder than you realise. It also makes a terrific bong if perchance you accidentally strike a chimney pot. The trouble was that

Sunbathing on the roof, early 1960s

once I was on the changing-room ridge the problems had only just begun. To get to the best chimney entailed a long traverse and, if I remember rightly, a stiff ascent of at least two chimneys before the summit.

It is also noteworthy that a small chimney from the ground becomes a very big chimney from the roof on a dark night, especially when you are hanging on to a metal dustbin that is making your hands lose all feeling.

Triumphant at last and the joke having disappeared long since, I made the the final push, only to find, horror of horrors, that there were two chimney pots and the wretched bin was not big enough to go over both. What to do now? Strength was almost gone; hypothermia was setting in.

There was only way round it – sit the thing on top and lash it down through the handles with the grappling iron rope.

Next morning hardly anybody noticed a very drunken dustbin at a strange angle on the chimney. Somehow word got round and just before games I was invited to Tusker's (Mr Tribe's) study. With a trace of a smile I was told this was an extremely dangerous thing to do and it would cost an awful lot of money to call in the fire brigade to get it down… unless of course another way could be found.

A short while later another way had been found.

The Rev. William Mather *(Forrester '63) is an Anglican priest working with Sharing of Ministries Abroad (SOMA) and is the author of the book,* Cry for Sudan.

William Mather's April Fool's Day escapade, 1962

A bed in the Round Pond

Secret lives, secret places

These days, I understand, studies are purpose-built (and standardised). In those days (with the notable exception of the old Glass Study block which was purpose-built, standardised and no one wanted to be in) studies were simply partitioned-off dormer spaces in the attics – above the woodworking and sculpture studios, in the Music Roof and above the Hardy House dormitories. All were irregular in size and shape. All were intensely personal spaces. And all were simply that: spaces. We ourselves took responsibility for furnishing them with carpets or rugs, scrounged from goodness knows where, with armchairs – which might have seen better days, with mattresses and loungers; we even added extra partition walls or redesigned the interiors.

In general our life in these private retreats was undisturbed: the only real constraint the weekly study-inspection to check that things were clean (-ish. Why was that always Ken Greenwood's task?). And in general life was perhaps much as might be expected for teenage boys: hours spent listening to the pop music of the time, posters, the occasional illicit drinking spree – but we were rarely bored. And it was by no means all a matter of booze and fags. Indeed we considered ourselves relatively civilised. Life was often a question of steak suppers and Roquefort, or pheasants in red wine with cranberries....

I remember I shared Hardy One with Will Andrewes and 'Moan' Simmons – and we struck up a close alliance in all things with our neighbours in Hardy Three

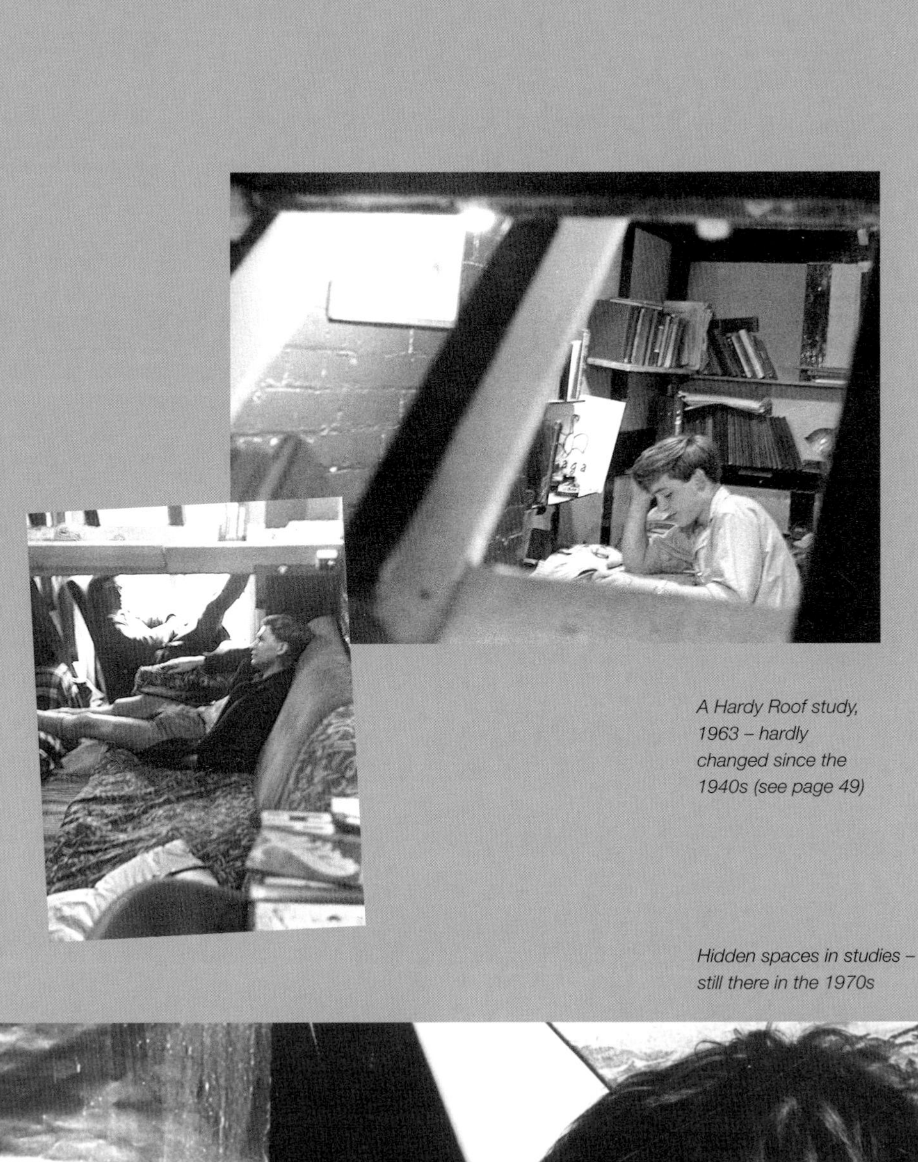

A Hardy Roof study, 1963 – hardly changed since the 1940s (see page 49)

Hidden spaces in studies – still there in the 1970s

and some of their friends from elsewhere within 'The Roof': Rupert 'Steam' Evans, Rog Pelly, Richard Hatfield, Carlo Pattinson.

We were fortunate also that we had all become very friendly with the main chef in the school kitchens, Harry Brett, and his wife Winnie. They were quite simply two of the best. Why they appeared to take such a liking to us I shall never truly fathom, but they took a keen interest and were always kindness itself. Harry it was who frequently 'obliged' with extra courtesies for us, like preparing us superlative steak dinners when we had somehow managed to miss the formal school meal, or cooking to perfection the pheasants we fairly frequently contrived to return with from our various expeditions. They were willing on occasion too, when we had no other obvious means of transport, to lend Steam Evans their own elderly Fiat.

It seems to me in retrospect that most of our diversions that year were engineered by Rupert, although in all fairness he almost always led from behind. But diversions we had in plenty. However delightful the Hardy Roof, we were always short of space and always short of real privacy. It was Evans who decided on the plan to provide Hardy One with a little more of both. Immediately outside the study stood three large cold-water storage tanks, presumably header tanks for some complex heating system floors below. But it seemed to Evans that not all these could possibly be needed to full capacity, so with a bit of careful plumbing we switched the intake from one so that it fed instead into its immediate neighbours, fitting a T-piece to link the outlets into parallel. Levers (and a study of *Theseus*) quickly turned the now redundant tank on its side with its open top against the study wall. Dummy piping was engineered so that to the casual observer all appeared as normal.

A door was cut through into the tank from Hardy One, which fitted flush and was covered with a wall-hanging when not in use. The tank itself was lined with a double mattress (it was sizeable!), and some bean bags; we also wired in electricity for a kettle socket and toaster. It was an excellent place to withdraw when one wished not to be disturbed.

Until the demolition (or modernisation) of the Hardy Roof studies some years later, the secret of this inner space was jealously guarded and passed down only from one set of incumbents to the next. I often pondered in later years if future generations ever wondered about the original creators of the tank-room and when, if ever, it was finally discovered by the authorities.

As a general rule, however, those authorities were relatively tolerant of our escapades (as long as these were themselves relatively harmless and didn't amount to the ultimate sin of being considered 'likely to corrupt others'). I remember once calling at my assistant housemaster's study door to seek permission for a late exeat. I wished to travel to Salisbury to take my then girlfriend out to a concert and to dinner – which required permission both to leave the school grounds, and to return late. Alan Shrimpton (for it was he) enquired as to the purpose of the trip and then asked how I intended to reach Salisbury. I explained that I could catch a bus.

'But,' he pointed out, 'you will be returning after the last bus, so how do you plan to get back? You know that hitch-hiking is against the rules.' (I did). 'I suppose,' he sighed with apparent resignation, 'you'll be going on one of those motorbikes you keep in the Old Stables,' and he waved me away. Actually, none of those motorbikes was mine, for I made other arrangements … but it was clear he knew more than we thought.

Others of our 'initiatives' were looked upon less kindly. Like the time we arranged to create something of a diversion in the middle of the School Dance with Wardour. This was a rather more elaborate enterprise which took some considerable coordination and planning. But the occupants of Hardy One and Hardy Three made quite a formidable team at times and possessed a remarkable array of very complementary talents (not all of which, like lock-picking, necessarily appeared in the formal school curriculum). Thus it was that at a pre-appointed time in mid-dance, one of our number picked the padlock to the electricity substation below the School and threw the mains power lever over, plunging the School and Dance Hall into darkness for three minutes, while those forewarned were able to escape with their girlfriends to somewhere that offered greater peace and privacy than the heavily chaperoned Dance Hall. At the same moment others, already stationed in the Drive, closed the school gates at Middle Lodge and the Main Gate, chained and padlocked them and disappeared into the gloom. When the three minutes were up the lights came back on, the electricity substation was wiped clean of prints and relocked and everyone simply assumed it was a 'normal' power cut … until the coaches came to leave and chaos reigned.

In many instances we were never caught out in these capers. In this case when the full facts emerged, I was suspected of masterminding the blackout. No one could ever prove it, for I was present at the dance throughout. Remember, I had a girlfriend in Salisbury and had simply joined the conspiracy to assist others. While I had a *very* interesting interview with Robson Fisher, headmaster at the time, no punishment ensued (for he was a fair man…). Indeed, throughout my time at Bryanston, despite bending many rules beyond breaking point, I only once received an 'afternoon run' and only once received School Punishment Number One. This last punishment was usually reserved for the more indiscreet of smokers. In my case it was awarded, I suspect, out of sheer frustration, or possibly on suspicion of heterosexual behaviour.

We were in the final stages of rehearsals for *Princess Ida* as the School Play, a joint production with girls from Cranborne Chase, one of whom, Alexa Turpin, had now become the new love of my young life. Both of us had finished rehearsing the parts in which we appeared, so we surreptitiously withdrew to the Hardy One tank. We did not foresee that we would be called upon for a further run-through of sections of the play we thought completed, and thus assumed we would not be missed.

The best-laid plans…. Ken Greenwood (for indeed, it was KPGG yet again) was dispatched with a prefect to find us; yet despite the most thorough of searches, never discovered us cowering silently in the tank. They never found us, they never found the tank (as far as I know) and, as I say, it was probably as much in irritation as anything else that full retribution was exacted on that occasion. Worse still I wasn't allowed to perform in *Ida*, either (the only part of the punishment that really rankled). Wardour's headmistress, Betty Galton, forgave me, however, and when I left Bryanston a few months later, elected me an Honorary Old Girl of Cranborne Chase; for, as she said, I had over the years spent considerably more time at the School than had many of her official pupils.

Rory Putman *(Hardy '68) is Emeritus Professor of Behavioural and Environmental Biology at Manchester Metropolitan University.*

The Citroën 2CV incident

One of the more amusing diversions when I was at Bryanston was the practice of breaking the night curfew, known as 'night wandering'. It was so easy to leave and re-enter the School at night that I sometimes wondered if the School simply decided to turn a blind eye to this

The 'Hit Squad' by the Citroën 2CV, Main Hall, 1981

activity. We would stuff pillows down the bed and sneak out, dodging the night watchman. Unfortunately this nocturnal wandering was brought to a close with the arrival of John Moore, hot from the Metropolitan Police and armed with a powerful police searchlight and a missionary zeal for stamping out smoking and other illicit behaviour.

However, I and a group of friends pulled off a spectacular finale to our night wandering careers at Bryanston one night in 1981 when we deposited 'Doc' Mike Adams' Citroën 2CV in the Main Hall of the School. We had been discussing and planning this stunt for weeks, and on the night in question we donned black clothes and makeshift balaclavas and went barefoot. We managed to lift the car with surprising ease and brazenly carried it through the front doors of the School, through the Jeffreys Room to deposit it on the parquet floor in the Main Hall. We even put newspaper under the wheels to protect the parquet. Before leaving we posed for a photograph as proof of our exploit. After nearly twenty-five years I think identities can now be revealed, and in the photograph Warren Andrews (right-hand side) and myself (left-hand side) can be seen 'bookending' each end of the car. Others involved included Paul Bliss, Charles 'Tav' McLeish, Bill Russell, Andy Barley, Will Blanchard, Ben Lyle and Jerry Hyde (the latter two can be clearly identified in the photograph kneeling at the front brandishing clenched fists).

The next morning word of the stunt travelled fast. The Dining Room was virtually empty for breakfast as most pupils and teachers gathered round the car itself and on the Shaftesbury House balcony above. Eventually word reached Mike Adams who nonchalantly circled the car with a wry smile on his face and then simply climbed behind the wheel of the car, reversing and driving it down the steps of the Jeffreys Room, 'Italian Job' style, and out through the main doors of the School. We later pinned the photo on the school notice board with a warning that the 'Hit Squad' had struck and would strike again. A few days later some of the younger teachers, led I think by Pete Hardy, responded by posting a photograph of themselves astride mopeds with a caption informing everyone that the 'A Team' would have their revenge on the 'hit squad'!

Matt Lambert *(Connaught '82) worked as a political assistant in the House of Commons before going into business, managing government affairs consultancies in Brussels and London. He is now Director of Government Affairs for Microsoft in the UK.*

EPILOGUE

A tale of five Heads

The new headmaster of Bryanston in September 1983 found a well-established co-educational school, secure in its liberal traditions but ready to face the future flexibly. It was a remarkably good school, tried in the fire of adversity, endowed with an exceptional staff and with a clarity of vision that owed a great deal to its fourth headmaster, his predecessor David Jones. Although the shortest-serving of the five heads the School had between 1928 and 2005, David defined, or, perhaps, redefined the School's position within the independent sector just as definitively as had Jeffreys and Coade. In doing so he built on a buoyancy sustained by Robson Fisher who manned the bridge in the most turbulent period of the School's history. The sixties and early seventies were years of student revolution and Bryanstonians, not surprisingly, were as well aware of the potential for radical action as any school pupils in the land. Whilst the business of teaching and learning, coaching and performing, recruiting and harvesting all went on as before, the general atmosphere was uneasy as schools and their inhabitants came through Cuba, Kennedy, Cohn-Bendit and Leonard Cohen.

Such shifting surfaces were, it turned out, the last shudders of the upheavals that had been at the centre of Thorold Coade's time at Bryanston. Whilst Jeffreys had been able to imagine and fashion a brave new school, Coade had to lead his staff and pupils through world war and its aftermath, an experience that cost Bryanston dear and that threw all into confusion. Thereafter, change grew from the ruins of Europe as people and nations rebuilt their lives and reoriented their intellectual and social maps. Issues like Health and Safety, league tables and staff car parking did not concern the first four headmasters unduly, but they will occupy a good deal of time in the life of the sixth! Parental attitudes to schooling, let alone boarding, the sheer cost of the operation, relationships within families, the overwhelming accessibility of raw information – these are all things that make the contemporary Bryanston very different from the School the first four headmasters ran.

Jeffreys must have been a man of extraordinary determination to have started the School and heaved it up from twenty-three pupils to more than 200 when Thorold Coade arrived. Jeffreys' faith could be seen in the appointment of so many staff for that first day, and his charisma must have been considerable to have attracted so large and so talented a Common Room. This was a courageous and significant new departure. Coade was charismatic, too, but in a completely different way. His oblique approach is sensed but tantalisingly out of reach in his collected writings. Reading *The Burning Bow* you are instantly aware of something unique and something remarkable, but without his voice, the cadences of his speech and, above all, his presence, the experience is incomplete. That presence was a constant affirmation of the School. The word Bryanston echoed the spirit of Coade, a spirit that spread abroad.

Robson Fisher joined the School in very different times. Materialism was replacing patriotism. 'You've never had it so good' rightly provoked a reaction in the thinking young people of whom Bryanston has always had its fair share. Their teachers, too, were not people for whom material benefits were the Holy Grail. Pupils of that era returning to Bryanston today are overwhelmed by the scale and luxury of the place, much as the first members of the School must have been when they laid hands on Lord Portman's gold-plated bath taps! Steering the School through the maelstrom of the sixties into the rapids of the seventies required a steady hand and a calm nerve.

Robson Fisher had vision to a highly developed level, as may be seen in the key buildings erected at Bryanston in his time, but his task was to keep the ship

JG Jeffreys

EM Forster's command 'only connect' would have been very appropriate for a school that connects people and seeks to connect individuals with their potential. JG Jeffreys was an undergraduate at Ormond College, Melbourne University (the alma mater of the fifth headmaster's father). Its motto, *et nova et vetera,* has been a guiding principle for a school seen by many as innovative, especially in its earliest years, yet aware of the significance of history. Jeffreys gave the School an Australian emblem, the rising and setting sun to be seen on Anzac cap-badges, and an Australian vigour. Like the eucalyptus tree, the School is evergreen and swiftly comprehensive in recovering from setbacks. Jeffreys was clearly flexible in that the first brand image of the School as an 'Empire School' seems to have moved seamlessly into a clearly progressive image and practice, culminating in the adoption of the modified Dalton system. Jeffreys' short reign, whatever the reasons for its brevity, was, surely, crucial. The concept and the place mattered greatly to him. 'The question of tradition is so intimately associated with our English public schools, that the newness of ours may seem to

afloat and on course, which he did. When David Jones arrived from Eton, there were many things to be done. Robson had opened Bryanston's doors to girls, having first allowed the change from short to long trousers. It was left to David to guide the School through the exploratory phase of co-education, leaving his successor a well-balanced community, happily encamped on the sunlit uplands of family life. The new facilities required by these developments rapidly became an avalanche in the budgets; growth, that great enemy of so many things that schools should be about, was becoming the objective towards which all businesses – and schools were now businesses – were expected to aspire. Bryanston was overstretched. Bryanston was, in common with many schools, uncertain of its place and purpose in a changing and changed society. The symbol of David Jones's headship, the proof of his vision, was the purchase of the ecclesiastical building in the grounds declared redundant by the Church of England but to become central to the School – Bryanston Church.

Were it not for the fact that we have a perfectly good motto that exemplifies the importance of relationships,

Thorold Coade

Robson Fisher

be a great disadvantage. However – each school has had to make a beginning. The tradition which is most worth looking after in the beginnings of a school, is the boy himself.… Let us rejoice in the fact that here, in this very lovely place, we have a heritage given us where the very finest and best things can grow and develop, so that when the time comes for us to depart into the wider sphere of life we shall be able to say quite sincerely, “It was good to have been there”.’

The choice of staff was his and his charisma drew to Bryanston young men of the highest calibre. One of these, Harold Greenleaves, lived close by the School and watched over it from its first to its seventy-fifth birthday. In the course of this extraordinarily long and loving association, Harold, like his fellow second masters Bunty Hunter and Bob Allan, acted as headmaster, exercising full responsibility for the School on behalf of the governors. Together, Jeffreys and his Rehoboamites used their lack of inhibition to implement the modified Dalton system and to establish a school that was a fertile ground for one of the great (if most understated) headmasters of the twentieth century, Thorold Coade. Although both men had been at Christ Church, the contrast between Jeffreys and Coade was marked. Nobody could ever have described Jeffreys as ‘wambly’, but Coade famously gave the impression of a certain vagueness. Like Jeffreys, though, he was both profoundly interested in education and more than ready to embrace unorthodox methods. It should, perhaps, be remembered how important orthodoxy – doing the right thing – was between the wars. Progressive ideas in education as well as art and music were vigorous and widespread but they grew from an orthodox soil.

Despite his unobtrusive appearance, Coade was an engaged and active headmaster. He plotted the School’s educational course with infinite care but, as a pastor, he drifted ubiquitously. He preached, wrote, appointed staff and established a national fame for the School and himself. Some of the most treasured memories of Coade were associated with the plays he directed, a pastime pursued at varying levels of The Drama by two of his successors. He acquired a high reputation in what seemed like a prolonged fit of absence of mind! Coade’s mind was, of course, not absent at all. It was elastic and it could be stretched to cope with great issues and trivia

David Jones

Tom Wheare

equally successfully. If a good schoolmaster's pockets are full of rubbish, perhaps a good headmaster's mind should be stocked with a catholic catalogue of ideas, information and impressions stored in a treasure-house held up by pillars of principle.

The fifth headmaster, like two of his predecessors, educated in part at Christ Church, came from an orthodox teaching background at Eton and Shrewsbury. A degree of continuity was provided by time shared with David Jones at Eton, and a more fundamental association came from the island continent of Australia. This trans-oceanic link was endorsed by the rapid establishment of the Harvard and University of Virginia Fellowships, first filled in 1984 and 1985 respectively and still going strong twenty-two years and sixty Fellows later. Bryanston had long provided education for children from abroad, in penny numbers not in massed battalions, a mix that suited parents, pupils and staff. This modest internationalism can be seen in the School's three European posts, graduate native speakers from France, Germany and Spain – often hockey players, a sport as pan-European as soccer.

Since 1983 the School has been a building site. Two all-weather hockey pitches; two new girls' houses (named after second masters Hunter and Allan); two new boys' houses; a dining hall extension; a Craft, Design and Technology building; squash courts in Harold Tarraway's Sports Centre; classrooms on the Plateau; an art building named after Don Potter; a series of studios linking this building to Coade Hall; and the first footings of a Science and Maths Centre.

Numbers, which rose by about ten per cent in the mid-1980s, have since remained fairly constant, but the gender balance has changed markedly both amongst the pupils and in the Common Room. The presence of so many brothers and sisters, husbands and wives, mothers and fathers in the School List demonstrated that a family school had been created. Loving principles guiding our conduct and the way members of the whole school family relate to each other also became a reality as well as an aspiration. The reduction of school rules to simple principles of common sense reduced tensions that might be thought inevitable in schools, and continuity of staff and governors as well as family dynasties have given the School a remarkable calmness.

That calmness, it may be asserted, owes much to the outstanding qualities of the five headmasters' wives. It is clear from everything that is said about May Jeffreys and Kathleen Coade that they were exceptional people who, like Sheila Fisher, Sue Jones and Ros Wheare, made their husbands twice the men they might have been and infinitely enhanced their roles as leaders of the School and as *patres familias*. The headmaster's wife is, necessarily, a shadowy figure. Caesar's wife, yes: Mrs Proudie, no! Yet they hear and see much that escapes their husbands, they are well placed to rein back intemperate responses and, like a cross between the Cheshire Cat and the Queen Mother, they are expected to be always in just the right mood with just the right degree of visibility and height of profile. The work these five women did was something their husbands could never have done and they deserve our loving thanks.

It has always been the policy of the Council of Governors to regenerate itself with youth! None of the five headmasters would wish his work to go unrelated to the work of governors, of whom three in particular should be mentioned – all Old Bryanstonians. Robin Pegna, currently chairman of the Finance and General Purposes Committee, was elected to the Board in 1973 and has seen the School through the financial challenges of plenty and of dearth. The School's present serenity and state of resource owe a great debt to him and to his predecessors managing the School's

On Tuesday, 24th January 1928, the School opened with twenty-three boys and seven teaching staff. In September 2004 it numbered 650 students and eighty teaching staff

finances. It is remarkable that there have only been two chairmen of governors since 1960, Geoff Udall and Nicholas Phillips. Their wise and loving presidency has been of extraordinary value to the School and its headmasters and, since they are former pupils, their virtues may be counted to the School's credit … or at least their parents' in choosing Bryanston!

All five headmasters have been committed Anglicans, if that is not a contradiction in terms! Perhaps, therefore, an Old Testament parallel would provide an appropriate closing picture of this varied quintet. The School Jeffreys founded was a bold and original venture that took root and blossomed extraordinarily quickly. Like Moses, Jeffreys led his little band into the promised land, an idyllic site for a school. Coade was our Solomon, wise builder of the Bryanston ethos, Fisher our Joshua when the tribes of student revolution threatened the stability of the state. David Jones was Isaiah, a visionary whose moral leadership withstood all adversities. In the years of Nehemiah, the temple has been rebuilt and we look forward to a Judith who will slay the Holofernes of twenty-first-century educational bureaucracy!

***Tom Wheare**, Headmaster 1983–2005.*

subscribers

GV Adams
Michael Adamson
M Aikin-Sneath
Simon, Christine and Tom Airey
Frederik Aldag
Candida Alderson (née Toller)
Loz, Ed and Riou Alexander
Crinan Alexander
Richard Allan
John Allan Connaught
Andrew Allan
Jan Allan
Caroline Allen (née Ferris)
Mr and Mrs RD Allan
Mark and Sophie Anderson
Lucy Anstey
Julian Arkell
Robin and Peter Ascher
Robert Ashley-Jones
Joanna Astor
Hugh Austin
Sooty Bain and Tony Vincent
Roger Baker
Tim Baker
Alexandra Balch
Jeremy Ball
Alec Bangham MD FRS
Prof David F Banker
Clive Barda
Aksinia and Miranda Baring
Ian Barker
CNR Barker
Jack Barkham and Ben Barkham
James and Liz Barnes
Rosemary Barnes
David Barker
Peter Barnitt
Jonathan Barton
Peter J Bartram
Alan Beattie
CFR Beauchamp
Bryony Beaumont
Eric Benedict
Martin Benham
Chloe Bentinck
Charlotte Bentley (née Suffield)
Charlotte Berens
William Bermingham
John Berry
John W Berry
Mick, Ruth and Luke Bettesworth
Dr James Bevan
Beth Bevan-Allen
Samuel JP Bigg
Edward Birch
Malcolm Black
Angus Blair
Stephen Blake
Cathy Blake
CC Blakey
Richard and Diana Blanden
R Blausten
Malcolm Boag
Alana Kate Boakes
Mark Bodley Scott
Philip Bodman
Alice Boileau (née Gumpert)
Peter Booth-Smith
Clive Borst
Alastair Borthwick
Dr and Mrs P Bosworth
David Bouchet
Professor Jonathan P Bowen
Simon Bowes
Oli Bowes
John Bowes
Rodney JC Bown
Daniel Braddell
Peter William Bradford
Xavier Bray
Andrew Bridge
Harriet E Bridges
David and Mary Briggs
Fiona Broad
BP Broad
Dr Gordon Brocklehurst
Henry Brockman
Jonathan Brooks
Jessica M Spickett-Brooks
AR Brown
Charlotte Browning
Jo Buckley
Bunty's sister
Solna Burnham, Mike Garrod and Ian Garrod
Bobbie Burns
Jonathan Burr
Richard Burton CBE RIBA
Richard Graham Bush
Patrick Butler-Madden
Jonathan WH Butterfield
DM Caldwell
Andrew MN Calvert and Jason MP Calvert
Adrian Campbell
Jonathan Capel
Stephen Carpenter
Susie Carpenter-Jacobs
Dr Clive Carré
Mr and Mrs David Carstairs
Dr Robin M Catchpole
John Cawood
Peter Chamberlain
Anna Chase
Nicholas Cherryman
The Chetwood Family
Jaquie Chirgwin
ME Chirgwin
Rory Chisholm MBE
Prentice W Claflin
Nick Clegg
Gwendal Collis and Rohanne Collis
Lady Conran
Miss Melissa Conville
Derek and Jennifer Coombs
Antonya Cooper
Frances Cooper
David Cope
Ian Corbett
Agnes and Joel Cordier
Paul Cornford
Tinks Corry, Pop Davies and Emma Corry
Brian Coulson and David Coulson
Antony Cox
Dr Michael J Cox
Douglas Cox
Quentin Craddock, Victoria Craddock and Tristan Craddock
Mr and Mrs JR Craft
David Craven
Dominic Crossley-Holland
Nicki Crush
Polly Culmer
JH Curtis
William Cussans
Gemma da Lunha
Peter Daniel
Adam Daum
AP David
Michael LM Davies
Naomi Davies
Mark Davies
NPA Davis
LSJ Davis
MJ Davis
John J Davis
Sam and Leo Dawkins
Mrs H Daynes
Ashley de Safrin
Wiek Merlyn De Vries
Andreas de Weerth
Timothy Denney
Mr and Mrs RG Denniston
Ben Derbyshire
Rodney Dingle
William Dobbs and Michael Dobbs
Mrs Tina Doble
Master James Dodd
Paddy and Sarah Douglas-Pennant
Mrs Victoria Downes
Nicholas Drake
Mrs LM Drew
Richard and Angela D'Silva
Rodney J Dukes
The Duncan Family
Phillip Arthur Simpson Dunnill
Sophia Durkin (née Jundi)
Maxi Jennifer Eckes
Mr and Mrs G Eggelhoefer
Joost Elias
Guy Erricker
Ellie Ervine
Jeremy Evans
David Austen Evans
Annabel Eyres
Merle Fahrholz
Simon Fairbank
Brian Falk
Natalia Farhi
Afsar Farman-Farmaian
Lawrence Fenelon
Sir Francis Ferris
The Ferris Family
MM and M Fianu
Rachel Field
David Filsell
Will Fitch and Henry Fitch
Dr Michael Flindt
Nancy and Thea Follett

Mr and Mrs SR Ford
Christopher Ford
Colum Forsyth
Jan Fortescue
Edward Fox
Freddie Fox
Simon Frampton and
Sharon Holloway
Amy Friend
Calum Frost
Peter Fryer
Mr and Mrs KRM Fuglesang
Sarah E Gale
Francesca Gardiner and
Josie Gardiner
JST Garfitt
Paula S Garvey and
Christopher C Garvey
Nick Georgano
Syne Georgulas
John W Gerrard
RO Gerrard OBE
David Gestetner
Peter and Annie Gibbon
Colonel and Mrs GK Gibbs
Family of Lucia Giles
Dr and Mrs KJ Gill
Ranulph Glanville
Mrs Elizabeth Godfrey
Ben Goodall
Richard and Francesca
Goodenough
Priscilla Goodfield (née Coade)
Nigel Goodman
Robin Goodman
Melanie and Francis Gordon
Eric Graham
Dr Leslie W Graham
Lucy H Graham
Edward G Grant
Mrs Janet Gray
Alex Gready
George and Carole Green
Malcolm Green
Colin C Green
Peter Greenhill
Betty Greenleaves
Mr Edward Greenwell
Kenneth Greenwood
Mrs E Griffin
Hugo Grimwood
Nigel and Diana Grimwood
Sophia and Fred Groom
Charlotte and Francesca Groves
Alp Guler
Francesca Ruth Zaple Gulliver
Rowan Gundry
Alexandra Haighton
Jon Hall
John Hall
Mr and Mrs Anthony Hallett
Edward Halsted
J Hamilton-Williams
Sue Handley-Merrick

George F Hanson
Richard Harding
TC Harding
Sara Harley
Sam Harper
Julian PH Harrison
Clive Harrison
Mrs MA Harthan
Dr Roy Hartnell
Colin Hastings
David Hay-Edie
Mark and Fiona Haynes
Agi and Anna Heale
Adrian Heath
Scott Hellewell
Trisha Hemingway
Nigel Hepburn
Angus Heron
Mr Hextall
Iain F Hicks-Mudd
Bob Hill
Tina Hillier and Charlie Hillier
Paul Hills
Ronald and Barbara Hird
Mrs E Hitchcox
Mrs Michael Hoare
Desmond and Philippa Hobson,
David and Geraldine Hobson
Desmond Hobson
Rachel Hodgson (née Gestetner)
Roger Hole
Suzy Hoodless
Paddy Hooper
Harry Hopkins
Richard and Poppy Horden
MS Horowitz
George A Hosford
Jeremy Houghton Brown
JC Huggler
Andy Hui
Mr and Mrs CR Humphry
Tomas Nicolai Hurcik
Mr and Mrs Jeremy Instone
Jake Irwin-Brown
Sevki Isin
Stuart Jackson
GT and MT Jacob
Neville Jacobs
Ronaldo Jacobs
Anthony and Diane James
Patrick James
Paul Jenkins
DH Jennings
Nigel Jennings
The Reverend David Jones
Richard P Joscelyne
Peter Jowitt
CRB (Chas) Joyce
Ralph T Kanter
Frank Kanter
Paul Kelly
Jessamine Batterham (Kemp)
Miss Thomasin E Kemp
Dorle and Eberhard Kempf

Alastair Kennedy ('Kenny') and
Family
Christopher A Key
Michael Kingerlee
Siena Knight Bruce and
Vita Knight Bruce
Laith Kubba
DM Ladd
Matt Lambert
J Ladd Gibbon
Justin Langham
Sheila Langley (née Cullington)
Karim Lari
Professor Bruce Laughton
Grant Laversuch
Marc Lazarus
Christopher Le Breton
Sarah A Lea and Adam JN Lea
Jeremy Lee-Barber
Elizabeth Allan (now Leicester)
Emma Lim
Stuart and Victoria Lindsay
Dr and Mrs DJ Lintin
Roy Lipski
JE Little
Guy Locke
Tamara Lodge
Toby Long
Graham Long
Anthony (aka George) Lowe
Huw Lumley
Edward Lumley
James Luther
Anthony Luttrell
David Lyons
Christopher Hugh MacAndrew
Malcolm Macdonald
A Macdonald Smith
Alan Nairne Macgregor
Seb Mackenzie Wilson
Ian Mackenzie-Kerr
Felicity Mackness and
Peter Mackness
Pippa and Charlie Madsen
Campbell Main
Ed and Lucy Makin
Colin Malcolm
Christina Malouf
Nick Mannering
GJ Margot
Tyrrell Marris
Peter Marris
Mr and Mrs Jeremy Marsh
Robert Marshall
Chris and Clem Martin
James Martin
George Marwick
Kaye Mash
David C Matcham
Reverend William Mather
Graeme K Matthew
Matthew Farrer
Henry C Matthews
Charles Maynard

Mrs Gill Maynard
Mrs Penny Mayson
AN McDonald
Victoria McDonaugh
Fiona M McKenzie Johnston
Tor McLaren Webster
Fiona McMillan
William McWilliam
Catharine and David Melville
Ernst Michaelis
Martin Miles
James D Millar
Sir Peter N Miller
Stephen Mills
Nick and Anna Milner-Gulland
Alexsandr Milton
Kate Milton
MR Minns
John R Moloney
Russell Molyneux-Johnson
Arthur Moore
Charles and George Moore
Giles Morant and James Morant
Mr and Mrs IP Morgan
Louise Morgan
Jeremy Morris
Rob and Jemima Morrison
Kay D Mottram
MF Murray
Isabel Murray and Simon Murray
Sarah and Kate Mynott
Timothy Neal
Aurélie Nedder
Peter Neumann
George, Freddie and Maddi Neville-
Jones
Patrick Newman and Rowena
Newman
Peter Newton
Roland Niblett
Rupert Nicholl
Charlie Norton
Nicholas O'Brien, Jade O'Brien and
Laura O'Brien
Mr and Mrs CE O'Dell
David and Rosalie Odgers
Georgia Oetker and August Oetker
William O'Hearn
Oli Margot
Jonathan Oppenheimer
Andrew Orme
Mr and Mrs Ratch Osathnugrah
Guy Osmond
Roger Otley
Mr and Mrs Nick Oundjian
Mr and Mrs Haig Oundjian
Jessica A Paddick
Neil Paffard
Justin Paige
Rosamund Pankhurst (née Barder)
Rupert Pardoe
Jenny Parkes
Michael Passmore
Christopher Patey

Fram Patuck
Chris Pawson and Jodi Pawson
NAR Pearce
Chris and Sally Pearson
Peter Pelly
Jemma and Emma Pengelley
Alasdair Peppe
Dr and Mrs GN Percival
Bart and Sam Pfizenmaier
Mrs Eileen Phillips
The Rt Hon The Lord Phillips of Worth Matravers
Mike Pigott and Rachel Pigott
John Pillar and Libby Howie
Madz Pinto
Pip Pirie
The Plimmer Family
Nick Poole
Dr Halcyon Pope (née Wood)
Michael and Penny Portman
Mary Potter
Roger Potter
RMC Potter
Dick and Sally Poulton
The Powell-Tuck Family
Selina Pratelli (née Faire)
Julian KS Pratt
Paul Pressland
Anna and Sarah Price
NB Pride
David Pugsley
Susan Purry
Janet M Coates Purry
Professor Rory Putman
Alice LB Pyne
Robin Pooley
Matthew and BJ Raben
Mr and Dr G Radcliffe
Robert and Scota Rakison
Leslie Rawlings
Ben Rea
Jonathan Rees
Tim and Linda Reeve
Megan Davies Reid
Simon Relph
Clive Renton
Jessie Reynolds
Catherine Rhys Jones
Emma Rice
Tim and Liz Richards
Matthew Richardson and Lydia Richardson
Louisa Richmond-Coggan and Grant Richmond-Coggan
Guy N Ridley and Max A Ridley
Jacqueline M Roa
Alistair GW Robb
TJL Roberton
Angela JS Roberts
William Roberts
Mr and Mrs Andrew Roberts
Michael Roberts
Dorothy Ruth Ashpole Roberts
John Robertson
AC Robinson
Jamie W Robinson
Nick Rocke
Dr Jack Rodgers
Keith Rodwell
Annabel Vetch Purbeck
Paul Rogers
Janie CL Rose
JDT and DM Rose
Rosenburg
Jonathan Rosenthall
Mrs Jean Ross Stuart and Anna
PT Ross
The Rowlands-Rees Family
David G Rowley
John Royds
Ben Royston
Mr and Mrs BC Ruck Keene
Charles Rudd
Roger Rustom
Marilyn Sadler
Lucy Sams
Benjamin Alexander Samuels and William Arthur Samuels
Gerald Sanctuary
Ms Julie K Saunders
Matthew Sayer
Patrick Scanlan
Robin Scoones
Robert M Scott Desrca
Jonathan Scott
Graham Scott
MJCS
Paul Searle-Barnes
Angus HTF Shapland
Roland W Shepherd
Mr and Mrs James Frank Shalmer Shon
Alan Shrimpton
Lucy Silovsky (née Henshall)
Anna Hunter Simmonds (Ross)
Dr Peter Simmons
Anne Singleton
John Singlieton
The Sketchley Family
The Skinner Family
Ann G Slaybaugh
Jason Rupert Slocock
Edward, Issy, Harry and Rosanna Smith
Simon JT Smith
Ollie Smith
Philippa Snellgrove (née Davies)
Cdr and Mrs MCP Snow RN
Ingrid Southorn
John D Spencely CBE
Hugh Spencely MBE
Kevin and David Stacey
Roger Stalman
Chloe and Archie Stead
Tal Stein
Mrs R Steinbach (née Toms)
Adrian D Stephens
Chris Stephens
Carole Steven-Fountain
Anna Steward and Alexander Hall
Caroline Stidston
Shelley A Stirling
Antonia Stocken
BS Stones
The Stonex Family
Mrs Emma Strange
Muir and Margaret Stratford
Mr and Mrs MJL Stratton
Joe Stirling
Michael Stuart
Rik Sturdy
John Sutherland-Smith
Helen Sweeney
Charles Swithinbank
Marianne C Sylvester-Bradley
Gareth Sylvester-Bradley
Jonathan Symons
Alastair Tanner
Dr Andrew Tanner and Mrs Christine Tanner
Dr Julian Tanner
Warwick Taylor
Linda and Barrie Teasdale
David Tew
Olivia Tew
Jeremy Thatcher
Mrs BJ Thompson
Mrs Karine Thompson
Edward Thompson
Donald Thompson
Mrs Anthony Thorp
Holly Thorpe
Anthony Thorpe
Heidi Thwaites
Joey Toller
Tony Toller
Rosamund and Richard Toms
Mary E Tonkin
JPL Tory
David Trick
James Twist
Brinsley Tyrrell
Barnaby Usbourne
John P van Montagu
PS van Someren
Edward Vandyk
Clayton Vernon
Andrew Vernon-Betts
Giles Vidgeon
The Wagstaffe Family
Michael Walker
Peter Walker
Peter B Wall
Janice Walters
Eric Warburg
Richard Warley
RI Warren
The Waterton Family
Kristin Watkins-Jones
Lucinda Watson
Roger and Anne Weatherly
Sue Webb (Rowe)
Mr and Mrs F Weinstein
Rob Weisberg
Dr and Mrs F Weller
Brenton West
RO Weston
Peter CE Wheadon
Elizabeth de Courcy Wheeler
Geoffrey D Whitaker
Nick and Jackie White
Robin Whitworth
Chris Wigglesworth
Daniel Wiles
David Wilkins
Terry Willcox
Oli Williams
Mrs E Williams
Peter RC Williams
Timothy R Williams
Brooke Lee Wills
PG Wills
Mr and Mrs P Wills
Nicholas AR Wilson
Jan Wilton
DC Winfield
Kate Winter (née Allan)
Christopher Wise
David Wood
Alan Wood
William Wood
John H Wood
Stephen and Mia Woodford
Mr and Mrs Mark Woodruff
Christine Worrall
Kate Worthing (Jones)
Nigel A Wright
James R Yates
Kent Yearsley
Steven Zielinski

index of names

Bold text denotes authorial contributions. Italics denote illustrations.

picture acknowledgements

Henrietta Van den Bergh
9, 13, 19 *below*, 31, 71, 77 *above*, 102, 105, 133, 145, 147 *below*, 148, 150, 157 *above*, 172

Harry Richards
6, 10–11, 18 *below left*, 19 *above*, 21, 41, 45, 75, 76, 77 *below*, 82–83, 85, 86, 91, 101, 111, 115, 123, 125, 127, 141, 142–143, 147 *middle*, 149, 156 *left*, 161, 169, 175, 187

We would also like to thank the many other people who have contributed images from their collections:
Mike Adams
Katie Birks
Peter Bradford
Eric Bramall
Dorian Brindler
Susie Carpenter-Jacobs
Clive Carré
Douglas Cox
William Cussans
Brian Falk
Jonathan Fisher
Ben Gaskell
John Gerrard
Jonathan Gooding
Lucy Graham
Malcolm Green
Kenneth Greenwood
Wendy Harwood
Nigel Hepburn
Desmond Hobson
Clare Kelly
Anthony Lowe
Malcolm Messiter
William Mather
Fiamma Montagu
Michael Owens
Steve Pallant
Rory Putman
Tim Roberton
Royal Commission on Historical Monuments
Alan Shrimpton
Roger Stalman
Harold Tarraway
Ian Whitcomb